CIRCLE OF FIRE

The story of the USS *Susquehanna* in the War of the Rebellion

By

Peter Barratt

To Michael
Best wishes
Peter Barratt

For my father. A sailor who never really left the sea.

First Edition

British Library Cataloguing in Publication Data.

A catalogue record for this book is available from the British Library.

Cover illustration and layout by Zoo Design

Printed in the UK

Published by Columbiad Press

ISBN 0-95-486640-1

ACKNOWLEDGEMENTS

This book could not have been completed without the assistance and encouragement of numerous individuals and institutions. I must first put on record my thanks to the archivists and researchers on the staff of The US Naval Foundation, The US Naval Historical Center (Photographic Division), Do-You Graphics, Maryland, The National Archives (Archives Reference Branch) and The Library of Congress (especially the Prints and Photographs Division), in Washington DC.

My special appreciation goes to Tim Dawson of Zoo Design for the cover design and page layout and Richard O'Sullivan, author of the regimental history of the 55th Virginia Volunteers, for taking the time to read the manuscript and for agreeing to write the foreword for this book. And finally, to my wife Jean, whose help and support was at all times invaluable.

Peter Barratt, August 2004

FOREWORD

"Circle of Fire" is more than the story of a Union warship during the Civil War. It is a glimpse into the inner workings of the blockade of the Confederacy told through the career of one of the Union Navy's longest serving work-horses, the USS *Susquehanna*. Whether it be the opening operations at Hatteras Inlet, the capture of the vital Port Royal Sound, the blowing up of the CSS *Virginia*, the blockade of Charleston and Mobile, or the capture of Fort Fisher and the closure of the South's last major port at Wilmington, the USS *Susquehanna* was there; exchanging shots with forts and shore batteries, overhauling blockade runners and struggling against mountainous seas and mechanical breakdowns.

In every action in which the *Susquehanna* participated it received unstinting praise from the admiral in charge. Its gunnery played a significant role in destroying five Southern coastal installations.

Landsmen will be grateful to the author for devoting a number of pages at the front of the book to a synopsis of the blockade and to the nature of life at sea. The narrative itself is firmly based on contemporary official reports and is given a human face through the recollections of Lieutenant John Bartlett and marine Amos Burton. It reaches an appropriate climax when officers, sailors and marines from the *Susquehanna* take part in the desperate and bloody assault on Fort Fisher.

The text throughout is profusely adorned with photographs, lithographs and maps and there are appendices containing a crew roster and a plan of the ship together with its technical specifications.

RICHARD O'SULLIVAN
London, July 2004.

CONTENTS

TO THE FORBIDDEN EMPIRE

Although this book is primarily concerned with the Civil War exploits of the *USS Susquehanna*, it would be remiss not to give a brief synopsis of her pre-war career. For this we must start on June 8, 1851 as three American warships cleared Hampton Roads and turned south on the first leg of a voyage to the Far East. The squadron's final destination being Japan, a country shrouded in mystery, with an almost pathological distrust of foreign 'barbarians', where feudal warlords reigned supreme. The flagship of this small flotilla was the spanking new side-wheel steamer *Susquehanna*. The United States Congress had been much impressed by the performance of her predecessor, the *Mississippi*, and authorized the building of the *Susquehanna* and a sister ship, the *Powhatan* based on the prototype but slightly larger.

The *Susquehanna* was laid down in 1847 by the New York Navy Yard and built in Philadelphia at a cost of $697,212. She was launched on April 5 1850. Classified as a side-wheel steamer, barkentine rigged, the first-class rated sloop's wooden hull was 257 feet in length and 45 feet in the beam. The ship was powered by two Inclined Direct-Acting engines manufactured at the Murray and Hazelhurst Vulcan Works in Baltimore, Maryland. Charles

W. Copeland designed her engines and the huge boilers needed to feed them. She weighed 2,450 tons fully laden and her draft was 20 feet six inches. The powerful paddle wheels could propel the vessel at a steady rate of eight knots with a top speed of twelve. The *Susquehanna*'s battery consisted of three 8-inch shell guns and six 32-pounder smoothbores. Her crew numbered 300 officers and men.

Accompanying the *Susquehanna* on the expedition would be the sloops *Plymouth* and *Saratoga*. The project was the brainchild of the 64 year-old commander of the *Susquehanna*, John H. Aulick. Born in Winchester, Virginia in 1787, he received his midshipman's appointment in 1809. Whilst serving on the Enterprise in the War of 1812 Aulick had tasted the smoke of battle during an engagement with the British ship *Boxer* on September 4, 1813. Following the latter's surrender the young Virginian was appointed her prize master.

By 1851 he had risen to the rank of commodore, and whilst with the East India Squadron had sailed to Japan, and it was he who suggested to President Fillmore early in 1851 the possibility of opening diplomatic relations with the Japanese. Aulick proposed negotiating a treaty with Japan that would have a twofold purpose: the establishment of trade between the two nations, and the siting of a coaling station on the coast of Japan. Following discussions with his cabinet, Fillmore endorsed the venture and placed Aulick in command of the expedition.

The *Susquehanna*, selected by Aulick to fly his pennant, had been commissioned by Aulick himself on Christmas Eve 1850. Following sea trials in January she returned to port to be victualled and to take on coal for her maiden voyage, sailing to join the East India Squadron, and then on to Japan. The squadron's course would take it via Rio de Janeiro – there to disembark three diplomats – and then across the South Atlantic to the Cape of Good Hope; on to Singapore and then China. Their stay in Rio was destined to stretch to two frustrating months while extensive repairs on the *Susquehanna*'s engines, paddle wheels and spars were carried out. Compounding these mechanical setbacks was Aulick himself.

An ill-tempered man, Aulick quarreled constantly with the *Susquehanna*'s skipper Captain William Inman and, worse still, with one of the VIP passengers on board, the Brazilian Minister to the United States the

The *Susquehanna* under construction at the Philadelphia Navy Yard. Unique photograph taken in July 1850.
Library of Congress

The *Susquehanna* under steam power; a wash drawing by Clary Ray.
US Naval Historical Center

The American fleet – including the *Susquehanna* – in rough seas in the Bay of Wodowara off the coast of Japan with Mount Fujiyama in the background. Tinted lithograph by Sarony & Co
US Naval Historical Center

Admiral Franklin Buchanan (CSN), took command of the *Susquehanna* in Canton, following Commodore Aulick's recall to America
Battles and Leaders

Chevalier S. de Macedo. These temperamental outbursts were fated to have dire consequences in the near future for Aulick. Finally on September 28, 1851, the squadron sailed for the Cape of Good Hope via Zanzibar. The passage was far from smooth and when the *Susquehanna* arrived in Table Bay, Captain Inman reported in a letter to the Navy Department dated October 17, that the seas "...were so high as to leave one paddle wheel eight feet or more out of the water while the other was buried in up to half of its depth."

Upon arrival in Hong Kong Commodore Aulick prepared for the final leg of the expedition, but it was a journey he was destined never to make, as he received orders to return to home waters. Although the official reason later released in a statement from Washington gave Aulick's ill health as the grounds for his recall, the most probable cause lay with the unfortunate incidents in the early part of the voyage.

In Canton, the *Susquehanna* received a new skipper, Captain Franklin Buchanan (later to command the Confederate ironclad *Virginia* in her epic clash with the *Monitor*). Once home however, Aulick demanded and got an official inquiry into his conduct which exonerated him. The commodore retired from the Navy in 1861, dying 12 years later at the age of 86.

On January 14, 1852, Commodore Matthew Perry received the following communication from the Secretary of the Navy. "Proceed to Washington and report to the Secretary of the Navy without delay. Report in person at the Department." Upon arrival in the capital Perry was informed that he was to take command of the Japanese expedition. This constituted something of a blow to Perry's aspirations as he had been promised command of the Mediterranean Squadron. Somewhat placated when told he could have the pick of the available vessels to strengthen the East India Squadron then awaiting his arrival in Hong Kong he subsequently raised his flag in the *Mississippi*. He sailed from Norfolk bound for China on November 24, arriving in Macao some four months later on April 6, 1853. With the squadron assembled in Shanghai, Perry transferred his flag to the *Susquehanna*, as her quarters were more commodious. Perry's re-provisioned fleet quit the China coast on May 17 cruising through the South China Sea and reaching Okinawa nine days later.

Perry's ships dropped anchor in Tokyo Bay on June 8 where,

following brief official ceremonies, the commodore presented the American governments' requests to Japanese officials. Within seven days the squadron set sail for the return voyage back to Hong Kong. Upon his return to China, Perry set up shore-based headquarters in a rented house and the fleet saw out the remainder of 1853 in Macao.

Perry received information that both France and Russia were contemplating expeditions to Japan. Determined that all his good work would not be undermined he sailed for the Land of the Rising Sun in the *Susquehanna* on January 14, 1854, arriving in Yedo Bay on February 11. After presents were exchanged and formal diplomatic conferences were completed to both parties' satisfaction, Perry left Japanese waters on March 31, the prized treaty signed by the Japanese government in his possession.

As for the *Susquehanna*, she sailed first for the South China coast then proceeded across the Pacific, rounding Cape Horn and putting in at Buenos Aires and Rio de Janeiro. She reached her home port of Philadelphia on March 10, 1855, being the first steam vessel of any nation to circumnavigate the world. Decommissioned five days later the ship lay at the quayside for almost 14 months before being re-commissioned into the service and sailing to take station with the Mediterranean Squadron. Arriving in July 1856 she became the flagship, fulfilling her duties until sailing for home.

Whilst on her homeward journey an outbreak of the dreaded Yellow Fever broke out. This highly fatal Mosquito-spread disease struck down officers and crew by the dozen. Putting in to Port Royal, Jamaica, the surgeons and nurses of the Royal Naval hospital worked tirelessly to care for 85 of the steamer's crew ferried ashore by launches of the British squadron. The *Susquehanna* sailed for New York; and with her went Assistant Surgeon Frederick A Rose of the Royal Navy who, at no little risk to his own life, continued to treat those of the crew who were too sick to leave the ship at Port Royal. This selfless act or heroism, combined with the prompt and skilled assistance provided by the surgeons, nurses and attendants at Port Royal, prompted a Congressional Resolution that ordered a medal struck; on one side was the image of President Buchanan and on the obverse an inscription which reads; 'For Kindness and Humanity to the Officers and Crew of the US steamer *Susquehanna*'.

Upon reaching New York, the sloop was laid up 'in ordinary' on April 18, 1858 until refitted and re-commissioned in August of 1860.

Hardly had the echo of the guns pounding Fort Sumter into surrender died away before the Federal Navy assumed the awesome task of enforcing a blockade of Southern harbors, from the Chesapeake to the Rio Grande. Likewise, their Confederate counterparts were busy organizing government chartered and privately owned steamers and schooners to challenge this threat to their vital trading links with the outside world. At the onset of hostilities the Stars and Stripes flew at the mastheads of 90 ships. However, sail alone powered half of these. Steam was slowly but surely making its presence felt, but the staggering cost of filling the coal bunkers of these craft was a major financial and logistical problem.

There were 13 modern screw-powered steam sloops plus five ship-rigged steam frigates and they carried batteries of up to forty 9-inch rifles on the gun decks plus larger pivot mounted weapons fore and aft on the spar decks. These particular vessels were the equal of any warships in the world; unfortunately many were out of commission in April 1861. Of the remaining vessels 40 had combined sail and steam power and these included four side-wheel sloops (the *Susquehanna* being one). These last had been at sea for more than a decade and their major drawback was the vulnerability of their boilers and machinery, situated as they were above the waterline. Throughout the war, ship-rigged steamers like the *Susquehanna* relied mainly on the energy of the wind as their main source of propulsion and treated steam power as an auxiliary.

Caught with his squadrons scattered across the globe – only three steamers were in home waters – and with many of its ships laid up 'in ordinary' Secretary of the Navy Gideon Welles and his assistant Gustavus Fox worked feverishly to create a naval force capable of mounting an effective blockade. Eight new ocean-going vessels and 23 gunboats had been ordered or were in various stages of construction. Also on the stocks were 47 'double-enders' – ship-rigged vessels carrying a rudder both fore and aft, with a pilothouse at each end of the ship. In the narrow confines of the rivers that flowed into coastal inlets they could change course simply by reversing their engines.

As the keels of new steam frigates and gunboats were laid in the navy yards, whalers, excursion steamers, tugs, fishing schooners, ferry boats, clipper ships and merchant steamers were bought or requisitioned and armed with whatever weaponry was available and sent south.

Manpower was also a problem. The coming of war tore the old Navy asunder. Of the highest-ranking officers, of which 93 were serving captains, 15 resigned, 12 taking up arms with the South. However, of 127 commanders 34 would send in their resignations, 29 accepting equivalent or higher rank in the secessionist Navy. From a total of 351 lieutenants, 89 sent in their papers and of these only 15 took no part in the war.

Among those who chose state above country were oceanographer Matthew Maury and the former captain of the *Susquehanna* Franklin Buchanan, who in 1861 commanded the Washington Navy Yard. Raphael Semmes, the 52 year-old future skipper of the famous Rebel commerce raider *Alabama,* also sent in his papers. Junior officers who would find fame under the Confederate ensign joined them; James McIntosh Kell, who would accompany Semmes on the *Alabama,* John Taylor Wood, Catesby ap R. Jones and John Maffitt, whose escapades as master of the Florida would strike fear into the hearts of Yankee shipowners.

In open defiance of the declared blockade and with impudent ease, blockade runners from Nassau and Cuba sailed virtually unmolested into Charleston, Wilmington, Mobile, Savannah, New Orleans and dozens of smaller inlets on the Atlantic and Gulf coasts, unloading their precious cargoes of arms, ammunition and medical supplies.

Among the handful of deep-sea vessels given the onerous task of hunting these daring ships was the side-wheel steamer *Susquehanna.*

THE BLOCKADE

"If ever a cool head, strong nerve and determination of character were required, it was while running through the American blockade of the coast of the Southern states." So wrote Augustus Hobart-Hampden, skipper of the blockade-runner *Don*.

There were rich rewards for surviving the hazardous journey past the blockade. A single successful run between Nassau and Wilmington could net a profit of $400,000 for a cargo of cognac, Madeira wine, Belgian silk, perfumes and cigars. On the outbound trip cotton purchased at eight cents a pound was sold for sixty cents in England. The master of a blockade runner, possibly a Royal Naval officer under an assumed name on 'extended leave', could expect a payout of $5,000 in gold for one trip between Nassau or St. George and the Confederate ports of Mobile and Wilmington. The lowliest crew member stood to earn $250.

The ink was barely dry on Lincoln's appeal calling for volunteers to restore the Union before Hobart-Hampden and other like-minded individuals embarked on their risky but profitable trade. In the hope of dissuading these cavalier sea captains and their wealthy backers, President Lincoln declared a blockade of Southern ports and harbors on April 19, 1861, six days after the United States flag was lowered on Fort Sumter's rubble-strewn parade ground. Under international law, a country at war with another was empowered to 'blockade' the ports of her enemy, but Secretary of the Navy Gideon Welles feared the implementation of such a measure would, in the eyes of the European powers, grant the Confederacy the status of a belligerent nation. This was just what Lincoln wished to avoid. Also, a 'paper blockade' was useless and held no standing unless sufficient warships, which the Union Navy at the time simply did not possess, could enforce it.

Instead, as the present rebellion was technically an internal insurrection, Welles suggested an Executive Order closing Southern ports to all foreign merchant ships. At first, Lincoln was in complete agreement but after word of the scheme reached Europe he was forced to revise his strategy. Great Britain in particular found the Executive Order unacceptable. As a neutral state, and one that depended heavily on the importation of Southern cotton, the British government announced it would refuse to recognize the edict, as in Parliament's eyes to respect such a ruling would appear to fully endorse Lincoln's war aims against the South. Her Majesty's Minister in Washington, Lord Richard Lyon, hinted that this mandate, if put into force, could lead to Royal Navy warships escorting British merchant vessels to ensure their unhindered passage into Southern ports, with the very real risk of direct confrontation with the Union Navy.

The 'mother country' actually preferred the declaring of a blockade. A formal blockade would allow foreign merchantmen to make for Southern harbors but with the attendant risk of being stopped and searched by Union cruisers and gunboats patrolling the waters offshore. If upon examination a vessel's papers aroused suspicion, and the master of the Union warship was also of the opinion that the cargo carried on board was bound for the Confederacy, he had the power to send the ship north with a prize crew in charge, for adjudication. If the decision of the prize court found for the Union authorities the ship and its cargo would be confiscated and auctioned off. After due consideration Lincoln resolved to call his measure a blockade

The Confederate government was convinced that whatever measures Lincoln's cabinet chose, the threat of a cotton shortage would eventually force

Britain and possibly France to intercede. In the hope of forcing foreign intervention the Rebel authorities even decided to impose an embargo on the export of the vital commodity in order to exaggerate the problem. One vital factor not taken into consideration was the amount of surplus cotton stockpiled in Europe. When this began to run low Egyptian and Indian cotton was imported, thereby gazumping the Confederate attempt to manufacture an artificial shortage, but the material was of such poor quality at this time that British manufacturers gave up trying to use it.

This led to appalling hardship in the mills of Lancashire with 350,000 workers laid off. By 1865 barely 46,000 people were employed in the factories of the North of England. Despite this, Britain remained neutral. The Confederacy had overestimated the power of the British mill owners. The cotton industry simply did not have enough political strength to dictate British foreign policy.

Legendary stories of famous blockade-runners such as the *A D Vance*, *Denbigh*, *Fingal*, *Banshee* and *Robert E Lee* abound. Although they and many of their consorts eventually fell victim to Yankee warships, they had repaid their investors many times over and had delivered tons of vital arms, munitions and medicines plus large quantities of luxury merchandise to the beleaguered South.

A high percentage of blockade runners were commissioned and built in British ports, especially Liverpool, where it is reputed that more Confederate flags flew than in Richmond. The fitting out of these vessels was paid for by prosperous British or Southern syndicates while the Confederate government purchased several direct. The skilled shipyard workers turned out slim, sleek, shallow-draft, ship-rigged steamers capable of carrying the maximum amount of cargo at maximum speed – a necessary feature as they carried no weapons with which to defend themselves and their only chance of salvation if spotted was to outrun the pursuing cruiser. A ship had to be able to attain a speed of at least 10 knots but many were capable of 14 and even 18 knots. Their hulls were usually painted light gray to further reduce their visibility to Yankee lookouts in the maintops of the blockading ships. Whenever possible they utilized clean-burning Welsh anthracite coal which, unlike the poor quality Southern rock, gave off little in the way of smoke from

The blockade runner *Robert E Lee*, formerly the *Giraffe*. After capture by the Union navy she was taken into service and renamed *Fort Donelson*.
Library of Congress

The old Navy Department, Washington DC.
Battles and Leaders

Standard naval 10 inch shell gun as mounted on Union warships such as the *Susquehanna*. *Battles and Leaders*

their raked funnels, thus improving their chances of escaping detection. Some of these smokestacks were telescoped, further diminishing the ship's outline.

A prime example of this type of purpose-built vessel was the steamer *Bat*, snared whilst making her maiden inbound run through the blockade in the fall of 1864. She was swift; capable of 13 knots and 230 feet in length with a beam of 26 feet. Her hold could take 850 bales of cotton and with a draft of six and a half feet the *Bat* encountered few problems clearing the shoals and sandbanks off the coastal inlets and estuaries.

Initially these swift ocean greyhounds had little trouble circumventing a mostly ineffective impediment and delivering their cargoes into Mobile, Charleston, Wilmington and Galveston. Indeed, during the first year of the war an estimated nine out of 10 vessels who attempted to run the blockade succeeded. As additional Union warships steamed to take up station off these harbors the subsequent tightening of the blockade adversely affected the frequency and ease of entry which the runners had up until now enjoyed. Under the purposeful drive of Navy Secretary Gideon Welles and his tireless assistant Gustavus Fox, the navy yards of the North worked flat out, adding some 200 ships to the blockading squadrons during 1861. The first of the brand new steam-screw sloops off the stocks, the *Tuscarora*, was launched on August 22, 1861. A proud Welles' boasted: "Her keel was growing in the forests three months ago." Initially, manpower was not a problem and some 24,000 recruits enlisted to serve on these vessels.

During 1862 Union naval strength rose from 264 to 427 vessels and by 1863 this figure had expanded to 558. In December of 1865 as Admiral Porter's fleet closed in on Fort Fisher, the Navy Department controlled a total of 670 ships of all types, from river-bound ironclads and gunboats, to modern deep-sea cruisers, served by more than 60,000 officers and men. In rounded figures, total Federal government expenditure on the wartime navy topped $123 million

In September of 1861 the blockading fleets were divided into a North Atlantic Squadron, covering the coastline from the Potomac to Port Henry, North Carolina and a South Atlantic Squadron, extending southwards to Key West, Florida. The East and West Gulf Blockading Squadrons covered the seas as far south as Matamoros, Mexico. Supporting these divisions other Union cruisers patrolled the sea-lanes of the Pacific and the West Indies, and even further afield to the Mediterranean and the coast of Africa. Their job was to protect American shipping from the jaunty Rebel commerce raiders, a needle-in-a-haystack task, which, apart from the taking of the *Alabama* and *Florida* reaped little reward. Estimates of the damage inflicted on American shipping vary from $15 to $25 million. The *Shenandoah* alone was responsible for over $2 million of this total. By 1865 the *Alabama, Florida, Georgia, Tallahassee* and *Shenandoah* had crippled the northern mercantile marine to such an extent, that it did not regain its share of the world carrying trade until 1913.

The task of the blockading squadrons was eased somewhat by the knowledge that only 10 secessionist seaports possessed rail links with the Confederate interior. Norfolk, Virginia; New Bern and Wilmington, North Carolina; Charleston, South Carolina; Savannah, Georgia; Fernandina and Pensacola, Florida; Mobile, Alabama. And the largest, and arguably the most important city of the South – New Orleans. Of these, only Wilmington, Charleston, Savannah, Pensacola and Mobile carried inter-state rail connections. It was against these ports and their fortifications that the main

Union offensives would be directed and by mid-1862 New Bern, Norfolk, Fernandina, Pensacola and New Orleans were in Federal hands.

The most difficult of Southern ports to stop up was Wilmington, situated some 17 miles inland on the banks of the Cape Fear River. There were two channel approaches to the river; New Inlet, north of Smith's Island and the Western Bar Channel, west of the island. 50 miles of ocean separated the two estuaries. Entrance to the Western Bar Channel was protected by Fort Caswell and the New Inlet Channel's custodian after 1862, was the mighty leviathan Fort Fisher. To cover such an expanse of ocean the Union warships were forced to divide into two flotillas and it was not until late in the conflict that sufficient Union vessels were allotted to mount a serious blockade. Even so, during the period 1863–64 as many as 230 ships knifed through the ring of Yankee gunboats into the Cape Fear River and on into Wilmington.

With the numbers of Union warships on the increase the flag officers commanding the squadrons off Mobile, Charleston and Wilmington were able to position an extra, outer ring of steam sloops and frigates which in theory doubled their chances of seizing blockade runners. To counteract this, their intended victims implemented a new strategy. The contraband-laden inbound steamers crossed the Atlantic and headed for the Bahamas and the bustling quaysides of Nassau and Bermuda. Here their merchandise was off loaded onto small schooners and light draft vessels, which drew no more than nine feet of water. Then followed the most dangerous part of the journey – the final leg across the open waters to the Confederate coast and a safe and profitable haven in a secessionist harbor. From Nassau it was 515 nautical miles to Charleston and 570 to the port of Wilmington. The run from Bermuda was 670 miles to Wilmington and a further 105 miles to Charleston. For the Gulf ports of Mobile and Galveston the schooners and small steamers set sail from the Cuban port of Havana.

Just how potent was the Federal blockade? It never became totally effective, it could never hope to be, and even as the war drew to a close there was still an even chance of evading the flotillas of Yankee warships guarding the approaches to the Confederacy. During the 12 months before the capture of Fort Fisher closed Wilmington, the final Rebel port on the Atlantic coast still open to the outside world, $65 million worth of cotton was exported from its docks. It has been estimated that although some 8,500 attempts at breaching the blockade ended successfully, 1,149 ships including 295 steamers were taken as prizes. As many as 355 ships were burned, sunk or driven ashore making a grand total of 1,504 vessels either destroyed or captured. In reality, the goods and supplies that reached the South were no more than a drip-feed and were insufficient to sustain the war effort of a desperate and ever declining Confederacy.

The success of the Rebel raiders' actions against the American merchant marine cannot be denied, but the hoped for withdrawal of Union cruisers from their blockading stations to pursue these lone-wolf warships across the world's oceans failed to materialize.

LIFE AT SEA

There was an old adage that it took three years to make a seaman. Unfortunately the Confederacy was not prepared to allow the United States Navy the time required. All told the Navy had 9,000 officers and men under arms in April of 1861. Many Southern born officers resigned to take up the Confederate cause and Gideon Welles' primary concern was to replace these 'traitors'. Merchant navy officers were induced to enlist with the offer of a volunteer commission and these experienced seamen would eventually outnumber their regular service comrades by four to one. The three upper classes at the Naval Academy at Annapolis, Maryland, which had been in existence barely a decade were ordered to sea, their studies would now continue in a more practical environment. The Academy upped sticks in May 1861 and removed itself to a safer location at Fort Adams close to Newport, Rhode Island and from there five months later to a hotel, the Atlantic House, where it remained for the duration of the war.

Patriotic fervor swept both North and South following the fall of Fort Sumter. Inspired by a desire to preserve the Union and the chance to earn glory, thousands of Northerners rushed to join the services. This at first ensured a steady stream of enlistments in the harbors and docks of the North. However, with the passing of time and the realization that this was going to be a long war, enlistment's abated to a trickle and, in parallel with the Army the Navy was forced into offering cash bounties to encourage volunteers.

During peacetime the Union Navy had conducted its affairs on the same strict principals adhered to by most navies and, come to that, armies of the period. Promotion was slow in coming and was usually based on a combination of long service and experience. The senior rank in the pre-war Navy was captain and it was fairly commonplace for lower grade officers to be stuck with the same rank for years, with little opportunity for advancement. With the coming of war these circumstances changed dramatically. Serving able seamen were offered a raise in stature to the rank of petty officer and junior commissioned officers found themselves with an extra ring on their sleeves.

Aboard the larger Federal vessels the *status quo* among the senior non-commissioned personnel was often maintained. The quartermasters, together with the captains of the foc'sul, were recognized as the most able seamen on the ship. They reported directly to the duty deck officer and during battle conditions their place was at the helm of the ship or on the quarterdeck where they were responsible among other duties for taking note of signals sent and received. In the regular pre-war navy, where the majority serving aboard were experienced seamen, the sub-divisions of the port and starboard watches carried the titles of foc'sulmen, foretopmen, maintopmen, mizzen topmen, afterguard and 'waisters.'

The chief petty officer was the master-at-arms, responsible for maintaining good order and discipline among the crew with two ship's corporals for assistance. Warrant officers included boatswains, carpenters, sailmakers and gunners. The remainder of the crew were divided into petty officers, able seamen, ordinary seamen, first, second and third-class boys and landsmen. These latter made up almost two thirds of the vessel's complement and few, if any had ever stepped onto a ship's deck. Only a handful progressed to a rank higher than ordinary seaman.

Unlike the Army, Negroes were first enlisted into the Navy in September 1861 and what's more received parity with their Caucasian shipmates where pay was concerned. Apart from Afro-Americans, the Navy welcomed many nationalities aboard its ships, mainly Northern Europeans such as English, Swedes and Norwegians. To enlist in the Union Navy, recruits below 18 years of age required parental consent, the minimum age accepted was 13 and in theory a man needed to stand at least five feet eight inches in order to sign articles.

Pay in the service commenced at $7 a month for a ship's boy third-class. An inexperienced landsman would be paid a starting wage of $12, ordinary seamen would earn $16, and seamen would be better off by $2. When at sea, a boatswain would receive $120 a month. All other ranks such as cooks, musicians and stewards received a monthly salary commensurate with their allotted tasks and length of service.

Volunteers were sent to receiving ships, usually outdated sailing frigates moored in harbor, for training and instruction into the duties expected of a seaman. Clothing issued consisted of dark blue woolen trousers and overshirt. This shirt featured a wide falling collar, which, along with the cuffs, was often hand embroidered with white tape. A large black neckerchief knotted in front and a flat visorless cap sometimes carrying a ribbon with the ship's name picked out in white or gold completed the outer uniform. Underneath the sailor wore a red or blue flannel shirt tucked into his trousers. Also supplied were underwear, socks and shoes, a hammock and two blankets along with a canvas bag to hold all his kit. For duty in the cold winters of the South Atlantic a thick blue double-breasted jacket was issued. In the semi-tropical heat of Southern climes the same style of uniform was worn but made of a lightweight white duck material, often topped off by a straw hat.

For the novice tar there was a myriad of information to assimilate regarding service procedures and the daily shipboard duties he would be called upon to perform. In combat he might be called on to board enemy vessels, or defend his own ship from a Rebel boarding party. For this he was taught to use cap and ball revolvers, cutlasses and even boarding pikes.

Naval etiquette was part of the education and the newcomer had to learn to identify the many and varied ranks and how to address and show respect to his officers, petty officers and of course his own messmates. During

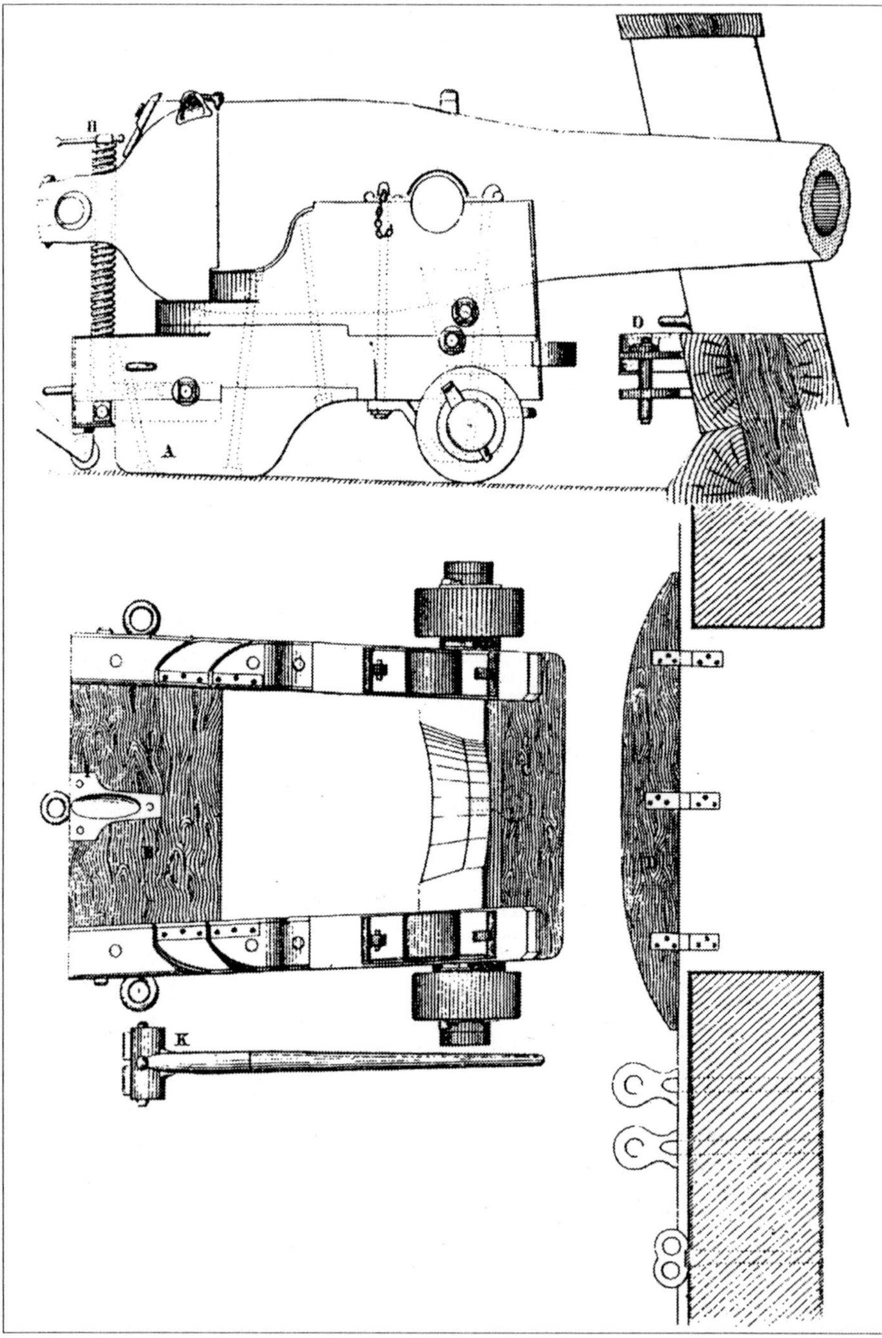

Diagram of a Dahlgren 9-inch smoothbore shell gun.
Standard broadside armament on Union warships
Ordnance Instructions 1860

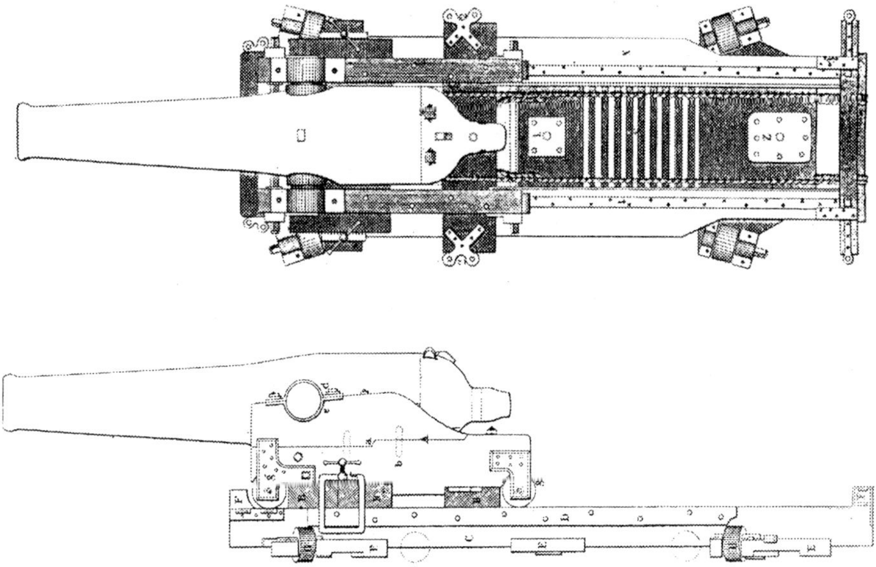

Plan and side elevation views of 11-inch Dahlgren smoothbore, mounted on pivot carriage.
Ordnance Instructions 1860

his time on the receiving ship shore leave was rare but the men were reasonably well fed and contented.

With the completion of basic training the new hands were posted to their vessels. Once on board they were divided up into port and starboard watches which in turn were split into divisions. Each seaman had to familiarize himself with his various stations and to know where he was supposed to be at all times; whether it was assisting with the gun crew he had been assigned to, or hauling at the lee main braces as the ship tacked to change course. It was the responsibility of the ship's master, via his subordinate officers and petty officers, to ensure ordinary seamen, landsmen and ship's boys received proper tuition in the duties expected of them while aboard ship. They were made familiar with the many and varied procedures and tasks; from basic seamanship and handling of the vessel, to the rudiments of navigation and the dangerous but necessary task of working aloft. Even mundane assignments such as the knotting and splicing of ropes and sewing and mending items of clothing had to be mastered. As was to be expected on board a warship, exercising with the gun batteries was a daily occurrence.

Large ships such as the *Susquehanna* carried among their complement a detachment of United States Marines, and if the stories are true there was little love lost between the two branches of the service as part of their daily duties included policing the ship. The Marine Corps muster rolls for 1861 showed a total strength of 1,892 officers and men. Although 50 per cent of its captains and three quarters of its lieutenants resigned their commissions to go south, within six months the Corps' strength had grown to 2,964. At the peak of their wartime service 4,167 men were serving in the Corps and in four years of duty 148 officers and men were killed in action and a further 312 died from other causes. In action their role was in assisting the working of the guns or picking off the enemy's crew with their rifle muskets. Marines also formed landing parties for shore based operations and in fact participated in most of the naval actions along the coasts and on the rivers. A detachment was even used as part of the force that quelled the New York draft riots in 1863.

Their uniform was similar to the Army pattern and consisted of a dark blue frock coat with a standing collar, the bottom edge of which was trimmed with scarlet piping, and sky blue trousers. Headgear was an army style kepi or forage cap. White pipeclay cross-belts were worn, holding a cartridge box and bayonet. Marines also carried a double-bag pattern knapsack with the letters 'USM' stenciled on the back. Full dress uniform included shoulder epaulets, white gloves and a shako topped with a red worsted pom-pom. Shipboard fatigue apparel comprised a four-buttoned blue pullover style flannel overshirt. Summer uniform differed only by the wearing of white linen trousers by enlisted men. In the winter months a blue-gray greatcoat was periodically supplied for sea duty.

A normal day aboard ship began with a marine bugler sounding reveille at 5am. In response the bleary-eyed matelotes turned out of their hammocks, encouraged on their way by bellowing petty officers. Their first chore was to stow away their sleeping gear. The blankets were rolled up inside the hammocks and then, in a routine which had not changed since Nelson's day, the canvas bundles were taken up on to the spar deck and stowed in special netting above the vessel's bulwarks. This was to give added protection from bullets and flying splinters should the ship go into action. Berth decks were then scrubbed with seawater. This task completed, attention switched to the main deck where all loose gear would be cleared away before the wooden planking was holystoned by parties of men under the eagle eye of a boatswain's mate. Hands would then be put to work scraping clean the guns and burnishing the ironwork. All brass fittings and other brightwork were polished, and sails, halyards and rigging were inspected for signs of mildew and wear. With these tasks completed the webfeet were permitted to shave and clean themselves up.

At 7.30am following ship's inspection by the master-at-arms, the boatswain's mate would pipe all hands to partake of the first meal of the day. Those assigned the job would unlock the mess chests and hand out the dishes and pots and pans. Each sailor was issued his own knife, fork and spoon. Breakfast consisted of pieces of salted beef called 'junk' washed down with a pint of strong black coffee. The noon meal varied little from breakfast but if the ship happened to be moored off Union occupied territory, local produce such as cheese, potatoes, eggs and rice made an appearance on the menu. The men consumed their meals in messes of eight or more shipmates. At around 4 o'clock in the afternoon the final meal of the day, a light 'supper', was prepared and eaten.

Official subsistence levels called for each man to receive daily one pound of salt pork with half a pint of peas or beans and a like measure of salt beef and half a pound of flour plus a quarter pound of dried fruit, raisins, apples or other substitutes. The staple ingredients varied little, but the pork or beef might be served up with half a pound of rice and a couple of ounces of butter and cheese with perhaps an issue of tea. Whatever was put in front of the hungry sailors it was usually accompanied by hardtack or baked biscuits. Officially, cranberries, pickles, molasses and vinegar were to be issued once a week to help combat scurvy but in reality this happened less frequently and the men suffered accordingly.

The cooks attempted to vary the daily intake by preparing the ingredients into more appetizing concoctions such as 'Dandy Funk' – a stew in which hardtack soaked in water was boiled up with salt pork and a healthy dash of molasses. Then there was 'Sea Pie', simply multi-layers of meat and pastry.

The Union Secretary of the Navy, Gideon Welles.
Battles and Leaders

In between the regular meal breaks, the remainder of the day would be spent in various gun drills, repairing damaged gear and sails, and inspections. Activities closed with a final muster around 6pm. The men then amused themselves with diverse recreational activities; writing letters home, repairing worn clothing or playing musical instruments such as banjos, guitars, fiddles, fifes and that cheap and cheerful favorite the Jaw's harp. Although gambling, especially card playing, was not permitted many tars were inveterate risk takers and were prepared to bet on almost anything, from the toss of a coin to the distance traveled by the ship that day. Many took physical fitness seriously and held foot races and took part in gymnastics and boxing contests. Sunday's were traditionally a day of rest unless duties decreed otherwise, and the men would take the opportunity to do their washing, spreading the garments to dry in the rigging.

The routine was not set in stone and could vary depending on the size of the ship and the circumstances and situations in which the vessel found itself. Chasing Confederate raiders, active duty on the blockade, or even the taking on of coal could completely disrupt the smooth running of the ship. Things as varied as the whims of the skipper or the seasons of the year could affect operations.

Bluejackets succumbed to the same health problems as their land-based compatriots. Dysentery, diarrhea, malaria and of course the traditional sailors disease scurvy, struck down many seamen. Records show that of a total of 132,000 Union seamen who served between 1861 and 1865, only 1,804 were killed in action or died as a result of wounds or injuries, but a further 3,000 sailors expired from various ailments.

Rules and regulations whilst on active service were strictly enforced. Although flogging was outlawed, punishments for everyday misdemeanors such as insubordination, negligence and fighting could bring demotion in rank, stoppage of pay and confinement in irons on bread and water. These types of incident were commonplace, and if the log of the *Susquehanna* is typical, not a day passed without some poor wretch incurring the wrath of a petty officer or somebody of a higher rank. For more serious crimes such as mutiny, desertion, refusal to obey orders and treason the accused would face a courts martial which, if the case were proved, could result in severer punishment being inflicted including dishonorable discharge from the service – even the death penalty could be invoked.

The root cause of disciplinary problems throughout the fleet was overindulgence in alcohol. The men were entitled to a daily ration of grog, consisting of one gill – four ounces – of whisky mixed with water. However, not all sailors drank, and those who did not either gave or sold their ration to those who did, the result being predictable. Finally on July 14, 1862, prohibition was declared, the Navy Department offering the men five cents a day in compensation for the loss of their liquor. Introducing regulations is one thing, maintaining them is another matter. Every opportunity to smuggle booze aboard ship was tried, even tin cans labeled 'oysters' and 'canned meat' was often found to contain something a little stronger than their advertised contents. Retribution for those found intoxicated was swift. If not immediately clapped in irons they were often as not hosed back into sobriety with ice cold seawater!

Eternal vigilance was the watchword aboard the blockading ships of the Union Navy, for it was at night and in inclement weather that the schooners and steamers of the Confederacy would attempt their speedy runs in and out of Southern harbors. In the hours of darkness noise was kept to a minimum, and other than a signal lamp on the designated flagship no other lights were to be shown. All vessels had to be ready to slip their cables in minutes in an effort to apprehend or sink these elusive craft. There also existed the remote possibility of being attacked by Rebel 'torpedo' boats. The fear of sharing the fate of the steam sloop *Housatonic*, sunk by the Confederate submersible *Hunley* off Charleston in the first successful foray in submarine warfare, ensured an alert 24-hour watch on all blockading craft.

Union warships differed considerably in size and fighting capability. Welles' campaign to seize control of the Southern coast was initially dependent on older ships such as the sailing frigate *Congress* and the combined sail and steam driven side-wheelers of the *Mississippi* and *Susquehanna* type. Gradually more modern steam powered screw sloops and frigates such as the *Hartford* and *Kearsarge* joined their consorts on blockade duty or headed off on long voyages to protect Yankee merchant ships and seek out Confederate privateers. Hard on their heels followed innovative ironclad steamers like the *New*

Ironsides and armored side-wheel gunboats like the *Sassacus*.

One of the most vital functions on any man of war involved the smooth and disciplined working of the ship's batteries. Gunner's mates and quartergunners were responsible for the weapons and their equipage. It required up to 16 men to load and fire the monstrous smoothbore and rifled pieces. Assigned to overall command for each gun would be a lieutenant assisted by a midshipman. Next in line came a gun captain, one second captain and two loaders. After each round left the bore, two rammers and spongers leaped forward to clean out any powder residue before ramming home the fresh charge. Four side tacklemen and five front tacklemen hauled the huge piece back into position following the recoil. A young powder monkey completed the gun crew.

The guns themselves were formidable and deadly weapons. The main armament on a conventional Union cruiser comprised 9-inch smoothbores divided into port and starboard batteries. To support these broadside-positioned pieces heavier caliber weapons were sited fore and aft. They ranged from mammoth rifled 200-pound cannon to sophisticated Parrott rifles with a reinforced breech band which could fire iron projectiles weighing between 12 to 150-pounds. The 11-inch Dahlgren smoothbore, pivot-mounted on steel runners set in the deck called 'Racers', could rotate 360 degrees. It weighed upwards of 16,000 pounds and could throw a 130-pound shell nearly a mile.

Normal rate of sustainable fire was three minutes per round but this could be cut to two minutes by a well practiced and proficient gun crew. Cutlasses, pistols, carbines or muskets and boarding pikes were stored in racks ready to be snatched up by the crew to repel boarders. Alternatively they would be issued to shore parties for land based operations. Fortunately, close quarter hand-to-hand fighting, at sea as well as on the battlefield, was a rare occurrence.

Despite the shrill blasts of the boatswains whistles summoning the crew to general quarters for daily gun drills, the constant exercises and inspections, in reality the biggest enemy by far was boredom. Captains tried alternative combinations of drill and varied the day-to-day formula where practicable. Even sailing to change station or taking aboard supplies and coal helped break the monotony. There were of course engagements with Confederate shore fortifications and the thrill of the chase as a brief smudge of smoke or a strange sail on the horizon heralded the possibility of prize money. There were recorded incidents of sea chases lasting up to four days before the issue was decided either by capture or successful evasion. A blockade-runner taken carrying contraband goods for the enemy could earn the crew that captured it up to $20,000. Vessels assisting in the pursuit or that were stationed nearby were also entitled to a smaller share.

Every bluejacket and marine looked forward with eager anticipation to spending time ashore, but opportunities were scarce and transpired only if their ship happened to be moored off a Union-held port such as Fernandina or Pensacola. Even better should the ship be sent north for refit and repair. As one sailor recalled: "Blockading was desperately tedious work, one made the best one could of it. The largest reservoir of anecdotes was sure to run dry; the deepest vein of original humor to be worked out. I remember two notorious tellers of tall stories being pitted against each other, for an evenings amusement, when one was driven as a last resort to recounting that 'Mary Had a Little Lamb'."

The war for the Union may have been ultimately decided on the bloody fields of Pennsylvania, Virginia, Maryland, Georgia and Tennessee. But without the tireless efforts of the Union Navy's never ending vigil of 3,400 miles of enemy coastline there is every possibility that Jefferson Davis's Confederacy may have held out long enough to achieve its dream of independence.

THE MEDITERRANEAN

The scene is the New York Navy Yard; it is August 17, 1860. Two years and four months of enforced inactivity have passed and a refitted *Susquehanna* awaits her ceremonial re-commissioning. Amos Burton, a 27 year-old private in the United States Marines, is about to embark on his first voyage. Born in Watertown in the county of Middlesex, Massachusetts in 1833 he enlisted in the marines at Philadelphia on May 9, 1860, listing his trade as that of 'laborer'. Lieutenant James Jones, the enlisting officer, catalogued his physical characteristics as follows: "Height five feet nine inches, a fair complexion with brown eyes and dark hair." Burton opened his account of service on the *Susquehanna* with the following description of the day's events.

"At 2 o'clock pm the United States steamship *Susquehanna* was put in commission, amid the hearty cheers of her crew. The Stars and Stripes floated in the breeze, and the pennant waved from her main royal masthead so proudly over us, assuring us that we were under the care and protection of the glorious Union."

Her commanding officer was Captain George Hollins, a 61 year-old veteran of the War of 1812. Born in Maryland in September 1799, he entered the service in 1814. Assigned as a midshipman to the frigate USS *President,* captained by Stephen Decatur, he was taken prisoner by the British when the *President* was taken in battle and sent to Bermuda until the end of the war. In 1815, again serving under Decatur, he saw action against Barbary pirates and received a Turkish saber from Decatur for bravery during the capture of an Algerian frigate. In 1824 was promoted to Lieutenant and by 1844 he had risen to the rank of Commander. He saw further action protecting American citizens in Nicaragua in 1855.

He spoke briefly to the assembled crew stating his intention to make the cruise as pleasant as possible and that he expected the men to do their duty. At noon, five days later, the vessel steamed gracefully downriver and anchored off the Battery. It was the beginning of an eventful voyage designed to "...pay courtesy and diplomatic calls at the different ports as needs and necessity required." A voyage that would take the ship first to Mexico and from there across the Atlantic to duty with the Mediterranean Squadron. A voyage that would end abruptly with the news of the fall of Fort Sumter and the threat to Burton's 'glorious Union' from the fledgling Confederacy.

On August 24, the *Susquehanna* weighed anchor and sailed for her first port of call, Vera Cruz, Mexico. Eleven days later she hove to and let go her anchor four miles from that city. For almost a month the *Susquehanna* idled at her moorings. During this time she was battered by a terrific storm, beginning on September 18 and lasting for four days. Gale force winds heavy seas and torrential rain buffeted the ship, causing the vessel to drag her anchors. On October 1 a seaman was court martialled for drunkenness, disobeying orders and using threatening language to a superior officer. He was found guilty and sentenced to a month's solitary confinement in double irons on bread and water plus the loss of one month's pay.

On October 8, following a medical inspection, nine members of the crew were pronounced as unfit for service and were put aboard the *Savannah,* which was bound for New York, sailing on October 19. The same day the *Susquehanna* steamed for Key West, Florida. After an eight-day stopover, during which the ship took on coal and supplies, the *Susquehanna* headed out into the broad waters of the Atlantic, bound for the Mediterranean. For several days the vessel passed through severe gales, these eventually dissipated and at midday on Wednesday November 11, the steamer ran past the Hamilton Lighthouse off Bermuda.

Four days later the bark *Release* bound from Boston with supplies for the Mediterranean Squadron was sighted and both ships hove to. The latest newspapers and letters were transferred to the *Susquehanna* and the vessels proceeded on their journey, the *Susquehanna* soon leaving the *Release* in her wake.

Religious worship aboard ship was mandatory, but many sailors openly embraced the religious services and instruction. Private Burton relates a typical Sabbath on board the *Susquehanna.* "At 10am the bell tolls – 'tis the hour for divine service; we all lay aft and what a scene meets our eyes. The capstan serves as an altar, there leans our chaplain in the attitude of prayer, his hair is white with the snows of sixty or more winters, while his countenance beams with manliness and Christian meekness, he loves the sailors' cause and strives hard to do his duty to them as regards their temporal and spiritual welfare.

"The service commences with reading a portion of Scripture. Then a prayer is offered up in our behalf, (not forgetting our beloved friends at home) also for our beloved country; then officers and men listen to an excellent discourse, after which a hymn is sung, accompanied by our band. Then books and papers are distributed, meetings appointed for the coming week, the doxology is sung, a benediction pronounced, and then all hands are piped down; the rest of the day is passed very quietly, and according to the inclination of all concerned. In the evening a few meet together in the Yeoman's storeroom, where a prayer meeting is held for our men, then all hands, except the watch, go to their hammocks. Thus ends a Sabbath at sea."

Eighteen days and some 3,700 miles from Key West, the Portuguese island of Madeira was sighted. A steady five hours cruising along its shores, with high craggy mountains forming a dramatic backdrop, ended with the *Susquehanna* dropping anchor off the city of Funchal. The crew were given 24 hours liberty and Burton took this opportunity to explore some of the island. He was suitably impressed by "...the streams of pure water running down the mountainsides...the well paved and clean streets." The chief curiosity of the town, a convent, contained a chamber, which was covered with the skulls and bones of all the holy men who had lived and died on the island.

Captain George Hollins. Upon returning to America he resigned his commission and joined the Confederate Navy.
US Naval Historical Center

One of the crew however, was fated never to leave Madeira. Michael Dean, a 35 year-old boatswains mate from New York, died from a severe bout of diarrhea and was interred with full military honors in the small cemetery adjoining the British-built Episcopal Church. With supplies replenished the *Susquehanna* sailed for Gibraltar on November 27. The anchor was let go in Gibraltar Bay in the forenoon of the 30th. 'The Rock' was the bastion of British influence in the Mediterranean; the fortifications mounted 1,800 pieces of artillery, ensuring it was virtually impregnable to direct assault.

It was a time of anxiety for many aboard the *Susquehanna,* the lack of news regarding the situation at home played on the minds of both officers and seamen. First Lieutenant James Jones, commander of the Marine Guard voiced his fears over the growing political crisis in a letter to his brother in Delaware:

"We are all very anxious to hear the result of the election. I cannot bring myself to believe that Lincoln will be successful. If he is, I am fearful that the South will begin to put her threats into execution. However, in a week or so, I suppose we shall get the news out here."

He would not have long to wait, for even as the sloop lay in the shadow of the Great Rock dispatches brought aboard informed Captain Hollins of the election of Abraham Lincoln to the Presidency. The South would be quick to react. Fearing the actions of a sectional Republican administration, many felt separation to be the only option. South Carolina was the first to act, signing an 'Ordinance of Secession' in Charleston, 'Dissolving the Union between the State of South Carolina and the Federal government.' As more states south of the Mason–Dixon line followed South Carolina's example, militia companies began mustering in towns and cities, determined to safeguard their new Confederacy.

Unaware of the war fever sweeping America, the *Susquehanna* weighed anchor on December 2, 1860, leaving Gibraltar behind and making for the port of Spezia in the Bay of Sardinia. Steaming past the islands of Minorca, Majorca and Ibiza and the island of Corsica – birthplace of Napoleon Bonaparte – the ship came to anchor at three in the morning on December 6. As was customary, the *Susquehanna* was boarded by the local health inspector who found one of the crew – an engineer named Hubbard – sick with cholera. Immediately a quarantine flag was hoisted and officers and crew were confined to the ship.

The following day whilst mooring ship a hawser snapped. The parting of the powerful line injured several seamen, one sustaining two broken legs. Such were the everyday hazards of life aboard ship.

On December 12 the flagship of the Mediterranean Squadron, the *Richmond* with Commodore Bell aboard arrived and dropped anchor, the *Susquehanna* firing the customary salute. A new surgeon joined the ship along with Captain Jones of the US Marines. Three sailors and one marine were invalided following a medical inspection and were shipped aboard the *Release*, due to sail for New York. And finally, after 11 days the yellow quarantine flag was hauled down, the *Susquehanna* having a clean bill of health.

On Christmas Eve at four in the morning in stormy weather, the *Susquehanna's* anchor chains rattled through the hawseholes as she set off for Naples, her next port of call. Christmas morning with the weather still thoroughly disagreeable found the steamer on course for the Neapolitan capital and the crew was given a ration of rum with which to 'splice the mainbrace.' By nine o'clock that night the ship had reached the bay of Naples and before them, dwarfed by Mount Vesuvius lay, according to Amos Burton "...the finest city on the station." Going ashore the Bostonian took in the sights, touring the city and the ruins of Pompeii and Herculaneum. The following day the ship was prepared for receiving visitors from the various British, French and Sardinian warships riding at anchor in the bay and salutes were fired honoring various flags and admirals.

New Year's Day 1861 was signaled with the ringing of church bells in the city. Many visitors ascended the tumblehome of the *Susquehanna* during the day and the ship's band played suitable airs. On January 8 a sudden squall blew up and the ship was caught with her sails hanging loose for drying. As the ship began to drag her anchor the command to "let go" the second anchor rang out, but still the vessel drifted towards the shore. The firemen below worked desperately to raise steam and with the ship just four feet from the breakwater and about to run aground on the jagged rocks the *Susquehanna* finally answered the helm. As Burton wrote later "...our noble ship steamed quickly out of all danger amid the hearty cheers of a multitude of witnesses on shore. We soon got our sheet anchors in readiness, and anchored in a safer position."

At noon on January 11 after 16 days in Naples, the ship weighed anchor in pleasant weather bound for a rendezvous with the *Richmond* at Messina, which haven was reached at eight the next morning. Those members of the crew who were not granted liberty while the *Susquehanna* was in Naples, disembarked for a spot of shore leave in Calabria. A reminder to all on board of the problems at home came with the recall to the United States of one of the Mediterranean Squadron's officers, a Captain Ingraham. His crime – expressing a little too loudly his secessionist sympathies. After a brief five days the ship headed out to sea again leaving the sloop *Richmond* at Messina. The *Susquehanna's* destination being Beirut, Syria.

Arriving at the Syrian capital after an uncomfortable six day voyage in heavy seas the ship paused for a week, departing on the last day of January during a storm, with the American consul, a Mr Johnson, on board. Captain Hollins' orders were to transport the diplomat to the island of Cyprus on official business and the *Susquehanna* came to anchor off the town of Larnica at noon the following day. The consuls of France, Great Britain and Sardinia joined Mr Johnson on the *Susquehanna* and a party was given for the ship's officers that evening at the French consulate.

The American consul was taken ashore at Latikia, Syria on the evening of February 3 for a brief visit. Upon his return the vessel proceeded to Tripoli, which place she arrived at 8am the next morning. Retracing her course the ship returned to Beirut where Mr Johnson took his leave of the *Susquehanna*. Departing the Syrian port in the early hours of the fifth, the sloop proceeded along the Syrian and Palestinian coast and Mount Carmel was sighted about 10am, and the ship came to anchor in the Bay of Acre. Here a party of sailors went ashore with the intention of visiting the holy city of Jerusalem but owing to heavy rains, which washed out many roads they only succeeded in reaching the town of Nazareth.

Within two days the *Susquehanna* lay at anchor in the Egyptian port of Alexandria where the American consul paid a brief visit to the ship. Alexandria was a busy, bustling port; its harbor crowded with the vessels of many nations and the large navy yard was a forest of masts. The warships were mainly French and British, both nations having strong commercial interests in the Middle East. On February 11 the ship took on coal. A grand party was held at the British consulate that evening and many of the *Susquehanna's* officers attended. Several spent their time ashore exploring the sights of Cairo and Suez.

February 22, George Washington's birthday and a national holiday. The ship was bedecked with bunting and flags of all nations. With all loose gear squared away on the quarterdeck, preparations were put in hand for a party to be hosted by Captain Hollins and his officers that evening. Guests began arriving at two o'clock that afternoon and with the band playing American, French and English airs the feasting and festivities continued until nine o'clock when fire-rockets lit up the night sky, signaling the conclusion of the party.

At noon the next day after more than two weeks in Alexandria, the ship sailed again for Tripoli. The short journey was not to pass without incident. Engine failure the next morning forced the *Susquehanna* to heave to for four hours while repairs were carried out and that same afternoon John Thompson, a seaman from Rhode Island died suddenly following a short illness. At midday on the 26th following the burial service conducted by Captain Hollins, Thompson's remains were consigned to the deep.

The *Susquehanna* arrived at Tripoli the following afternoon and after a two hour stopover during which the American consul came on board for a brief meeting with Captain Hollins, was under way again, destination Malta. There the steamer dropped anchor in Valetta Harbor on the afternoon of the February 28, after giving and receiving the customary salutes from the British shore batteries and ships. Burton logged an unfortunate accident that evening involving British seamen from the *Caesar.* Apparently a small party, probably the worse for drink "...were returning from shore in a small boat, when a quarrel sprung up between them, upsetting the boat and drowning three of them. Our boats were lowered and went to their assistance and saved all but the three mentioned; their bodies were found and buried on the island."

On March 6 the *Susquehanna* was ordered to Messina, Sicily, encountering rough weather throughout the voyage. Italy was embroiled in its own civil war, and the Neapolitan forces of King Bomba were fighting a losing battle against Garibaldi's revolutionaries, championing the cause of King Victor Emanuel. The crew of the *Susquehanna* which had dropped anchor

The *Susquehanna* and the *Congress* in Naples Bay, Italy in 1857. The *Congress* would be destroyed by the Confederate ironclad *Virginia* in Hampton Roads in 1862.
US Naval Historical Center

A view looking forward, of the crew of the *Susquehanna* exercising at the guns.
Library of Congress

near the American flagship *Richmond,* had a grandstand view as the Sardinian fleet sailed in to attack King Bomba's troops holding the forts which guarded the Straits of Messina. The bombardment was spectacular but caused few casualties, but at daylight on March 14 the garrisons in the strongpoints capitulated.

Yet another entry in the ship's log recorded the death of a shipmate five days later when Joseph Cardona, an engineer's steward expired from what Burton termed "...stricture of the bowels." Coincidentally the deceased had relatives in the city and his body was turned over to them for burial. Sailing next for Naples the *Susquehanna* came to anchor in the bay on March 21, landing some broken machinery from the *Richmond* for repair.

When expected orders to sail for home failed to materialize, Hollins next steamed for the Sardinian port of Spezia, coming to anchor near the gunboat *Iroquois* on the 25th. On the last day of the month, a beautiful Easter Sunday, many of the crew attended a church service ashore. The *Iroquois* left that evening for Naples. The *Susquehanna* also quit Spezia four days later for the short run to Genoa on the Italian mainland. Genoa's famed architectural delights, including its opera houses, theatres, public gardens, squares and promenades much impressed Amos Burton. Sailing from Genoa, the *Susquehanna* arrived at Leghorn on April 12, 1861.

In the early hours of that morning, half a world away, the guns ringing Charleston Harbor opened fire on the outnumbered and outgunned Federal garrison in Fort Sumter. Rhetoric had given way to rage. As the iron projectiles rained down on the fort, all chances of a peaceful settlement of the sectional differences between North and South disappeared. The issue could no longer be settled with compromise, only with blood and fire. News of the fall of Sumter reached the ship on May 3 together with orders for Hollins to report to Commodore Bell at Naples. In compliance with these instructions, the ship ran out to sea at 9am, arriving the same evening.

Burton wrote in his journal "...arrived at this port at 5.30pm, and our worst fears are realized. Our orders are to make a cruise, for the purpose of delivering orders to the gunboat *Iroquois,* and then return to the United States with all dispatch. It was with feelings of sorrow that we heard of the distracted state of affairs at home; we hoped ere this that a civil war would be averted.

We remained only one hour at Naples; weighed anchor and took our leave of this beautiful city. The weather is stormy, the sea rough, but off we go!" Indeed, the conditions were so bad that all other vessels were confined to the port, but the *Susquehanna,* her powerful paddles churning through the waves beat out to sea. Arriving at the Spanish port of Cadiz on May 13, she coaled and provisioned for the homeward journey, sailing from Cadiz five days later. This would be her last touching point before reaching America, and Burton hinted at the troubles on the horizon when he wrote "...started for the United States, but with unpleasant feelings, as each day has revealed secessionist principles among a large number of our officers. A large number will be likely to resign when we reach home."

The air of gloom and despondency aboard ship deepened when a fatal accident occurred below decks claiming the life of George Brown, a fireman. He slipped and fractured his skull on a beam while passing through a part of the ships' engine room. The 27 year-old from Flushing, Long Island was buried at sea and Burton eloquently recounted the sombre ritual of the burial service. "The body is carried to the quarterdeck, covered with the Stars and Stripes. Our band plays a funeral dirge, after which the burial service is read by the Executive Officer and at the words 'we commit his body to the deep' the corpse is raised, a gentle push causes it to glide into the dark blue waves; a splash, then a few bubbles, caused by the body going down, and the remains of poor George disappear from his shipmates; all hands are piped down, the ship moves on and our companion of yesterday sleeps his last sleep amid the coral and seaweed of the ocean. The waves shall sing his requiem!"

On May 24 a schooner was sighted bound from Halifax to Jamaica, but upon being hailed, her captain had no news of importance for Hollins. At midday on June 4, amid humid and showery conditions off Sandy Hook, the vessel took aboard a pilot who reported to Captain Hollins with orders for the *Susquehanna* to make for Boston and not as originally intended, New York. Two days later, to the cheers and huzzahs emanating from the crews of the steamers moored at the wharf, and from soldiers in volunteer encampments and the crowds ashore, the ship entered Boston Bay, and by 9.30am was anchored off the Charlestown Navy Yard.

Burton closed this part of his journal with the following. "To me, a Boston man I felt proud, and although a wanderer in foreign climes and Italian scenes I now fully realized the expression. 'There's no place like home' ...we have cruised 24,585 miles, entered 25 different ports and extended the cruise as far as Syria, in the Holy Land. There have been many changes among the crew; two of our shipmates have found a grave in foreign land, and two others have been consigned to a watery grave; a few have deserted from the ship, and a few more have been discharged.

"With few exceptions the general health of the crew has been good. Our officers, with few exceptions, have been uniformally kind and obliging to the ship's company. But deplorable as it is, secession principles are rank among a large number of our best officers, and they will probably resign. Should we meet them again it will be in open hostility. We experienced severe storms and heavy seas, yet our noble ship carried us safely through, and we feel grateful for all blessings bestowed."

In the months to come the fortitude and patience of the *Susquehanna's* crew would be tested often. Their duties would not just be confined to the seaman's constant battle with the elements, but against a brave and determined foe and the wily skippers of the blockade-runners supplying their enemy's wants and needs.

INTO BATTLE!

Amos Burton's misgivings regarding the loyalty of certain of the *Susquehanna's* officers proved accurate. Her commanding officer Captain Hollins, Lieutenant J. N. Barney, Felix Senlac (the ship's paymaster), four forward officers and four midshipmen resigned from the Navy. All would take up arms with the Confederacy. For Hollins, a well-liked and much revered officer, it must have been a heart-breaking decision.

On June 12, 1861, Captain John A. Chauncey received orders from the Secretary of the Navy, Gideon Welles, directing him to proceed to Charlestown Navy Yard, there to take command of the *Susquehanna*, which by July 1 had been thoroughly overhauled and made ready for sea. From there he was to proceed for duty with Flag Officer William Mervine's Gulf Blockading Squadron. The warship's batteries now consisted of fifteen 8-inch smoothbores plus two 12-pound and one 24-pound howitzer.

As to the *Susquehanna*'s new skipper, Burton wrote: "Of our captain and executive officer we know nothing, but it is said that coming events cast their shadows before them. We are reminded, by the introduction of four new sweat-boxes, that a new mode of punishment is on hand for all victims falling under their displeasure."

The *Susquehanna*'s new commander had joined the Navy on New Year's Day 1812. He first served as a midshipman aboard the *Peacock*, attached to Commodore Porter's West India Squadron. In August 1822 the *Peacock* captured several pirate schooners off Bahia Honda, Cuba and Chauncey was placed in command of one of these prizes. It almost proved to be his undoing. An outbreak of Yellow Fever carried off more than 40 of the crew, Chauncey being the only officer to remain on duty. Following this narrow brush with death, he received a commission as acting lieutenant from Commodore Porter and transferred to the schooner *Grampus.* In 1824, Chauncey found himself on board the sloop *Ontario* and as a full lieutenant served for two years with the Mediterranean Squadron.

On September 8, 1841 he received his commission as commander, taking charge of the sloop *Vandalia* sailing with the West Indies and Home Squadrons. There followed a spell of shore duty as Inspector of Ordnance in Washington from 1847 to 1850. He was promoted to captain on September 14, 1855. A strict disciplinarian, the new skipper was to prove a hard taskmaster and would be the cause of much resentment among the ship's company with his martinet ways.

Also joining the *Susquehanna* was Lieutenant John Bankhead, coming aboard as Chauncey's executive officer and Washington Irving the new Paymaster. At seven in the morning of July 3, the *Susquehanna* sailed under sealed orders, the weather was pleasant but cool, and as the steamer slipped from her berth Burton noted that "...our ship was cheered on all sides, and promptly responded to by our gallant tars." The following day being Independence Day, it was celebrated aboard with the firing of a national salute at midday and by splicing the mainbrace in the evening.

Two days later at four in the afternoon the starboard water wheel shaft snapped without warning. As the ship slewed to a standstill, the anchor was immediately let go. Throughout the night the ship's firemen worked to make running repairs sufficient to allow the vessel to be towed into Hampton Roads. Chauncey reported the incident to his immediate superior, Flag Officer Stringham commanding the Hampton Roads Blockading Squadron, and suggested the ship sail for New York as soon as possible to affect a speedy repair. However, in a communication from the Navy Department to Stringham dated July 15, it was decided to send the *Susquehanna* instead to the navy yard at her home port of Philadelphia. In accordance with these instructions the ship sailed from Hampton Roads two days later.

Propelled by one paddle wheel, Chauncey's crippled vessel came to anchor opposite Fort Miflin on the Delaware River where the *Susquehanna*'s powder was off loaded, then on to Philadelphia which place was reached on July 19. The journey had not been without incident and two vessels were stopped and boarded. The bark *Pericles*, out of Boston and carrying a cargo of guano from Callao and the brig *J. Rhoades* of New York, bound for Fortress Monroe laden with government stores. Chauncey endorsed the papers of both vessels and the ships were allowed to proceed.

For seven weeks the *Susquehanna* was laid up while a new shaft was fitted and other mechanical repairs were carried out. It was while languishing in Philadelphia that Chauncey's ill temper rose to the surface. The mood among the crew blackened as the actions of this petty martinet threatened to destroy the morale of the ship's company. The Marine Guard suffered more than most, with Chauncey assigning them to duties that were normally the province of the sailors. Many transfer requests were written and submitted to the officer commanding the *Susquehanna*'s marines, Lieutenant Philip Fendall, but Chauncey refused to endorse them. Eventually, four marines took matters into their own hands. On July 23 they took advantage of a day's shore leave and made for Washington where Marine Colonel Commandant Harris listened to the men's grievances and reported their complaints to Secretary Gideon Welles at the Navy Department.

Harris also wrote to Lieutenant Fendall, initially authorizing the men's transfer requests. But Welles, whilst sympathetic, felt that he could not agree with the marines' transfer, stating: "I am apprehensive that this action will tend to demoralization in the service. That the men have cause for their conduct may be true but discipline and order must be maintained." The marines were ordered to report back to the *Susquehanna*.

Worse was to follow. At a summary court-martial, two marines and two seamen were sentenced to 30 days' solitary confinement. Normally this would have been spent in the ship's brig. However, for the four unfortunates,

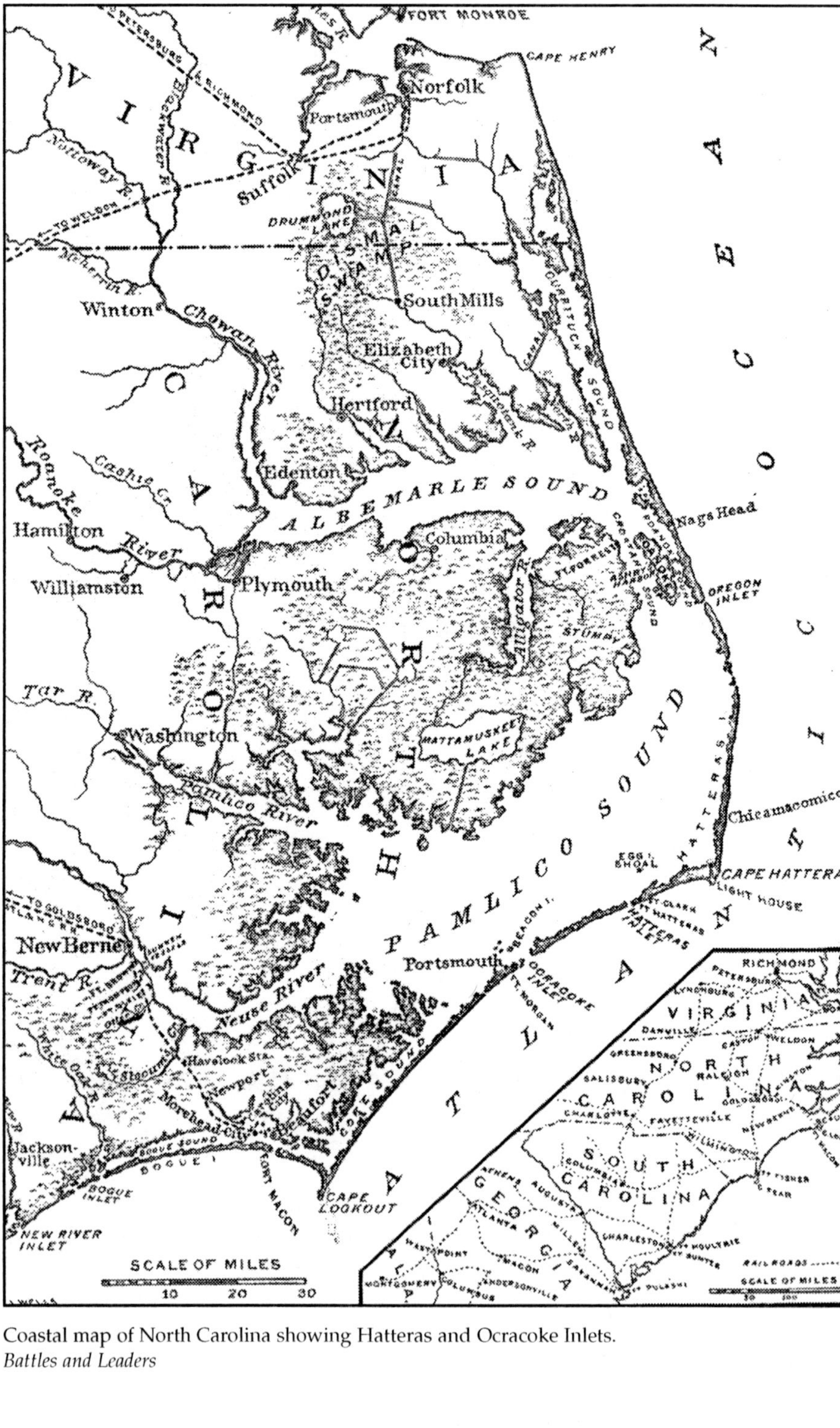

Coastal map of North Carolina showing Hatteras and Ocracoke Inlets.
Battles and Leaders

Rear-Admiral Silas Stringham, commander of the Hatteras expedition.
Battles and Leaders

Federal troops land and form up on the beach at Hatteras Inlet while the Union fleet opens fire on the Rebel works The *Susquehanna* appears on the right of the engraving.
Battles and Leaders

it meant 16 hours a day incarcerated in Chauncey's iron sweat boxes.

As Burton wrote: "Our new captain, on account of his unfortunate and disagreeable disposition, has made himself very unpopular with the crew: so much so, that complaints were sent to Washington, in consequence of which a court of inquiry has been held. The results of which have not been made known. He is to go out with the ship."

On July 31, Chauncey received fresh instructions from Washington; he was now to make for Hampton Roads as soon as the *Susquehanna* was ready for sea. There the warship was to form part of Flag Officer Stringham's squadron which was making preparations for a combined operation with 880 Union troops under the command of Major-General Benjamin Butler; their task was the seizure of two Confederate forts on Hatteras Inlet. On August 24, the *Susquehanna* weighed anchor and headed for the open ocean once more, pausing only to take on powder at Fort Miflin and then on to Fortress Monroe which she reached on the 27th, only to discover that the fleet had sailed two days earlier.

Off the Cape Henry Light the *Susquehanna* hove to in order to allow the captain of the *Quaker City*, a large schooner rigged side-wheel steamer of 1,600 tons, to clamber onto the quarterdeck with a dispatch from the commodore. The *Susquehanna* was to proceed with all haste to join Stringham, currently lying off Hatteras Inlet with his fleet of warships and transports, making preparations to attack the two Confederate forts.

The origins of this operation lay with General-in-Chief of the Army, Winfield Scott. Reluctant to commit half-trained and ill-prepared armies of volunteer soldiers to an all-out invasion of the South, he formulated a strategy that called for a two-pronged Northern offensive. Scott envisaged a river campaign along the Mississippi, designed to split the Confederacy in two, coupled with a naval blockade of Southern sea ports, denying the Rebels the importation of much needed supplies and munitions and the reciprocal exportation of cotton, tobacco and rice to pay for these goods.

The so-called 'Anaconda Plan' if pursued rigorously, would slowly but surely strangle the South. To carry out this grandiose scheme and enforce the blockade of over 3,400 miles of enemy coastline was an impossible task for the Federal Navy of early 1861. Its handful of modern, ocean-going warships were scattered on various stations all round the world and even with the recall of most of these vessels, the Navy was still woefully understrength in ships and men. However, President Lincoln convened a board of officers to determine a plan of operations to reduce and capture Confederate fortifications and harbors. This board consisted of Captain Samuel Du Pont and Captain Charles Davis of the Navy, Major John Barnard of the Army, and Professor Alexander Bache of the Coast Survey.

They faced an awesome task. The Atlantic coast from the mouth of the Rio Grande to Chesapeake Bay was riddled with inlets, many protected by natural shoals and sandbanks which the large Union cruisers could not enter for fear of grounding. In June 1861 the board presented their findings to the President. They had graded their targets, taking into account their geographical peculiarities, the strength of their defenses and their value to the Southern cause.

They chose as their primary target Hatteras Inlet, North Carolina. It was guarded by two log and earthwork redoubts, both still under construction. They were sited on the tip of a 40-mile long by half a mile-wide

The *Susquehanna* in the thick of the action as the Union fleet pours in fire on Forts Hatteras and Clark, the sloop is second from the right.
Battles and Leaders

A wartime sketch showing Fort Hatteras.
Battles and Leaders

strip of barren land, which commanded the entrance to Pamlico and Albermarle Sounds. These in turn opened out into the rivers Neuse, Roanoke, Pamlico and Chowan, giving easy access deep into the interior to the constant stream of shallow-draft schooners and steamers carrying their vital cargoes to the Confederacy.

Fort Hatteras, a 250 foot-square redoubt protected the eastern side of the channel and mounted twelve 32-pounder smoothbores; roughly one and a half miles to the east the smaller Fort Clark, with five 32-pounders and two small 6-pounders faced directly out to sea. Both forts boasted bombproof shelters, and with the approach of Stringham's fleet, the garrisons had been reinforced. Almost 700 men commanded by Flag Officer Samuel Barron of the Confederate Navy, whose headquarters were in Fort Hatteras, stood ready to defend their posts.

Silas Stringham's squadron consisted of the steam frigates *Minnesota* (flagship) 46 guns, *Wabash*, also 46 guns, the sloops *Cumberland*, 24 guns and *Pawnee*, 10 guns and the gunboats *Harriet Lane*, 5 guns and *Monticello*, six 8-inch guns. At 10 o'clock on the morning of August 28, the *Susquehanna* arrived

Fort Clark. A sketch made after the capture of the fort.
Battle and Leaders

off Hatteras to the sound of gunfire. Stringham's fleet was already in action. Chauncey signaled the *Susquehanna*'s arrival to the flagship reporting that she was "...ready for service." Preparations for battle were evident, as Burton recorded, "...from the busy movements of the gunner and his mates it is evident that there is some work ahead that we have not yet experienced."

By 10am the *Wabash* and the *Cumberland* had approached within range of Fort Clark and began pouring in rapid and accurate broadsides. The *Susquehanna* soon joined the action, opening fire with her starboard battery. Burton recalled: "All hands were called to general quarters and as we came up to where the fleet lay we were signalized to join in the bombardment... our position taken close in, we opened fire at 11am. Our first shot went into one of the ill-fated forts. The firing was continued at intervals during the day... the forts did not return a brisk fire. A few of their shots passed over us and many fell short." At 11.30am, covered by the guns of the fleet, General Butler attempted to land his men some two miles above the forts. They disembarked from the transport vessels *Fanny*, *Adelaide* and *George Peabody* into launches and cutters supplied by the fleet. However, Stringham had not taken into account the powerful Atlantic surf crashing onto the beach, making the landing of small craft extremely hazardous.

Consequently many of the launches and iron surfboats were swamped and it was only with great difficulty that some 300 soldiers splashed ashore soaked to the skin, with no provisions and with their munitions rendered almost useless. Attempts to land the remainder were aborted until the morrow. Observing the Army's problems, Stringham's fleet closed with the forts and employed a tactic used successfully by the Allied fleets against Russian fortifications in the Crimean War seven years earlier. Stringham kept his ships in constant motion, passing and repassing the enemy's works at differing ranges, thereby rendering the task of the Confederate gunners to lay down an accurate counter battery fire almost impossible.

The defenders of Fort Clark having expended their ammunition were driven to the safety of the bombproof by the sustained fire from the fleet. Just after midday, with the flags of both forts shot away, the garrison was observed fleeing from their batteries towards Fort Hatteras. An hour and a half later those Union troops who had made it ashore occupied the deserted works. Their tenure was short-lived, as shells from the fleet whistling overhead towards Fort Hatteras, were landing in close proximity to the fallen Fort Clark. Deciding prudence outweighed a comfortable billet, the soldiers withdrew to pass a miserable night without food, water or shelter on the narrow beach. Compounding the hapless soldiers predicament the weather worsened, forcing the covering gunboats to withdraw to the safety of deeper water leaving the Union troops without their support and vulnerable to attack should the Rebels decide to sortie out from Fort Hatteras.

At 8am on the 29th, in perfect weather conditions, the Federal fleet resumed the bombardment on Fort Hatteras, the *Susquehanna* being the first vessel to open up. Firing at extreme range, the initial shots from the fleet fell short, but the problem was solved by elevating the pivot guns to maximum height and sending a plunging fire down into the fort, dismounting two pieces of heavy ordnance. The Rebel gunners were soon driven from their weapons and sought shelter in an earthen bombproof. Burton witnessed the terrific deluge of shot and shell raining down on the Confederate position. "The gunboats moved in close, and gave a raking fire. The fort returns the fire slowly – then falters – while the entire fleet pours in torrents of shells upon them. The *Susquehanna* did splendid execution with her pivot guns, having moved as near to the beach as the depth of water would permit. The enemy directed most of his shot towards this ship, but fortunately without doing any injury. Many of them passed through the rigging over our heads, while others fell short."

A Confederate officer inside the battered fort recounted: "The shower of shell in half an hour became literally tremendous, falling into and immediately around the works not less, on an average, than ten each minute, and, the sea being smooth, the firing was remarkably accurate. One of the officers counted twenty eight shells, and several others counted as many as twenty falling a minute." One shot pierced the bombproof in which most of the garrison had taken shelter. The men panicked and scrambled out into the daylight, fearful of the consequences should a Yankee shell ignite the fort's magazine, separated from the shelter by a thin wall of earth. As the defenders emerged, they were faced with the maelstrom of incoming rounds from the Union fleet; bursting over their heads or plummeting down to explode inside the fort.

The result of this one sided fight was not long in doubt. Following a hurried council with his subordinate officers, Barron decided to seek terms for capitulation. At 11am a white flag appeared over Fort Hatteras, the Federal fleet immediately ceased fire. Faced with Stringham and Butler's demands for unconditional surrender, Barron had little choice but to accede. Confederate gunboats in the sound observing the fall of the fort, fled upriver as Butler's bedraggled bluecoats took possession and the Stars and Stripes were soon flying over the captured post.

The entire Confederate garrison fell prisoner and were taken on board the *Minnesota* which sailed for New York, there the Rebels were confined on Governor's Island. Despite the ferocity of the bombardment damage to the forts was limited and casualties remarkably light. The Confederates lost four men killed and approximately 25 wounded while the Union squadron emerged largely unscathed and suffered no casualties.

In his report written after the engagement and while a prisoner on the *Minnesota*, Flag Officer Barron paid due testament to the performance of the

Federal fleet. "During the first hour the shells of the ships fell short, we only firing occasionally to ascertain whether our shots would reach them, and wishing to reserve our very limited supply of ammunition until the vessels might find it necessary to come nearer in; but they, after some practice, got the exact range of the 9, 10, and 11-inch guns, and did not find it necessary to alter their positions, while not a shot from our battery reached them with the greatest elevation we could get. This state of things – with shells bursting over and in the fort every few seconds – having continued for about three hours, the men were directed to take shelter under the parapet and traverses, and I called a council of officers, at which it was unanimously agreed that holding out longer could only result in a greater loss of life..."

The next day with Colonel Hawkins' New York Zouaves garrisoning the fallen works, several of the *Susquehanna*'s officers were rowed ashore to inspect the forts and hunt for souvenirs. Lieutenant Bankhead returned with two battle flags and Burton describes them thus; "...one of them, a colour standard made of heavy twilled silk, fringed with gold. The colours were red and white, the Union blue, having a star on each side. One of the sides had the following inscription: 'Presented by the Ladies of Shiloah, Camden County, to the North Carolina Defenders'. Over the star was 'May 20th 1775' and underneath 'May 20th 1861'. The letters and stars were of gold gilt and very beautifully executed. The other trophy was a silk flag, bearing the following inscription; 'Independent Greys, Aug. 1st, 1859'. The Union bore nine stars, being the number of states in the Confederacy at that time."

There was a sad postscript to the expedition for the crew of the *Susquehanna*. That afternoon the *Harriet Lane* had run aground on a shoal and attempts were being made to free her using boats and cutters manned by sailors from the fleet, one of these small boats was the first cutter from the *Susquehanna*. The weather was foul with a heavy sea running and a seaman named Simon Huttleson, from Rhode Island, was swept out of the cutter and drowned. The stranded vessel finally floated clear but only after all her ordnance except one 11-inch gun; all her coal and most of her provisions had been cast overboard.

COASTAL PATROL

With the fall of the forts, Hatteras Inlet was closed to blockade-runners and Confederate privateers. It would provide the Federal Navy with a base on the enemy coast where supplies and coal would be available for the blockading ships, thus enabling them to maintain station at sea for longer periods. The battle had demonstrated that naval gunfire alone was capable of reducing shore batteries and the speed and skill which Stringham's squadron exhibited in reducing the forts without incurring a single fatality paved the way for future actions against sea-coast fortifications.

Both Butler and Stringham headed for Washington, each keen to gain the kudos for the success of the engagement. Both overlooked some pertinent facts. The weakness of the rebel works – neither was finished; both were badly sited in exposed positions and were poorly armed – the old smoothbores in the forts were outranged by the guns of the Federal fleet. Barron's powder had been badly affected by the moist conditions of the coastal region, so much so that it would hardly propel the charges Also, in this first combined operation, the Army had proved more of a hindrance than a help, and against a more determined foe, Butler's stranded and unsupported troops might have faced defeat and capture, thus jeopardizing the whole expedition.

Stringham ordered Chauncey to patrol the vicinity of Cape Hatteras with a view to afford assistance and protection should the Confederates attempt to recapture the two forts. From her station off the inlet the *Susquehanna* also beat out to sea daily in search of blockade-runners. On 9am on September 1, a ship was sighted and the *Susquehanna,* together with the gunboat *Monticello* sailed in pursuit, overhauling the vessel at midday. She proved to be the *Abie Bradford* from Boston. Taken by the Rebel raider *Sumter,* she had been recaptured by the *Powhatan,* and with a prize crew from the Union warship aboard, the vessel was now making for Philadelphia. Two further ships were challenged and boarded that afternoon, both proved to be Union merchantmen.

That evening the *Susquehanna* returned to Hatteras Inlet. The next day all was activity and bustle ashore. The Federal soldiers were busy making good the damage to the forts and remounting the guns. Some 200 local citizens appeared to take the oath of allegiance, while officers from the *Susquehanna* brought back a 68-pound solid shot fired from the forward pivot which had dismounted one of the enemy's guns during the fight, also wounding several men.

On the 4th one of the ship's company had a lucky escape. Burton recalls: "Thomas Goulding fell from the foreyard this morning, but fortunately into the water: he was soon rescued without suffering any injury." The next morning the ship proceeded down the coast to the Rebel town of Portsmouth near Ocracoke Inlet. In a bid to confuse shore-based observers she approached flying English colors. Heaving to off the town, the *Susquehanna* hauled down the foreign flag and ran up the Stars and Stripes. A shot from one of the pivot guns was fired in the general direction of the hamlet and a small steamer was seen to rapidly make tracks into the shallow waters of the sound to seek refuge. The acting master of the *Susquehanna* was sent to take soundings and reported that up to one mile from the beach the depth of water reached four fathoms. Her mission completed, the *Susquehanna* returned to Hatteras Inlet.

At daybreak on the 5th, the warship captured her first blockade-runner. Burton left the following account. "Weighed anchor at 5 o'clock this morning and steamed south-west; at 10 o'clock three sails were reported, we went in pursuit; overhauled the schooner *Prince Alfred*, from Antigua, boarded her, and not finding her papers correct, made a prize of her sending her to Hampton Roads, under charge of a prize crew and taking her own crew aboard this ship. She was loaded with sugar, salt, coffee and fruit."

That same afternoon the schooner *Louisa Agnes* from Lunenburg was overhauled. She carried a cargo of fish. Chauncey spent several hours examining her papers, and although deeply suspicious of her true intentions, gave her the benefit of the doubt and allowed her to proceed, with a strong warning not to again be seen south of Hatteras Inlet. Both vessels had been displaying English colors. On the 7th the *Susquehanna* bespoke the English corvette *Rinaldo*. Her captain was invited on board the *Susquehanna* and while in conversation with Chauncey, stated that there were two ships loading with cargo at Beaufort, North Carolina, awaiting their chance to make a run for the open sea. After an hour, the Englishman headed north, taking with him the *Susquehanna's* mail. At 6pm Chauncey's vessel came to anchor off Fort Macon, North Carolina.

The steamer continued the perpetual search for vessels attempting to slip into and out of the small estuaries along the coast. On Tuesday the 10th, a sail was sighted just before noon and the *Susquehanna* gave chase. It turned out to be a fruitless effort, the vessel was the schooner *Yarmouth*, and she was under the guns of the Union gunboat *Cambridge*. The Yankee warship had taken her as a prize and as her crew was transferred aboard the *Susquehanna*, Chauncey was not too surprised to find the captain and crew of the *Louisa Agnes* among the prisoners. Her skipper had obviously ignored Chauncey's advice and his ship had been snapped up by the *Cambridge* while attempting to pass through the blockade.

The latter part of the day was to prove an eventful one for the *Susquehanna*. A steamer was sighted and a warning shot from Chauncey's ship halted the stranger. She proved to be the *Rhode Island*, out of New York and bound for Key West, she carried mail for the warship, which was gladly received by the crew. Then, at approximately nine thirty in the evening off Beaufort, the *Susquehanna* collided with the gunboat *Flag*. Such was the force of the collision, those below decks thought the frigate had run aground. All was confusion as officers and men on both ships attempted to ascertain the damage. Boats were lowered and closer inspection showed both vessels to have sustained a hard knock, with the *Flag* coming off worse. Neither captain would accept blame, although Burton had little doubt that the fault lay with his ship. Both vessels returned to Hatteras Inlet the next day and the *Flag* was ordered north for repairs.

In the forenoon of September 13, the *Susquehanna* claimed her second victim, the British schooner *Argonaut*. Sighted near Hatteras Inlet the vessel was overhauled and boarded by a small prize crew under the charge of master's mate Crozier. She claimed to be from Westport, Nova Scotia bound for Key West, Florida. Her miscellaneous cargo consisted of fish, shoes, soap, coffee, cotton goods and tea. Chauncey was delighted with her capture as evidenced by his report, written that day: "...the vessel was discovered last evening at sundown standing in for this place with a free wind, but tacked seaward as soon as he discovered this ship inside of him.

"It being dark, I laid in wait till daylight, when I discovered him standing in to leeward. She was boarded by a boat from this ship, and, upon examination of his papers, I have decided to send her in for adjudication. She is one of a number of vessels under English colours, ostensibly clearing for Key West, but without doubt intending to evade the blockade in order to supply the Rebels on this coast, the cargo universally being of such articles as they stand in need of and bringing high prices. The *Argonaut* was evidently bound into this place. The master gives as an excuse for being in this neighborhood that he is short of water and light, and that he did not now where he was, although he was close in with Hatteras Light-house.

"I have placed a master's mate and three men on board as a prize crew, with orders to proceed to New York, sending two of her crew as witnesses...I may state that the *Argonaut* has no register and no certificate of ownership."

The crew were kept busy the next day, the *Susquehanna* stopped two ships but finding their papers in order allowed them to continue. On the 15th the crew was called to muster and Chauncey read out a letter of thanks from the Secretary of the Navy complimenting them on their gallant actions during the capture of the forts at Hatteras. The captain added his congratulations before entertaining his officers with dinner in the wardroom.

The celebrating Yankee officers were however, unaware that Stringham, stung by criticism from Washington on his conduct of the blockade, coupled with the knowledge that his ideas and methods had been rejected by Navy Secretary Gideon Welles and the Blockade Board, Captain Stringham, victor of Hatteras Inlet, offered his resignation. Welles readily accepted. In his opinion, echoed by the Blockade Board, the lengthy Atlantic seaboard was too vast for one officer, and an elderly one to boot, to administer effectively. Therefore two blockading squadrons would be established commanded by two younger flag officers; Captain's Samuel F. Du Pont and Louis M. Goldsborough.

Also on the 15th, Chauncey received a communication from Commander Rowan, master of the 3,000 ton single screw sloop *Pawnee* requesting Chauncey's assistance in preventing the Rebels from removing heavy guns from fortifications on Beacon Island and at the town of Portsmouth. The next morning the *Susquehanna* weighed anchor and ran down the coast and soon stood off the bar at Ocracoke Inlet, ready to support the expedition, which was to land, and spike the enemy's guns. Two launches and two cutters from the *Susquehanna,* filled with 26 marines and two howitzers attempted to make a landing. Towed by the tug *Tempest,* the boats found it impossible to get over the bar due to high northerly winds and heavy surf. Consequently they returned to the ship.

However, the boats from the *Pawnee,* under tow from the tug *Fanny* fared better. Making a successful landing they hoisted the national colors over the deserted works and destroyed one 8-inch 63-hundredweight piece and thirteen 32-pounders, the buildings in the fort were then put to the torch. Moving on to Portsmouth they found four 32-pounders which they put out of action as well as burning a small boat with a quantity of stores on board. On September 18 the small squadron returned safely to their anchorage in Hatteras Inlet.

Over the next few days the weather turned foul. On September 19 a terrific gale battered the ships off the inlet and the *Susquehanna* was forced to drop both port and starboard anchors to prevent being driven ashore. The gunboat *Flag,* now repaired following her brush with the *Susquehanna* arrived with a large and most welcome delivery of mail for Chauncey's ship.

The destruction of Fort Ocracoke on Beacon Island, on the North Carolina coast on September 17 1862 - the *Susquehanna* assisted in the operation.
Library of Congress

Encountering the storm on her outward journey two of the *Flag's* seamen were swept overboard and drowned. Yet another gale blew down on the estuary on the evening of the 27th and Chauncey decided to run out to the open sea to ride out the storm. Heavy seas carried away the woodwork about the ship's head and her spar and berth decks were deluged with water as the pitch darkness was split with vivid flashes of lightning.

By first light the weather had moderated and Chauncey headed back to Hatteras. While off Ocracoke Inlet, a strange sail was reported. The crew immediately went to general quarters as the *Susquehanna* began the chase. The vessel flew no flag and showed no inclination to heave to, even after a warning shot was fired in her direction. Propelled by her giant paddle wheels gouging the water the warship gradually gained ground on her quarry, and with escape impossible, the schooner finally hoisted the American flag and hove to. She proved to be the *San Juan* of Elizabeth City, North Carolina, sailing from Anguilla for her home port loaded with contraband salt, sugar and gin. A prize crew was put aboard with orders to make for Hatteras, from there the *San Juan* would be sent to New York for adjudication in a prize court.

Another day dawned, and with it yet another catch for the *Susquehanna*. At about nine in the morning of the 29th the Yankee sloop overhauled the schooner *Baltimore* of Elizabeth City. She was in a bad state of repair, barely seaworthy, the water having all but ruined her cargo of salt, sugar and coffee. Judging her unsafe to make New York, a prize crew sailed her into Hatteras. Low on coal after five weeks at sea Chauncey made for Hatteras to replenish the *Susquehanna's* bunkers.

The capture of the *Baltimore* was to be the last action Captain Chauncey would see with the *Susquehanna*. The decision of the court of inquiry, convened before the *Susquehanna* sailed for the Hatteras expedition was to relieve Chauncey of command and he was ordered to report to Washington.

The previous day Captain James Lardner received orders from Flag Officer Goldsborough detailing him to sail from Hampton Roads on the *Stars and Stripes* for Hatteras Inlet. There, he was to relieve Chauncey of command of the *Susquehanna*. The communication instructed him to: "...follow out the instructions given to Captain Chauncey in relation to the blockade and rendering assistance to our people at Forts Hatteras and Clark. A memorandum of vessels which intend to violate the blockade with instructions in reference to neutrals etc. is herewith furnished you."

The 59-year-old Philadelphia-born Lardner had spent his entire adult life in the Navy. Appointed midshipman in his 18th year on May 1, 1820, he served with the Pacific squadron on the 80-gun flagship *Franklin* from 1821 to 1824. In August of the following year he escorted the famous General Lafayette back to France in the frigate *Brandywine* before reporting for duty with the Mediterranean Squadron. From October 1826 until June 1830 Lardner sailed with the Pacific Squadron in the schooner *Dolphin* and ship *Vincennes*, on which vessel he served for three years as her navigating officer, circumnavigating the globe in the final year of the voyage.

Promoted to lieutenant on May 17, 1828, Lardner spent the next 25 years sailing the oceans of the world, serving with the Mediterranean and

Brazilian Squadrons and whilst aboard the 60-gun *Independence* he visited Russia and England. Lardner completed a three-year tour with the Pacific Squadron on the flagship *United States* in 1844 and from 1845 to 1848 he commanded a receiving ship in Philadelphia. In May 1850 he sailed in command of the brig *Porpoise* on an expedition to the coast of Africa in command of that vessel and the sloop-of-war *Dale*, returning to Boston in April 1853. Elevated to the rank of commander in May 1851, by the summer of 1855 he was Fleet Captain of the West India Squadron.

In 1860, with the secession crisis looming, Lardner was ordered to return to the Philadelphia Navy Yard where on May 19, 1861, just over a month after the fall of Fort Sumter, he was promoted to captain. Now, four months later he was to take over command of the *Susquehanna* from Chauncey.

At break of day on the morning of October 1 the gunboat *Monticello* steamed into Hatteras Inlet towing a schooner, carrying as a passenger Captain Lardner who boarded the *Susquehanna* with orders officially relieving Chauncey of command and instructing him to report to Washington. That night a storm broke over the inlet and one of the prize schooners parted her cable and drifted a considerable distance but was safely returned to her anchorage the following morning.

On October 2, Chauncey bade farewell to the crew of the *Susquehanna,* Burton wrote of his departure: "Captain Chauncey took leave of the ship's company...he was not mourned after by any of the crew; who think his absence very good company. Captain Lardner then took command, and immediately, on announcing his intention, he received three hearty cheers; he has the reputation of being a good officer."

Late on the afternoon of October 4, Lardner was requested by Goldsborough to make for Beaufort to keep watch for the two English vessels reportedly awaiting favorable conditions to attempt to run out past the blockade. However, before Lardner could comply with this order he received a communication from Lieutenant Werden, commanding the *Stars and Stripes* informing him that Confederate troops had landed at Kinnakeet and Chickamicomico and attacked 300 Union soldiers.

These men were part of Colonel W. Brown's 20th Indiana Volunteers sent by Colonel Hawkins, commanding the forts at Hatteras, to observe

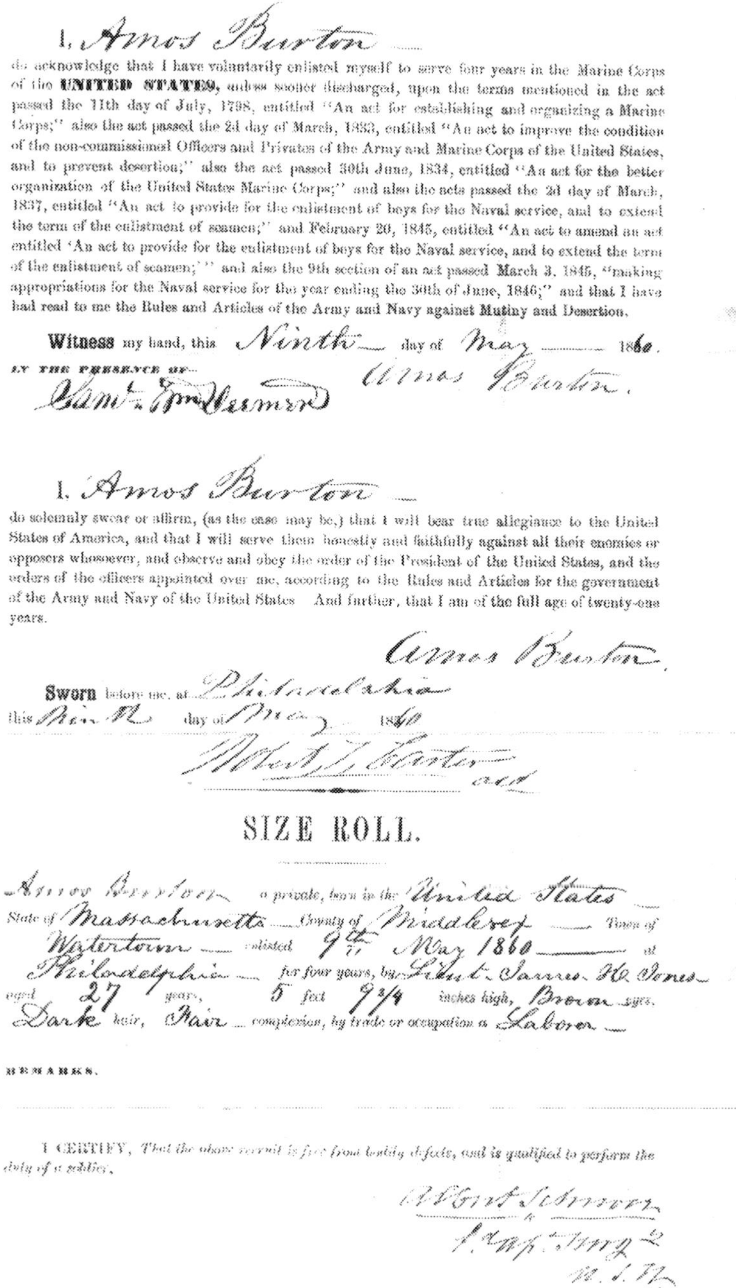

I, Amos Burton

do acknowledge that I have voluntarily enlisted myself to serve four years in the Marine Corps of the **UNITED STATES**, unless sooner discharged, upon the terms mentioned in the act passed the 11th day of July, 1798, entitled "An act for establishing and organizing a Marine Corps;" also the act passed the 2d day of March, 1833, entitled "An act to improve the condition of the non-commissioned Officers and Privates of the Army and Marine Corps of the United States, and to prevent desertion;" also the act passed 30th June, 1834, entitled "An act for the better organization of the United States Marine Corps;" and also the acts passed the 2d day of March, 1837, entitled "An act to provide for the enlistment of boys for the Naval service, and to extend the term of the enlistment of seamen;" and February 20, 1845, entitled "An act to amend an act entitled 'An act to provide for the enlistment of boys for the Naval service, and to extend the term of the enlistment of seamen;'" and also the 9th section of an act passed March 3, 1845, "making appropriations for the Naval service for the year ending the 30th of June, 1846;" and that I have had read to me the Rules and Articles of the Army and Navy against Mutiny and Desertion.

Witness my hand, this Ninth day of May 1860.

IN THE PRESENCE OF—

Saml. Wm. Weimer Amos Burton.

I, Amos Burton

do solemnly swear or affirm, (as the case may be,) that I will bear true allegiance to the United States of America, and that I will serve them honestly and faithfully against all their enemies or opposers whosoever, and observe and obey the order of the President of the United States, and the orders of the officers appointed over me, according to the Rules and Articles for the government of the Army and Navy of the United States. And further, that I am of the full age of twenty-one years.

Amos Burton.

Sworn before me, at Philadelphia

this Ninth day of May 1860

Robert L. Carter

SIZE ROLL.

Amos Burton a private, born in the United States State of Massachusetts County of Middlesex Town of Watertown enlisted 9th May 1860 at Philadelphia for four years, by Lieut. James H. Jones aged 27 years, 5 feet 9 3/4 inches high, Brown eyes, Dark hair, Fair complexion, by trade or occupation a Laborer

REMARKS.

I CERTIFY, *That the above recruit is free from bodily defects, and is qualified to perform the duty of a soldier.*

Albert Schriver

Asst. Surg.

U. S. N.

Marine enlistment document of Amos Burton.
National Archives

Confederate troops engaged in erecting batteries on the south-western shore of Roanoke Island, covering the entrance to Albermarle Sound some 40 miles north of Hatteras. Loaded onto two steamers, the *Ceres* and the *Putnam*, they sailed for Chickamicomico on September 29. Anticipating revictualling the troops using six tugboats, Hawkins was dismayed to learn that only two were available, and Lardner had detained these at Charleston. In desperation the Colonel sent the *Fanny* northwards with supplies for the soldiers, but as she was unloading her cargo into small cutters, three Rebel gunboats stationed in Pamlico Sound and commanded by Captain William Lynch CSN steamed into view.

They were the *Curlew*, carrying one 32-pounder rifled gun and one 12-pound smoothbore, the *Raleigh*, two 6-pounder howitzers and the *Janaluska*, one 16-pounder. Although the *Fanny* put up a fight she was completely outgunned and was driven ashore and captured, along with her 49-man crew.

The Yankee soldiers were in a desperate situation. The Confederates planned a simultaneous attack; whilst a portion of their forces would move against the 20th Indiana on land, the remaining Rebels would embark on a flotilla of schooners and small streamers and land below the Union troops, cutting off their retreat and ensuring their capture. The triumphant Confederates would then take to their vessels and attempt to recapture the forts at Hatteras. Before this audacious plan could be put into action, the 20th Indiana received orders to retreat. With over 40 miles of marshes, inlets and sand to cover and a tenacious enemy snapping at their heels, this was no easy task. Luck was with them however, and before the Confederates could land troops in front of their line of march the Indianians neared the safety of Hatteras, although some 40 Yankees had fallen into Confederate hands.

In response to a request from Lieutenant Braine, commanding the Union gunboat *Monticello*, Lardner had run the *Susquehanna* inshore above Hatteras Inlet to cover the retreating Federals, and near sundown he made contact with the fleeing Union forces now encamped on the beach. The night passed with no sign of the pursuing Rebels and the next morning he sent a boat ashore loaded with provisions for the weary troops. Lardner ordered the *Monticello* to seek out the enemy and an hour after she sailed, heavy firing was heard in the distance.

Braine had sighted a Confederate regiment retiring northwards, looking for Union stragglers. The Confederates were shelled out of their positions and fled towards nearby schooners and steamers from whence they had landed. Several Union prisoners took advantage of the confusion and attempted to escape. One, a Private O'Haver of the 20th Indiana, was picked up after swimming to the *Monticello* and told Lieutenant Braine that during the bombardment, he had seen two shells from the Union gunboat blow apart two sloops full of Rebel soldiers causing many casualties. The plucky private, who claimed to have shot a Confederate officer while affecting his escape, directed Braine to the spot where the Rebels were waiting to embark onto six schooners and steamers, including the recently captured Union tug *Fanny*. Braine placed some well-aimed rounds amongst them and claimed to have scored at least one hit on the *Fanny*. With the Confederates now in full flight, this action brought to an end any threat to the Federal forces at Hatteras Inlet.

On October 7, the *Susquehanna* sailed for Hampton Roads to take on coal and provisions. Arriving the following morning their entry into the roadstead was delayed for an hour by dense fog, but by noon they had dropped anchor and after the crew had partaken of a meal they commenced coaling the ship. Amos Burton described his surroundings. "I noticed no change since we were here before. The fortress and its grey, sombre walls look the same. The Rip Raps are still unfinished. The same number of white tents are to be seen above the fortress, and the flag of treason waves over Sewell's Point. There is a large fleet lying here, which gives to this place quite a mercantile appearance. Among them are quite a number of men-of-war. Steamers and sailing ships are coming and going constantly."

Rumors abounded of the imminent appearance of the feared Confederate ironclad *Virginia* – formerly the Union frigate *Merrimack* – although it would be another five months before the former US Navy frigate sallied forth from the Elizabeth River to wreak havoc among the wooden sailing vessels lying in Hampton Roads. Nevertheless, at 9pm the men of the *Susquehanna* were called to quarters and the ship put in readiness for action. No hammocks were allowed and the men not on watch slept on the decks. During the night a sudden squall blew up stopping the coaling of the

Susquehanna.

At 9am fresh orders to prepare for action were received and general quarters again reverberated about the ship; hammocks were lashed and stowed in their places; guns cast loose; screens set down; powder and shell whips put up; decks wet down and sanded. Within 20 minutes the ship was cleared for action. All this frenetic activity was of course to no purpose. Yet one thing was certain, the Union naval commanders were a pretty spooked bunch.

Lieutenant Bankhead, the ship's executive officer, having been promoted to command of the gunboat *Pembina,* left the ship. An efficient and popular member of the crew, he was given a rousing send off by the webfeet of the *Susquehanna* who manned the rigging giving three cheers. Lieutenant Jonathan Young took over the position vacated by Bankhead as acting executive officer.

On October 12 Goldsborough informed his subordinate officers that the fleet in Hampton Roads would be divided into two squadrons; one to operate north of the point at which the coasts of North and South Carolina meet, and the other to take station south of it. The *Susquehanna* would form part of the South Atlantic Squadron under Flag Officer Du Pont, and with the coaling and revictualling of the ship completed by Sunday October 13; Lardner reported the readiness of the *Susquehanna* for sea. He was told to steam south and maintain station off Charleston harbor. In obedience to these instructions the vessel got under way at noon on October 16, running past Hatteras Inlet the next morning. The brig *Champion* making for Boston from Havana with a cargo of sugar was overhauled midmorning the next day and reported several vessels loading in Havana, no doubt with the intention of running through the blockade. A week at sea, the small brig had suffered its share of misfortune with an outbreak of Yellow Fever aboard which had carried off four of the crew.

Contending with heavy seas and high winds, the *Susquehanna* dropped anchor in Rattlesnake Channel on the evening of the 19th, within sight of Forts Sumter and Moultrie, sentinels of Charleston Harbor. Also on station off the port were the gunboat *Flag* and the frigate *Roanoke,* which vessel the *Susquehanna* was to relieve. She left for Hampton Roads the next day. The lookouts needed to keep a keen eye as ships were continually running in and out of the harbor. Only a few days prior to the *Susquehanna's* arrival the *Flag* had run a schooner ashore, forcing the crew to abandon ship before burning the vessel and destroying its cargo of blankets, salt and other goods.

Problems now surfaced for Lardner. The ship's engines were in a poor state, with a cracked pillar-block and one shaft in bad condition. Emergency repairs were made and on October 23 they were tested as the *Susquehanna* ran up and down the coast for a distance of some 10 miles. Although able to function, it was obvious to Lardner that the ship's machinery was in dire need of a major overhaul. On the evening of the 27th, the gunboat *Alabama* came in to reinforce the blockade and along with mail for the ship she brought Lieutenant Clark Wells who would be joining the *Susquehanna* as executive officer.

At 1pm on September 28, general quarters were sounded and the crew exercised at the guns for an hour. This was the first exercise since Lardner had taken command and as Burton recounted, "...he declared himself well pleased with the efficiency of the crew." On the morrow, a clear beautiful autumnal day, Lardner ordered the 3rd cutter inshore to take soundings. The small craft, under the command of acting master George Bradbury crept near to Fort Sumter, too near for Lardner's liking and he ordered a gun fired to signal the craft to return. As the cutter turned back for the ship Fort Sumter opened fire, fortunately the shots fell short of their target.

At four in the morning on the last day of the month, four runaway Negroes clambered up and over the bulwarks of the *Susquehanna*. Taking advantage of the darkness they had slipped away from their masters in Charleston and paddled out to the Union warship in a leaky old boat. Signed on as part of the ships crew these 'contrabands' soon became accustomed to life at sea and were accepted by the crew of the *Susquehanna*. That same evening the French man-of-war *Proney* approached the harbor and her captain came aboard requesting permission, granted by Lardner, to send in dispatches to the French Consulate in Charleston.

On the morning of November 1 a raging storm arose. Conditions worsened as the day wore on, forcing the *Susquehanna* to seek the safety of deep water. The tempest continued unabated through the night and the *Susquehanna* ran before the wind under shortened sail. Mountainous seas broke over the deck carrying away the woodwork about the head and the bowsprit. The leaden skies finally clearing during the morning of the 2nd, and by late afternoon the sloop was back on station off Charleston, just in time to spy the Rebel steamer *Carolina*, flying the French flag at her mizzen mast, heading out from the harbor.

A warning shot from one of the *Susquehanna's* pivot guns brought her to, and it was then discovered that she was carrying the French consul, bound for the *Proney* with dispatches for home. Lardner allowed her to proceed, and with her task completed, the *Carolina* returned to the safety of Charleston.

The tedious spell of blockade duty was about to end for Lardner and his crew and with it would come their chance to participate in one of the most successful Union naval actions of the war. The ferocious storm they had just passed through a matter of hours before was perhaps the omen of a more deadly tempest awaiting them just a few days hence.

CIRCLE OF FIRE

Weeks of constant sea duty exacted its toll on both men and ships. Storm damaged upperworks, broken spars, sailcloth shredded and torn from the yardarms by ferocious gales and mechanical defects that could not be rectified at sea meant vital weeks lost from blockade duty. Ships that could not be spared were forced to sail hundreds of miles to far northern ports when in need of repair or refitting. The resulting gaps in the blockade were fully exploited by the sleek craft standing off the Southern coast awaiting the opportunity to run in and unload their cargoes of military stores and luxury goods. Driven by the need to reduce the time ships were away from their stations and emboldened by the success gained at Hatteras, the Union high command now turned its energies towards establishing a deep-water haven on the South Atlantic coast. A base where Union cruisers could take on coal and provisions and where workshops could be constructed enabling repairs to be carried out, thereby allowing ships to resume their patrol duties in a matter of days, not weeks.

Four possible targets were considered. Bulls Bay, Port Royal, Fernandina and Brunswick. Eventually after much deliberation, Port Royal,

South Carolina was chosen. It was to be another joint operation, but on a much larger scale than Hatteras Inlet. Samuel Du Pont was ordered to assemble a fleet of warships and sufficient transports to carry 12,000 Federal troops under the command of Brigadier-General Thomas Sherman. The expedition was due to sail in early September 1861 but following the Union defeat at Bull Run on July 21, Sherman's men were ordered to Washington to defend the capitol. The city's inhabitants were in turmoil, fearing an onslaught from the victorious Confederate army following the rout of the Union forces at Manassas. However, the expected Confederate onslaught failed to materialize.

Anxious for the operation to proceed, President Lincoln sent communications to both the War Department and the Secretary of the Navy urging them to be ready by October 1 or as early as possible that month. The expedition now became bogged down with logistical problems. General Sherman experienced great difficulty in procuring sufficient weapons for his troops while Du Pont was obliged to work tirelessly in an attempt to amass adequate shipping at Hampton Roads. A dozen or more small gunboats were then under construction in Northern shipyards and vessels of every size, from a canal steamboat to the largest coastal steamers, were purchased and fitted with batteries, shell rooms and magazines. If the coming expedition succeeded, these ships would have a second purpose; that of establishing, maintaining and extending an effective blockade of Southern ports. By the end of October, the largest fleet ever assembled by US forces, consisting of over 70 craft, including 15 warships and 31 transports was finally ready to sail.

On October 19, Du Pont left New York on the steam frigate *Wabash,* accompanied by numerous warships, among which were the new gunboats *Unadilla, Ottawa, Pembina* and *Seneca,* 'ninety-day gunboats' – so called because their contracts stipulated that they be built and ready for service within that time. Despite every effort to keep the fleet's objective a secret, word leaked out and Confederate Secretary of War Judah Benjamin telegraphed both the governor of South Carolina and General Drayton, commanding the Rebel forces at Port Royal warning that an attack might be imminent. Benjamin also suspected that Du Pont might be intending to capture Fort Lowry on the Rappahannock River as a first step to occupying Fredericksburg, Virginia. This uncertainty suggests that while he knew a powerful fleet was assembling, Benjamin didn't know for sure where the blow would fall.

Du Pont finally quit Hampton Roads on October 29. The fleet, sailing in an inverted 'V' formation, stood down the coast for Port Royal. For two days the weather remained calm with fair winds, then at midday on November 1 the ferocious storm the *Susquehanna's* crew would endure that same night off Charleston, screamed down on the Union fleet as it neared Hatteras Inlet, still over 300 miles from its destination. The skies darkened and the wind from the southeast rapidly grew to gale force, and at 2.30pm Du Pont signaled the fleet to disregard the order of sailing. While the storm lasted, each ship was to look out for itself. By nightfall, his huge armada of warships and transports had been scattered to the four points of the compass.

Daniel Ammen, a future rear-admiral then serving on the *Seneca* wrote of that night: "In the drifting mists and rain, it soon grew dark. The greater part of that night I stood under the lee of the weather bulwark, near the wheel, casting glances to windward, to be in readiness to bear away should a vessel be seen coming down upon us. It was a long, weary and anxious night. On peering to windward, the rain drops pelted the face like sleet, and the phosphorescent spray broke over us in superlative grandeur."

Many of the flat-bottomed transports, not built to withstand the rigors of deep-sea service, came near to foundering during the darkness. These vessels were loaded to the gunwales with Union troops who, having suffered a night of hell emerged the next morning bruised, battered and thoroughly seasick. The storm-lashed ocean claimed several victims. The *Union*, carrying large quantities of gunpowder had sunk as had the *Peerless*; and the quartermaster ship *Ocean Empress* had been wrecked and her crew taken prisoner as they struggled ashore. This loss was to prove costly as the vessel carried much of the Army's artillery, ordnance stores and three million rounds of small arms ammunition. The transport *Governor*, carrying a complement of marines sustained such severe damage that she would also founder the next day; fortunately all save six were saved from a watery grave. By daybreak not a single sail could be seen from Du Pont's flagship. Undeterred, Du Pont sailed on, counting on the wind-blown warships and transports to make their own way to the rendezvous point off Port Royal.

Commodore James Lardner, as he appeared when skipper of the *Susquehanna* in October 1862.
US Naval Historical Center

Rear Admiral Samuel Du Pont, Union naval commander at Port Royal.
Battles and Leaders

November 3 dawned calm and clear, and the crew of the *Susquehanna* was treated to a splendid view. The horizon was dotted with the sails of those Federal ships which had managed to rejoin Du Pont, heading southward. The gunboat *Seneca,* detached from the passing fleet, brought the steamship not only her mail, but orders from Du Pont for Captain Lardner. He was to detain those vessels of the expeditionary force that had reached Charleston until nightfall, in order to decoy the Confederates into thinking that Charleston was the target for attack. They were to sail the next day to join him off Port Royal Sound. By ten in the morning of November 4 the *Susquehanna* had sighted the fleet and dropped anchor near the *Wabash*. Twenty-five ships had arrived and more were appearing hourly. Du Pont determined to take no aggressive action until the greater part of his fleet had reassembled.

Probably the finest natural harbor on the South Atlantic coast, Port Royal was also reputed to be the best defended although Du Pont was ignorant of the exact strength of the two earthwork forts which the Confederates had built either side of the entrance to the sound. Fort Walker sited on Hilton Head was the stronger of the two and mounted two 6-inch rifled guns, twelve 32-pounders, one 10-inch and one 8-inch columbiad, three 7-inch seacoast howitzers, one 8-inch howitzer and two 12-pounders: in all 22 pieces of ordnance. Brigadier General Thomas Drayton's garrison consisted of two companies of South Carolina Militia artillery and 600 infantry. Outside the bar his brother, Commander Percival Drayton, captained the Yankee warship *Pocahontas*.

Originally designed to mount seven 10-inch columbiads mounted en barbette to be separated by earthen traverses offering protection from enfilade fire, the serious shortage of heavy coastal guns forced the Confederates to compromise with the artillery pieces they could muster. In order to gain maximum firepower from the more numerous but smaller caliber weapons, the traverses were dispensed with, leaving the guns and their crews vulnerable to flanking fire.

Two and a half miles across the roads on Bay Point lay Fort Beauregard. Like Fort Walker this smaller, open earthwork was still incomplete on the eve of battle. It possessed five 32-pounders, one 10-inch and one 8-inch columbiad, one 6-inch rifled gun and five 42-pound seacoast guns.

The distance between the two forts meant that only Fort Beauregard's rifled piece had the range to support her sister fort on the other side of the bay. Outside the main walls and sited so as to cover the landward approaches were three 32-pounders, two 24-pounders and two 6-inch Spanish guns. Fort Beauregard was manned by 150 men of the Beaufort Volunteer Artillery commanded by Captain Stephen Elliott. The Confederate Navy was represented by Commodore Josiah Tattnall's tiny flotilla of three lightly armed gunboats; the steamer *Savannah*, Lieutenant John Maffitt (destined for fame as the commander of the commerce raider *Florida*); the *Samson*, Lieutenant J. Kennard; and the *Resolute*, Lieutenant Pembroke Jones. Each vessel carried two 32-pounders but Tattnal had no intention of risking direct confrontation with such a mighty force.

To Du Pont's annoyance, the Rebels had removed the buoys indicating the safe channels over the bar into the inlet. However this caused little delay as with the assistance of a representative of the Coast Survey a new channel was marked out and the shallower draft gunboats anchored inside the bar on the afternoon of the fleet's arrival. Now came a series of irritating delays, which tried Du Pont's patience to the limit. On November 5 the signal was given for the larger warships of the main battle fleet to head into the sound and take up positions prior to attacking the forts. The *Wabash* took the lead, followed by the *Susquehanna*. As the flagship slowly maneuvered into the shallow Port Royal Sound, she ran fast aground on Fishing Rip Shoals. By the time the flagship was floated clear it was too late in the day to commence the assault and Du Pont ordered his ships to anchor out of range of the enemy's guns.

At dawn on the 6th, Tatnall's ship *Savannah* dashed out of Skull Creek. The Rebel commander's ploy was to lure the Yankee warships into pursuit and onto the shoals, thereby giving the gunners in the forts stationary targets. His ruse almost succeeded as the *Wabash* ran her stem onto a sandbank. Fortunately for Du Pont, she managed to work her way clear before the Confederates could get her range. The Federal warships now opened a concentrated fire on the tiny Rebel gunboat and an 11-inch shell from the *Susquehanna* passed straight through her pilothouse without exploding. Dipping his colors to the enemy, the cocky Tatnall retired to the safety of Skull Creek.

Du Pont now held a conference aboard his flagship with his senior officers including Lardner, which, among other things, revealed the sorry state of Sherman's troops. With little ammunition and their landing craft lost in the storm, they could offer no real assistance in reducing the forts – the Navy was on its own. Du Pont, from the outset reluctant to commit his wooden-walled ships to attacking the forts, was left with little option other than to make ready his fleet for battle against a resolute and desperate foe who had been allowed ample time to prepare for an attack

Du Pont's flagship, under Commander Rogers, would lead the assault. A ship's length behind her would be the *Susquehanna* followed by the sloops *Mohican,* Commander Godon; *Seminole,* Commander Gillis and *Pawnee,* Lieutenant Wyman. The gunboats *Unadilla,* Lieutenant Collins; *Ottawa,* Lieutenant Stevens and the *Pembina,* commanded by Lieutenant Bankhead – the *Susquehanna's* old first officer were in support. Finally the sailing sloop *Vandalia,* Commander Haggerty, this last vessel being under tow by the steamer *Isaac Smith* under Lieutenant Nicholson. Altogether 10 ships, their formidable batteries amounting to 123 guns were set to take on the Rebel forts.

Du Pont's tactics, loosely based on those employed at Hatteras, envisaged the main flotilla steaming in line ahead formation northwards up the center of the channel passing and firing into Fort Beauregard on Bay Point. When a point two and a half miles above the fort was reached the fleet would steer south round by the west, heading back down the sound and close with Fort Walker on Hilton Head. When the squadron was clear of Fort Walker the battle line, following the *Wabash,* would turn to port heading back up the channel to close to within 500 yards of Fort Beauregard. The earthwork would receive its share of high explosive shells and solid shot as each ship passed it in turn. A veritable circle of fire.

This elliptical maneuver would continue until the forts were blasted into submission. As at Hatteras, with the Yankee ships on the move and with the range constantly varying it was anticipated that the return fire from the Confederate artillerists would prove ineffectual. In fact the only danger to Du Pont's ships while in the center of the channel would come from the rifled pieces in the forts.

Complementing the main flotilla were five gunboats, the *Bienville,*

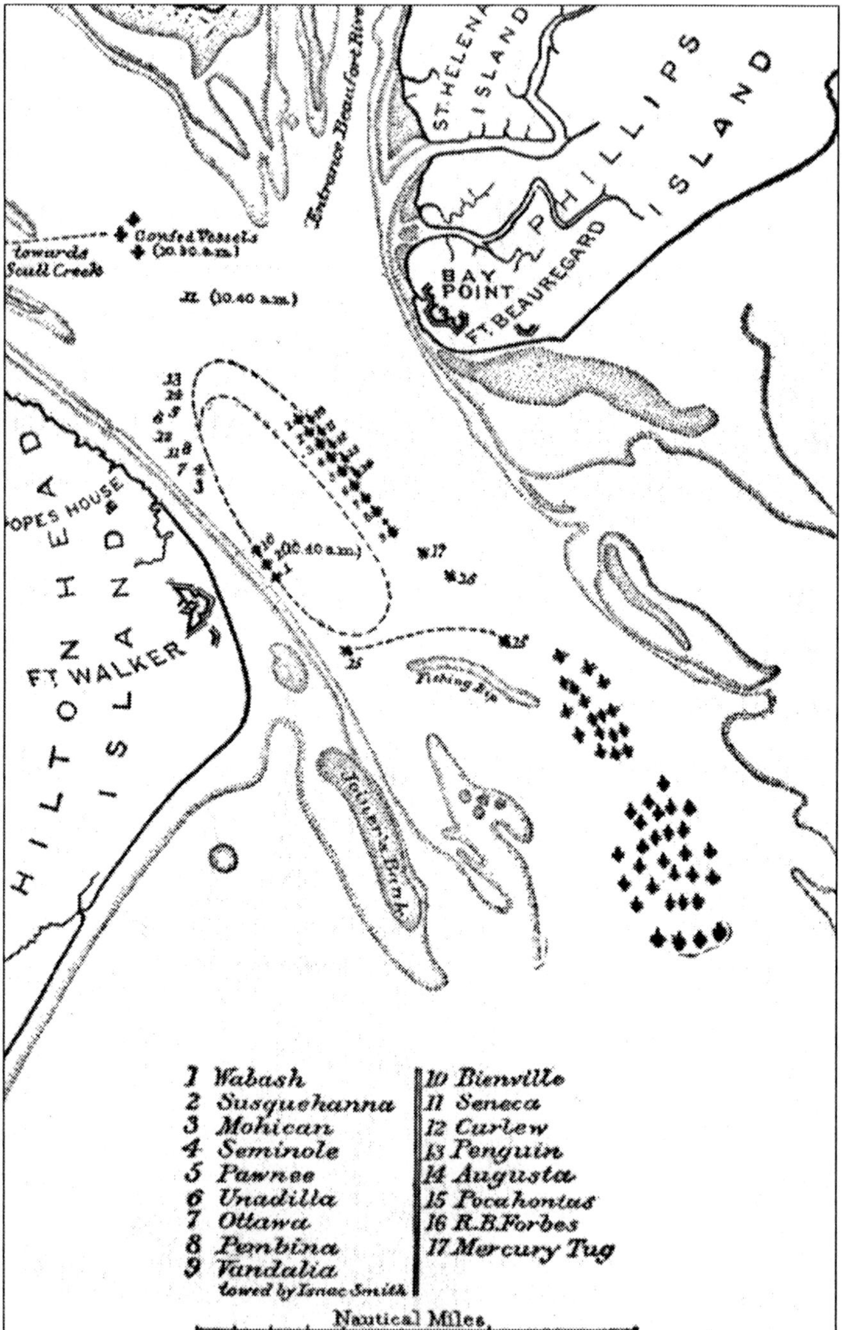

Map of the action at Port Royal showing the Union battle plan. The *Susquehanna* is second in the line of battle directly astern of the *Wabash*.
Battles and Leaders

A wartime sketch of the *Susquehanna* astern of the flagship *Wabash*, blazing away at Fort Walker, sited on Hilton Head and Fort Beauregard on Bay Point: the Confederate posts defending Port Royal, South Carolina.
Battles and Leaders

Brig. General Thomas F Drayton, commander of the Southern forces at Port Royal.
Battles and Leaders

Another view of the Union fleet in action against the Rebel forts...

...with the hoisting of the National colors over the captured forts at the conclusion of the fight.
Battles and Leaders

Two views of Fort Beauregard on Bay Point after capture by Union forces.
Battles and Leaders

Seneca, Curlew, Penguin and *Augusta,* and their task was to steam up the channel on the starboard flank of the squadron. Having reached the point where the squadron made the turn southward, the gunboats, as Du Pont stated in his report, would be "...thrown off on the northern section of the harbor to engage the enemy's flotilla and prevent them raking the rear ships of the main line when it turned to the southward, or cutting off a disabled vessel."

Yet another early winter gale sprang up making an attack impossible and adding to Du Pont's frustration and the remainder of November 6 passed with the fleet preparing for action the next day. Fortunately the 7th broke calm and clear. Burton recalled that "...our preparations were complete, and on a large scale, and our jolly tars in high spirits and confident of success; 'God defends the right'"

At 8am the signal for close order was flown from the flagship and the fleet got under way, steaming at a steady six knots making for the west, or Hilton Head side of the sound. The Confederate commander General Drayton left a vivid description of the approaching Union fleet. "At last the memorable 7th dawned upon us, bright and serene; not a ripple upon the broad expanse of water to disturb the accuracy of fire from the broad decks of that magnificent armada about advancing, in battle array, to vomit forth its iron hail, with all the spiteful energy of long-suppressed rage and conscious strength."

Within half an hour the battle line fell within the extreme range of Fort Walker, which fired the first shot of the engagement at 9.26am, Fort Beauregard soon joined her. In reply a thunderous broadside roared from the *Wabash,* followed almost immediately by the *Susquehanna's* starboard battery. The rush of shells arrowed down on Fort Beauregard. Precise fire from the pivot guns dismounted cannon while red hot iron shards from the exploding shells cut down the Rebel gunners. Gallantly the Confederates replied and Du Pont's ships took many hits from Fort Beauregard as they passed up the sound. Burton witnessed the courage of the *Susquehanna's* senior officers first hand during the fight. "Our brave and noble Captain Lardner and Lieutenant Clark Wells, took their position on the hurricane deck... the enemy then opened fire upon us from both forts; our ships continued pouring shells into the forts like hail; yet the enemy's shot came thick and fast, and well directed."

Meanwhile the Confederate flotilla made a brief appearance and opened up on the Yankee ships, but the *Seneca* and the *Pocahontas* soon drove them back into Skull Creek. By 10am the fleet reached the turning point and Du Pont ordered the column to close up for the return down-channel pass where the main target was to be Fort Walker. However, only three ships were destined to carry out the order, the remainder maintained their positions supporting the attack with deadly enfilading fire into the Confederate bastion. This left the *Wabash,* closely followed astern by the *Susquehanna* and the *Bienville* to press home the attack against Fort Walker. As they drew abreast of the earthwork at a range of 800 yards the three ships commenced to pour in a most devastating and accurate fire. As the smog of battle covered the *Susquehanna,* rounds from the Rebel batteries smashed gun carriages and spars, shredded standing and running rigging and ripped through canvas. Men were hurled to the dampened and sanded decks as deadly splinters tore through clothing and flesh as the Confederate defenders exhibited a courageous resistance.

Commander Drayton in Fort Walker later wrote "...in spite of our fire, directed with deliberation and coolness, the fleet soon passed both batteries apparently unharmed, and, then returning, delivered in their changing rounds a terrific shower of shot and shell in flank and front. Besides this moving battery, the fort was enfiladed by two gunboats anchored to the north of the mouth of Fish Hall Creek... this enfilading fire on so still a sea, annoyed and damaged us excessively, particularly as we had no gun on either flank of the bastion to reply with, for the 32-pounder on the right flank was shattered very early on by a round shot."

At 11am the *Wabash,* having reached the spot in which the ellipse had started began her turn to port ready to retrace her passage past Fort Beauregard for a second run up the roads. Again the Confederates felt the fury of Du Pont's firepower. Twenty minutes later and the flagship and her consorts were once more level with beleaguered Fort Walker with the range closed to 500 yards. The deadly profusion of shells fell with unerring precision into the Rebel works, dismounting cannon and maiming gun crews. For nearly half an hour the *Susquehanna* stood before the fort, the sweating

Photograph taken inside Fort Beauregard on Phillips Island by Timothy O'Sullivan.
Library of Congress

gunners pumping in round after round from the starboard battery, the huge pieces recoiling after every shot against their restraining blocks and tackle. Near midday an eyewitness remembered "...the ships were again enveloped in a dense cloud of white smoke, and a few seconds later the shells were bursting in the battery in a splendid manner. The sand was flying in every direction, and it seemed impossible that anyone in the battery could be saved from death. The Confederates now worked only two guns, but I will give them the credit of saying that they worked them beautifully."

Almost 200 rounds had plowed into the hapless fort. Amos Burton wrote "...we lay twenty one minutes before the fort, completely enveloped in smoke, their shot whizzing over and around us: it was then that we experienced what a close action was. The enemy's fire grew weaker, and poorly directed; it was now one o'clock, and our third hour; we felt ourselves completely exhausted: we passed the fort; a signal from the flagship gave the order to rest; then followed eating, drinking and smoking for a few moments. The flagship again gave the signal to renew the attack; we stood before them again, fire commenced, and was kept up till two o'clock pm. A white flag was seen flying from the fort. The fire from the enemy had ceased, and as the smoke cleared away the enemy was seen fleeing in all directions. A signal from the flagship caused all firing to cease after a hard fight of four hours duration."

The climax of the fight was near. The scene in Fort Walker was one of disorder and turmoil. The garrison consisted in the main of untried militiamen, who nevertheless had put up a creditable performance. Their cause was not helped by the fact that much of their ammunition was of poor quality and even the wrong caliber. Several guns became inoperable due to mechanical faults after firing only a few rounds. With only three cannon serviceable the garrison, carrying their small arms and field artillery, decided to quit the fort and retreat to the mainland.

It was now a little after midday as Du Pont commenced a third northerly run past Bay Point and a desultory fire was received from Fort Beauregard which was soon smashed into silence by the guns of the small flotilla. Just after one o'clock Du Pont was about to commence a third run down the channel to finish off Fort Walker. The gunboat *Ottawa,* which had remained anchored near the turning point and had been sending in a steady enfilading fire into the place, reported that Confederate soldiers were apparently leaving their guns and abandoning the post. By 2.30pm the waiting transports had off-loaded 100 surfboats that were soon crammed with Sherman's troops awaiting the signal to land.

The *Wabash* steamed cautiously past silent Fort Walker and fired a single round into the earthwork. Receiving no reply, Du Pont ordered the fleet to come to anchor and a small cutter with Commander John Rogers put off from the flagship carrying a flag of truce. The men of the fleet held their breath as the whaleboat grounded on the shingle beach and the small group of figures vanished inside the fort. Suddenly Commander Rogers was spotted scrambling onto the ramparts carrying the National colors; tremendous cheers broke out from the tired but jubilant seamen. A small party of marines was next ashore and by nightfall Sherman's troops were in occupation. By sunset Fort Beauregard was also found to be deserted. The Confederates having witnessed the fall of Fort Walker spiked the guns and set fire to the magazine before retiring on Beaufort, and on the morning of November 8 the Union banners were floating over Bay Point.

Burton later wrote: "It was an exciting time. The enemy's shot came thick and fast from both sides, around and over our heads; some striking the ship causing it to shake like a reed before the wind, cutting away iron stays, ropes and running, also heavy shrouds, which fell to the deck with a crash. One of their shot passed through the starboard bow and fell on the berth deck; another striking the main yard, embedding itself some three feet into the wood. Numberless others falling in the water close to the ship's sides."

Confederate losses amounted to 59, of whom 11 were killed. Among the casualties in Fort Beauregard was the post surgeon Dr Buist, his decapitated body would be discovered after the battle, a surgical instrument clutched tightly in his lifeless hand. Du Pont listed Federal casualties as eight dead and 23 wounded. The crew of the *Susquehanna* had not escaped untouched from the bloody carnage. John Clark, a seaman from Portsmouth, New Hampshire and William Price, a fireman from Philadelphia received wounds which would prove mortal, both expired that same evening. Young Samuel Smart, first-class boy had fallen severely wounded and two gunners, Patrick Dwyer and Samuel Holbrook were also hit but only slightly injured.

A Union officer told of the damage caused to Fort Walker. "On the line along the front three guns were dismounted by the enfilading fire of our ships. One carriage had been struck by a large shell and shivered to pieces, dismounting the heavy gun mounted upon it and sending the splinters flying in all directions with terrific force. Between the guns and the foot of the parapet was a large pool of blood mingled with brains, fragments of skull and pieces of flesh evidently from the face, as portions of whiskers still clung to it. This shot must have done horrible execution, as other portions of human beings were found all around it. Another carriage to the right was broken to pieces, and the guns on the waterfront were rendered useless by the enfilading fire from the gunboats on the left flank. Their scorching fire of shell, which swept with resistless fury and deadly effect across this long water pond, where the enemy had placed his heaviest metal *en barbette* without taking the precaution to place traverses between the guns, did as much as anything to drive them from their works. The fort was plowed up by shot and shell so badly as to make an immediate repair necessary. All the houses and many of the tents about the works were perforated and torn by flying shells, and hardly a light of glass could be found intact in any building. The trees in the vicinity showed marks of heavy visitation. Everything, indeed, was in ruins."

Brigadier-General Thomas Sherman whose troops, through no fault of their own, had played such a passive role in the reduction of the Rebel works, also visited Fort Walker and depicted the interior. "The beautifully constructed work on Hilton Head was severely crippled and many of the guns dismounted. Much slaughter had evidently been made there, many bodies having been buried in the fort, and some twenty or thirty were found some half-mile distant...the number of pieces of ordnance that have fallen into our hands is fifty two, the bulk of which is of the largest caliber, all with fine carriages etc., except eight or nine, that were ruined by our fire, which dismounted their pieces."

With both forts and the harbor now secure, the threat to the South posed by Du Pont's victory became clear. The Union Navy now possessed a first-class base on the Southern coast, located midway between Charleston and Savannah, from which Yankee cruisers could threaten the landing places all the way from Charleston to Cape Florida. After Hatteras and Port Royal, the Confederates abandoned all minor coastal installations, and resorted to placing obstructions in these channels and inlets as their only means of defense.

Amos Burton later put on record that he and his shipmates had been impressed by the courage of their foes. "We lay before them for three days prior to the attack, so they must have been fully aware of what they had to contend against. The Rebels could have evacuated their strongholds and left nothing but ruins behind them; they chose to stand their ground and bid defiance to our fleet. They fought well, but we drove them from their strongholds and achieved a glorious victory!"

The day after the battle for Port Royal, all was hustle and bustle aboard the *Susquehanna* as carpenters, engineers and sail makers set to with a will to repair the battle damage. During the engagement the ship sustained 10 hits in the hull and 20 rounds had damaged spars and rigging. In reply the frigate had fired off 852 rounds at the enemy. In his written report to Du Pont, Lardner stated that, "The officers and crew began the fight and went through it with the greatest enthusiasm."

On the afternoon of November 8 the somber duty of burying those seamen killed in action the previous day was carried out. Boats from the flagship *Wabash, Susquehanna, Pawnee, Mohican* and *Bienville* carried the dead to the shore. Burton wrote a moving description of the event. "This afternoon the killed of yesterday were conveyed in boats from the *Susquehanna, Pawnee, Mohican* and *Bienville,* alongside the *Wabash* when the body of Thomas Jackson (Third Assistant Engineer on the *Mohican,* and the only Union officer to lose his life) was lowered over the ship's side. The flags were at half-mast. The boats formed in line led by the whaleboat, which contained the *Susquehanna's* band. It was a solemn sight to witness the boats moving slowly along, while the band played funeral dirges. From the landing the coffins were borne by messmates of the deceased to the place of burial. At the grave the chaplain of the flagship read the funeral service. A squad of marines from the *Wabash* and

Union gunboat *Seneca,* Captain (later Admiral) Daniel Ammen's ship at Port Royal.
Battles and Leaders

the *Susquehanna* fired three volleys. Each grave was marked with a headboard, stating name, age, and place of residence and date of decease. There they were left to rest, on the bank of a gentle stream which courses its way through the meadows and empties into the bay."

During the next two days troops and supplies were landed at Hilton Head and Bay Point as General Sherman's men consolidated their positions. The evening of the 9th was enlivened by a rocket display and melodies, both patriotic and lively from the various bands drifted across the bay. At 10am the next morning the crew were mustered aft to hear congratulatory messages from the flag officer, one of which was addressed personally to Lardner and the men of the *Susquehanna.*

Wabash, off Hilton Head, S. C. Port Royal bay, November 9th 1861

MY DEAR LARDNER: – I enclose a general order to be read to the officers and crew of the *Susquehanna*, and I take pleasure in saying, that your noble ship, throughout the whole battle, was precisely what I wanted her to be, and doing precisely what I wanted her to do; and that your close support of this ship was a very gallant thing.

Signed Truly your friend

S. F. Du Pont

This was followed by a more formal address, a copy of which had been received by every ship in the fleet.

GENERAL ORDER No. 2

Flag ship *Wabash*, Hilton Head, Port Royal, S.C. Nov. 8th, 1861.

It is the grateful duty of the commander-in-chief to make a public acknowledgment of his entire commendation of the coolness, discipline, skill and gallantry displayed by the officers and men under his command, in the capture of the batteries on Hilton Head and Bay Point, after an action of four hours' duration

The Flag Officer fully sympathises with the officers and men of his squadron in the satisfaction they must feel at seeing the ensign of the Union flying once more in the state of South Carolina, which has been the chief promoter of this wicked and unprovoked rebellion they have been called upon to suppress

Signed *S.F. Du Pont*

Flag Officer commanding South Atlantic Blockading Squadron.

On the 10th, a series of comings and goings aboard the ship saw the executive officer, Lieutenant Jonathan Young transferred to the sloop *Jamestown*. A well-liked and respected officer, the crew manned the rigging to cheer him on his way. Also departing the ship was William Grozier who had received promotion to acting master and took up an appointment on the sloop *Vandalia*. Two acting master's mates, Adams and Baldwin, reported for duty on the *Susquehanna* as the frigate weighed anchor at noon, bound for Charleston and a resumption of her blockading chores.

As she slowly passed the *Wabash*, the crew of the flagship gave her three cheers and a 'tiger'. Soon after crossing Martin's Industry the vessel was forced to anchor by a dense fog bank, and did not get under way again till 4.30pm. Arriving off Fort Sumter at eight o'clock the next morning Lardner took command of the forces outside the harbor which consisted of the gunboats *Flag* and *Alabama*. The *Flag* however sailed for Port Royal at 4pm that afternoon.

As a final addendum to the battle, the ships carpenter Mr Doughty cut from the main yard a 32-pound sold shot which had struck the *Susquehanna* during the close quarter fighting with Fort Walker off Hilton Head.

CHARLESTON AND FERNANDINA

Early in the forenoon of November 12 the Union frigate *San Jacinto* arrived off Charleston. She carried two unwilling passengers, Confederate emissaries James Mason of Virginia and John Slidell. of Louisiana. They were on their way to Europe to plead for recognition for the South, and had been abducted in mid-Atlantic from the British mail steamer *Trent*. They were now bound for New York as prisoners. The *San Jacinto*'s captain, Charles Wilkes, would be lionized in the North for this act of bravado, but 'tweaking the Lion's tail' almost resulted in dire consequences for Washington. The enthusiastic officer had acted illegally in stopping a neutral merchantman in international waters and removing the Rebel commissioners, and the British government's reaction was swift and predictable. While diplomatic letters were exchanged the Royal Navy was put on full alert and British troops were mobilized on the Canadian border. Unwilling to fight more than one war at a time, Lincoln's cabinet climbed down and the pair were released.

The *Susquehanna* settled in to the mundane routine of blockade duty. Frequently sighting sails and giving chase only to find the vessels, when overhauled, to be other Union warships or friendly merchant vessels. On November 14 the steamer *Connecticut* approached Charleston, hove to and sent on board a large delivery of mail and supplies before departing for Port Royal.

The next morning the gunboat *Penguin* presented herself for duty with Lardner's flotilla and reported that Beaufort, North Carolina was now in Union hands. Lardner ordered her to maintain station off Eddystone, some 20 miles from Charleston. Saturday the 16th and the English warship *Immortalité,* 50 guns, arrived after an eight-day trip from New York with dispatches for the British consul in Charleston. The usual formalities ensued with Lardner granting permission for communications to be opened with the shore. The Sunday church service had barely finished on the *Susquehanna* when the Confederate schooner *Caroline,* flying English colors, was spied heading for the *Immortalité* which was in the act of getting underway. As the Royal Navy frigate moved to meet the Rebel ship the *Susquehanna* fired a blank warning shot which caused the small schooner to heave to. Lardner sent a boat alongside and the consul was taken off and conveyed to the English man-of-war. Returning to the *Susquehanna* he spent an hour with Captain Lardner before embarking on the Rebel schooner and sailing back to Charleston.

Thanksgiving passed quietly but the following day the gunboat *Penguin* appeared along with a schooner she had taken laden with saddles, bridles, salt and fruit. She was the *Albion,* built in Maryland and bound from Nassau sporting English colors. The *Penguin* seized her as she attempted to run into Edisto. The *Penguin's* skipper repaired aboard the *Susquehanna* to give his report to Lardner. That evening the gunboat sailed to take up her station while the schooner, with a prize crew aboard, made for Philadelphia. The bluejackets were treated to a welcome change to their diet thanks to several members of the crew who took the second cutter and the whaleboat on a successful fishing expedition.

On the morning of the last day of the month several sails were reported out to sea and the side-wheeler set out in pursuit only to discover them to be cargo ships chartered by the Navy to bring supplies to the Union forces at Port Royal. Returning to Charleston the next day the captain of the Union bark *Roebuck* informed Lardner that four Rebel steamers had put out from the harbor. In all probability they had sought to take advantage of the *Susquehanna's* absence to have a crack at the small Yankee sailing ship. But upon sighting the returning frigates' sails they quickly put about for the safety of Charleston.

The old year was drawing to a close. On December 2 the *Bienville*, one of the *Susquehanna's* companions at the Port Royal fight dropped anchor near Lardner's ship and transferred much needed powder, shot and shell to the *Susquehanna,* although she brought neither provisions nor news. That evening a severe gale commenced and came near to forcing the ship out to sea.

The gunboat *Florida* came in from Port Royal on the 4th to report for duty under Lardner. She brought with her a mail delivery and dispatches for the *Susquehanna's* captain, including a letter of congratulations from the Secretary of the Navy thanking the officers and men for their efforts in the late engagement at Port Royal. The following missive was read out to the crews of the various ships the next day.

Copy of General Orders

NAVY DEPARTMENT, 12th NOV. 1861

The Department announces to the Navy and the country its highest gratification at the brilliant success of the combined Navy and Army forces, respectively commanded by Flag Officer S.F. Du Pont and Brigadier General W. T. Sherman in the capture of Forts Walker and Beauregard, commanding the entrance to Port Royal Harbor South Carolina. To commemorate this signal victory, it is ordered that a National salute be fired from each navy yard, at meridian, on the day of receipt of this order.

Signed *GIDEON WELLES*, Sec. of the Navy

On December 6, the English sloop *Racer* arrived and the captain requested permission to communicate with the British consul, which Lardner granted and once again the Rebel schooner *Caroline* glided forth from Charleston on her diplomatic mission. As the *Racer* set course for Port Royal the *Florida* brought in a Swedish bark carrying ballast, but she was allowed to sail on after Lardner had checked and endorsed her papers. Better luck was enjoyed by the *Augusta*. At midday on the 7th she appeared with a fully rigged

English ship snared while attempting to run in further down the coast with a cargo of stores, small arms and ammunition. The next morning with a prize crew manning the yards she set her course for New York.

Acting upon orders received from the *Florida,* Lardner weighed anchor at 10am on the 9th, destination Port Royal. The *Augusta, Florida* and *Roebuck* were left on watch outside Charleston.

Sighting the Federal fleet that afternoon the *Susquehanna* dropped anchor off Martin's Industry, a small shoal lying east of the main inlet for the night. Passing through the harbor entrance the next morning the ship finally came to rest near the *Wabash.* Amos Burton was visibly impressed not only by the change in the environs of Port Royal Sound but in the energetic forays subsequently mounted by the Union occupation forces. "The harbor presented a decidedly mercantile appearance while Hilton Head looks like a large town ...our gunboats have reconnoitered in every river and inlet, where there was water enough for them to go, within five miles of the city of Savannah. The country is deserted by all the white inhabitants leaving splendid residences, comfortable homes, highly cultivated plantations, rather than remain true to the flag which has so long protected them. A large number of contrabands have been left behind, which are now cared for at Hilton Head; a post office and express office have been established at Hilton Head. The Secretary of the Navy has changed the name of Fort Walker to that of Fort Seward, and that of Fort Beauregard to Fort Wells."

Orders from Du Pont received on Monday, December 17, instructed Lardner to sail for St Simon's off the Georgia coast, there to assume blockading duties, keeping a close watch for several English craft which Union intelligence sources believed were on their way from Britain, determined to breach the blockade. Lardner in turn requested Commander Steedman in the *Bienville* to cover Fernandina and Commander Lanier's *Alabama* was to cover Wassa and Ossabaw Inlets.

The *Susquehanna* was piloted out of Port Royal Sound by the *Pembina* and arrived on station on the afternoon of the 18th, only to run aground on St Simon's Banks. A changing tide allied with three hours of sheer hard work hauling on hawsers saw the steamship float free, finally coming to anchor around midnight. The *Susquehanna* began her patrol the next morning and soon sighted the *Alabama*, which came alongside to report the running on shore and subsequent destruction of a schooner obviously laden with a contraband cargo. The *Susquehanna* dropped anchor that night off the entrance to Brunswick Bay, some 60 miles from Savannah. Two strong sand and earthwork batteries defended the bay.

Heading on a southerly tack the *Susquehanna* sailed at 7am on the 20th and four hours later hailed the gunboat *Bienville* which ship passed on additional welcome news. Captain Steedman had chased a schooner and after forcing the ship aground had burned her, destroying the cargo of oil, turpentine and cigars. Following in the wake of the *Bienville*, both vessels arrived off Fernandina, Florida and proceeded along the enemy coast making observations and taking soundings. The *Susquehanna* returned to her moorings off St Simon's Bay that evening.

Christmas Day found the sloop lying at anchor and Amos Burton in a depressed mood, a feeling no doubt shared by his messmates. "Christmas Day, and how dull to be laying on such a blockade as this – no little delicacy to be had for love or money, consequently our Christmas dinner is made up of pork and bean soup. Music by the band, and target practice with small arms, are the little amusements we enjoy to pass the time; what a contrast between this and our last Christmas on board this ship. We were then on our way from Spezia to Naples. None can forget the pretty view of the city and bay, and also of Vesuvius by moonlight. The rebel commodore, George Hollins, was our captain then; we were proud of him and thought there was none better, but he has forfeited our respect by trampling on that flag under which he was raised to honour and position. Today he lies in wait at New Orleans in the ironclad boat *Manassas*, and would destroy this ship and her gallant crew that were once proudly praised by him. This evening our band plays its liveliest airs, and all who choose may join in the dance up till 9 o'clock, then the watch goes below and our Christmas on the blockade ends."

The crew celebrated the opening day of the new year in similar fashion to that of Christmas Day. For several uneventful weeks the ship continued her patrols but failed to add to her tally of captured vessels. On January 13, 1862 Lardner's ship sailed for Hilton Head coming to anchor at 5.30pm the next evening. Returning from a hunting trip in one of the

The *Susquehanna* rides at her moorings.
US Naval Historical Center

whaleboats on the evening of the 20th, acting master Zeraga accidentally discharged his musket, severely wounding ordinary seaman J. Hyatt, the ball passing through his arm at the elbow joint.

With Hatteras Inlet and Port Royal secure, Du Pont now turned his attentions on the network of interior waterways extending along the coast of South Carolina, Georgia and Florida, from Bull's Bay to Fernandina. Two flotillas were formed, one commanded by Captain Drayton sailed to investigate and take soundings of the northerly inlets at St. Helena Sound and North and South Edisto, while Commander's John and C. P. Rogers explored Tybee Roads, Wassaw and Ossabaw Sounds to the south. Virtually all the Confederate fortifications in these areas were found to have been abandoned, with the exception of Fort Pulaski on the Savannah River and, it was believed, Fernandina slightly further to the south.

Therefore Fernandina and its neighboring posts were to be the next targets for Du Pont and preparations for this new expedition were begun. On March 26, a severe gale hammered the gathering fleet, and as the storm's velocity grew Amos Burton recalled, "The prize ferry-boat *St Regle* parted her cable and was driven by the wind and tide down against the flagship. Clearing herself, she dashed on to our ship, striking across our bow, carrying away the martingale. Sweeping along the starboard side, her woodwork caught on the wheelhouse. Before she could be extricated the upper part of her woodwork was considerably damaged. The steamer *Mercury* came alongside attached a hawser to the runaway and hauled her off, towing her to a safe anchorage.

As night came on the storm increased in violence. At 9 o'clock pm., our ship dragged her anchors. Having steam up, we were able to keep clear of the *Wabash,* which was close astern of us. Weighed anchor, moved up the bay; let go the port anchor – in a few minutes the cable parted, and we were again adrift. By good management we succeeded in getting a safe anchorage into the shore."

The next afternoon the steamer's boats swept the channel for the lost anchor but with no success. Further searching was abandoned when the squadron received orders to make sail. Following in the wake of the *Wabash* the fleet headed out to sea. Once clear of the bar they anchored for the night. At 7am on the 28th, the *Wabash,* with the fleet following in line ahead formation, set her course due south. Around midday off Tybee Island the sloops *Pawnee* and *Pocahontas* joined the squadron.

Du Pont arrived off Wassaw Sound in the early evening where a further five gunboats joined the fleet, and at 8pm with the ships showing a profusion of blue and white lights the expedition proceeded on its way, coming in sight of the entrance to Brunswick Bay on the morning of March 1. All appeared quiet, and while the large steamers rode at anchor several smaller gunboats slipped into the entrance to the bay only to find the batteries deserted and the guns removed. At 1.30pm the fleet got under way again and arrived off St. Andrew's light, the upper entrance to Amelia Sound where the squadron dropped anchor.

Bright and early on the morning of the 2nd, 20 marines from the *Susquehanna* under 30 year-old Lieutenant Philip Fendall Jr., together with marines from the *Wabash,* transferred aboard the *Keystone State* to assist the land forces under General Wright. With Du Pont now flying his broad pennant in the gunboat *Mohican,* the gunboats and transports headed into Amelia

Sound coming to a halt some two miles inside. At 9am the *Susquehanna's* paddles threshed the surface of Amelia Sound and the frigates' crew went to battle stations. Three hours later the Confederate bastion of Fort Clinch, a part casemated work capable of mounting 150 guns, was sighted with a small Rebel ship lying close under her lee.

A clever ruse that morning involving the Union ship *Onward* had resulted in a Rebel officer and six men being taken prisoner. The *Onward* had been lying off Amelia Sound and her captain ordered French colors and a pilot jack to be hoisted aloft. In answer to this, a small cutter carrying the unsuspecting Confederates put out for the *Onward*. Once aboard however, the foreign colors were lowered and the Stars and Stripes raised, the bemused secessionists being informed they were on board of an American volunteer and were now prisoners of war!

That afternoon the yacht *Rebecca* sailed close into Fort Clinch to take soundings and although well in range of the guns, the fort remained strangely silent. The results showed the depth of water would prevent the warships closing with the Rebel works and only the pivot guns of the fleet could be brought to bear with any effect.

During the night of the 3rd with the weather cooling and a blustery wind rising, brilliant flames suddenly lit the dark sky in the vicinity of the fort. As dawn broke, officers on board the fleet could discern through their telescopes the buildings in and around the fort burning furiously. Under way by 7am, the *Susquehanna* stood in closer to the shore and opened fire with her forward pivot gun. This action solicited no response from Fort Clinch and it appeared a safe assumption that the Rebels had evacuated the post.

The fort had been considerably strengthened comprising a garrison of 5,000 men and the addition of sand, masked and water batteries capable of mounting a further 90 guns, yet they had chosen to abandon the place, destroying a railroad bridge and railroad depot. As the Confederates piled onto railway cars they opened fire with small arms on the Union gunboat *Ottawa*. Stung into action by this act of bravado, the gunboat sent several rounds of canister into the boxcars causing considerable damage to both the cars and their passengers.

Du Pont had received information that the Confederates were also abandoning Fernandina and Lardner was requested to cut off the retreat of any Rebel vessels attempting to sneak out to sea. Accompanied by the *Rebecca*, Lardner reached Fernandina on the afternoon of March 3. After sending in the yacht to take soundings and investigate the batteries mounted at the entrance to Amelia Sound, Lardner moved in on the Rebel positions the next morning. The *Susquehanna* loosed off several rounds but it proved a waste of ammunition, the works had been abandoned.

The Confederates had left little in the way of equipment and arms. Seventeen guns and a small steamer loaded with women and children fell into Du Pont's clutches. Of the handful of Fernandina citizens who remained to welcome the Yankees Amos Burton was informed that, "...a few were Union, but the women were rank secesh." Fernandina had now been added to the roll of Union prizes. Additional forays soon set out from Fernandina. Federal forces occupied both St. Augustine and Jacksonville to the south and Brunswick and St. Simon's Island to the north. The Union fleet now claimed domination of the Southern coastline from Port Royal to the St. John's River, Florida.

On March 5 1862, the *Susquehanna* ran down the coast to Nassau Inlet where the *Keystone State* and the *Onward* were on blockade. Although the Confederates had constructed batteries to protect the estuary these positions stood abandoned. The purpose of the trip was to recover the detachment of marines taken from the *Susquehanna* and the *Wabash* who had gone ashore via the *Keystone State* to assist the Army in occupying Fernandina. The sloop put back to that harbor the same evening, relaying the flagship's contingent of marines to the *Wabash* upon her return.

Orders from Du Pont detailed Lardner and the *Susquehanna* for temporary assignment at Port Royal, there to superintend the day-to-day activities of the roadstead. However, if all was quiet and Lardner felt his presence at Port Royal was not required, he was to sail to Charleston and take command once again of the blockading vessels off the harbor. Du Pont would reinforce Lardner's flotilla with as many vessels as could be spared including the *James Adger* and the *Bienville*. The *Augusta* and the *Sumpter*, at present off Charleston, were to remain on station. Consequently, on the afternoon of the 7th, the *Susquehanna's* capstan hauled the protesting anchor chains through the hawse holes, and the fore and main topmen scrambled aloft to loose the weathered canvas and make ready to sail for Port Royal.

The weather had turned extremely cold and Amos Burton wrote, "This is the coldest day we have experienced since winter set in; it is impossible to keep warm forward of the main mast, while our ward rooms and cabin are provided with stoves." Sighting a strange sail the next morning the steamer attempted but failed to overtake the vessel and arrived at Port Royal at midday.

On March 10 the warships *Mississippi* and *Maratanza* arrived at Port Royal with transports packed with General Benjamin Butler and 3,000 Union troops. The soldiers were to assist in the attempt to capture New Orleans in a combined expedition with a Federal fleet under the command of Flag Officer David Farragut. The vessels had encountered rough weather on the passage from Hampton Roads and the *Mississippi* had grounded on Frying Pan Shoals. As a consequence of this Butler had placed her master, Captain Fulton, under arrest charged with disloyalty. On the morning of the 13th Butler's expedition got underway, passing the *Susquehanna* whose band were playing national airs while her cheering crew manned the rigging. The soldiers on the passing craft returned the salutations while General Butler, with head uncovered, stood on the quarterdeck surrounded by his staff.

During a week overseeing activities in the harbor, news came of the disaster that had befallen the Union vessels lying at Hampton Roads. The *Virginia* had finally emerged to give battle, sinking the *Cumberland,* running the *Congress* ashore leaving her a blazing wreck, and forcing the frigate *Minnesota* aground to be finished off on the morrow, along with any other wooden-walled Yankee warships foolhardy enough to interfere. The Rebel ironclad's plans were thwarted by the appearance of the *Monitor*, and the ensuing battle between them, the first duel between two ironclads, ended in a standoff with the *Virginia* withdrawing up the Elizabeth River.

A dispatch to Lardner dated the 19th arrived from Lieutenant Collins, master of the gunboat *Unadilla* in Wright's River, South Carolina. He informed the *Susquehanna's* skipper that two Confederate deserters had assured Collins that Rebel naval forces based in Savannah were planning an imminent attack on Yankee batteries sited on the Savannah River. This

Fort Sumter, defender of Charleston harbour and symbol of Southern defiance.
Battles and Leaders

information was backed up by a dispatch from General Viele, the officer commanding the threatened Union positions. With no gunboats to send, the only assistance Lardner could offer was the steamer *Pettit* and two of the *Susquehanna's* launches, each fitted out with a howitzer and manned by 38 volunteers under Lieutenant's Wells and Gillis.

On the 21st, and 22nd the launches made investigative trips up the New River and Wright's River. One of the boats was fired into by mounted Confederate pickets. One round from the howitzer crashed out in reply, scattering the gray-clad horsemen. No losses occurred among the Union seamen resulting from this skirmish, but the day was to have a tragic ending for one of the *Susquehanna's* men. That night as the crew of one of the boats assigned to picket duty at the junction of Pull-and-be-Damned Creek and the Cooper River landed to pitch their tents they were fired on by Federal soldiers, also on picket duty. One of the hastily aimed shots found a target and ordinary seaman George Collins of Smyrna, Delaware, pitched lifeless to the ground.

The sailors had obviously been mistaken for Confederates. They returned the fire and ran for the launch where they turned the howitzer on the 'enemy'. The soldiers returned to their camp while the *Susquehanna's* boat, with the body of the unfortunate seaman made for the gunboat *Unadilla*. He was later interred at Hilton Head alongside those who had been killed in the Port Royal engagement.

Operations along Wright's River continued and on March 26, reinforced by 250 men of the 6th Connecticut Volunteers, the *Susquehanna's* launches, towed by the *Pettit* and *Mercury*, made a 12-mile incursion upriver but finding no sign of the enemy returned to the *Unadilla*. The threat to the Yankee positions on the Savannah River, if it had ever existed, was ended and the men of the *Susquehanna* returned to their ship totally exhausted from their efforts, having spent eight days in open boats exposed to the elements.

Over the next three days two officers were transferred from duty with the *Susquehanna.* On March 28 Lieutenant Gillis, one of the officers just returned from the Wright's River patrol assumed command of the gunboat *Hale* lying in Mud Creek. Lieutenant Clark Wells the ship's executive officer, was dispatched to take over the sloop *Vandalia* then off Tybee Island, whose captain had been relieved, suffering from a debilitating illness. Wells was added to the list of promising young officers who had proven their worth while aboard the *Susquehanna* and he would not be the last. Several were destined for their own commands and would gain further honors. Wells left the ship on the last day of March. Lieutenant A. W. Weaver superseded him.

While on patrol off Georgetown, South Carolina on the 12th, the Federal bark *Gem of the Sea* stopped and boarded the British schooner *Fair Play* listed as from Halifax, Nova Scotia. She was carrying a mixed cargo of fish, soap, candles, shoes, brogans, boots, leather, blankets and blue flannel. The Union skipper, not satisfied with either her captain's explanation or his papers sent the schooner with a prize crew to Port Royal with orders to report to Lardner. While on the *Susquehanna*, evidence of the *Fair Play's* true profession came to light. Four witnesses, lately escaped from Charleston, recognized her master as a Captain Thayer, previously employed not only as a police officer in that city but also as the master of the quarantine boat running between the city and the medical segregation area. They also stated that with the outbreak of war he had; "...adopted the secession uniform." Armed with these facts Lardner provisioned the schooner and ordered her back to the *Gem of the Sea.* She then sailed for Philadelphia for adjudication in a prize court.

April 1862 started promisingly enough. At 7am on the 1st the sloop made the short trip to take up station off Charleston. Whilst on patrol on the 3rd, the British schooner *Coquette* came under the *Susquehanna's* guns some two miles off the bar. Her papers showed Nassau registered as her home port and her cargo, listed by Lardner as "...suitable for and in great demand in a southern port", was sufficient for Lardner to order the schooner to Philadelphia under a prize crew commanded by master's mate Cooke. Two days previously, a vessel similar to the *Coquette* and carrying a like cargo had been stopped by the *Onward* but allowed to proceed after investigation. Later that same evening, while trying to run into Charleston she had been pursued by another warship that succeeded in forcing her ashore on Sullivan's Island where she became a total wreck. The Union gunboat *Huron* fired into the stricken schooner finishing her off on the morning of the 3rd.

On April 12, running before the wind in the teeth of a vicious squall a ship attempted to slip past the blockading squadron. The *Susquehanna* spied her and Lardner ordered the *Huron* and *Sumpter* in pursuit. Opening fire on the hapless schooner they drove her close inshore where she ran fast aground. Abandoned by the crew and left to the elements she was pounded into matchwood on the rocks.

On the 18th the bark *Restless* brought a mail delivery for the tars aboard the *Susquehanna* and also news of the fall of the Rebel Fort Pulaski following a bombardment of 26 hours. The *Pocahontas* arrived that afternoon confirming this latest success together with reports of the taking of some 357 Confederate prisoners.

Further ships fell prey to the vigilant Yankee cruisers, including two schooners making the run out to sea laden with cotton. The *Susquehanna* was ordered to return to Port Royal and Lardner weighed anchor on the night on the 20th, arriving the following afternoon.

The war for the Union had so far accomplished much at sea, with the fall of New Orleans the latest success. At dawn on April 24, Flag Officer David Farragut's fleet ran the gauntlet of Forts Jackson and St Philip, the Confederate strongholds guarding the mouth of the Mississippi. Two days later the Crescent City surrendered to Farragut without a shot being fired.

Ashore, it had been a different story. In the West the Union cause had flourished, with Ulysses Grant advancing down the Tennessee River capturing Forts Henry and Donelson in late February. However, overconfidence bred contempt and on April 6 Grant's troops were caught unawares by a surprise attack whilst encamped on the banks of the Tennessee at Pittsburgh Landing by General Albert Sydney Johnston's 40,000 strong Confederate Army. The culmination of two days' savage fighting at Shiloh ended with Johnston killed and his army retreating on Corinth – but it had been a near run thing with a dreadful casualty list totaling 23,000 for both sides. Following the debacle at Manassas, Lincoln had appointed George Brinton McClellan as commander in the eastern theatre. 'Little Mac' – a sobriquet coined by his adoring troops – was a West Point graduate and a superb logistical organizer, he threw himself into restructuring the Federal army. McClellan gave his army a new title, one that it would carry until the war's end – the Army of the Potomac. He forged the green recruits and demoralized soldiers into a disciplined, well-trained force of over 100,000 men.

Persistently urged on by Lincoln to take the field against the Rebel forces still entrenched at Manassas, McClellan refused to be rushed. At last in mid-March of 1862 the Union Army was on the move. McClellan's plan called for a primary amphibious operation whereby his army would be ferried to Fortress Monroe on the tip of the Virginia Peninsula. From there they would advance upon Yorktown then, supported by Union naval forces, strike on up the Peninsula to the gates of Richmond – and the end of the war!

IN FEAR OF THE IRONCLAD

The *Susquehanna*, still lying at Port Royal, would figure in the preliminaries of the campaign. Du Pont had been requested by the Navy Department to send the sloop to Hampton Roads, there to join Flag Officer Goldsborough's fleet. Du Pont was far from happy with this situation and in a communiqué to Washington written from his cabin on the *Wabash* on April 27 he stressed the importance of the *Susquehanna's* role on the Charleston blockade. In his opinion: "It would be doing an injustice to the public interests here and to myself did I fail to say that the withdrawal of this ship and the officer in command is a serious inroad into the efficiency of this squadron.

"I had prepared to shift my flag to her on Tuesday, for the purpose of visiting Charleston, and to see for myself if it was possible to place the blockading ships in more effective positions. Captain Lardner's experience made his presence there very important to me. The *Susquehanna* is the only vessel, by her armament, which could cover the large force of weak vessels now off that port."

In an attempt to placate the irate commodore, a reply was sent from the Navy Department. It assured him that it was of the greatest importance to the war effort and a genuine emergency, which necessitated the *Susquehanna's* transfer to Hampton Roads. She would be returned to his squadron as soon as was deemed practicable.

Accompanying the orders detaching the *Susquehanna* for service with Goldsborough, Du Pont sent a personal letter to Lardner which ended "...I think it is due to you and to myself to express my most unqualified appreciation of the zeal, efficiency and devotion which have marked your services with this fleet, and I trust they will not be overlooked by the Department."

Du Pont's chagrin was understandable when borne out by the evidence of the effectiveness of Lardner's squadron as presented to him by the *Susquehanna's* commander. In the first three weeks of April five blockade-runners were either captured or destroyed by Lardner's flotilla while endeavoring to find a way through to Charleston. Nevertheless, having coaled and received back on board a rifled howitzer borrowed by the *Hope*, the *Susquehanna* departed Port Royal at midday on March 28. Cracking on all sail the frigate reached Hampton Roads on the evening of the 29th.

The intimidatory presence of the *Virginia*, now moored above Sewell's Point, had led to the reinforcing of the Union warships riding at anchor in the roads. Besides the newly arrived *Susquehanna*, Goldsborough's force consisted of the frigates *Minnesota, St Lawrence, San Jacinto, Seminole* and *Dacotah*. These were complemented by the ironclads *Monitor, Galena* and *Naugatuck*. If the former Union frigate did venture out to try her mettle, the *Virginia* could be assured of a warm reception.

A Union tug, nosing her way slowly up the Elizabeth River on the afternoon of May 2, glimpsed the *Virginia* with steam up. Assuming her intention was to run down to confront the commodore's squadron the tugboat's skipper turned back towards Hampton Roads and alerted Goldsborough to the danger. The commodore immediately ordered his warships cleared for action and signaled the transports to make for the open sea. Sure enough the Rebel ironclad was soon sighted, but she came to a stop under cover of the Rebel batteries at Sewell's Point, and around 4pm retraced her course back up the Elizabeth River. That evening the *Susquehanna* took on board two 100-pounder rifled Parrot guns. In her role of supporting

McClellan's advance up the Peninsula, the frigate would be operating on the York River.

Bogged down for days before Yorktown, McClellan had constructed elaborate siege works, bringing heavy guns and mortars to bear on the Confederate lines. Convinced that the Rebels greatly outnumbered him 'Little Mac' had spent precious time laying siege to the town. However, McClellan's timidity in front of Yorktown brought vital time for the main Confederate forces to consolidate outside Richmond and prepare the counterattack which would ultimately push the Army of the Potomac back down the Peninsula in ignominious defeat. On May 4, heavy firing could be heard from the direction of Yorktown by the crew of the *Susquehanna* and a signal was received informing the fleet that the town had been evacuated and was now in Union hands. Lardner's orders to prepare for action on the York River were countermanded with the fall of the town.

The 7th brought a flurry of activity in nearby Fortress Monroe, with the visit of President Lincoln. The Chief Executive and his party went sightseeing to Fort Wool on the Rip Raps and at noon Commodore Goldsborough accompanied by two officers climbed aboard the *Susquehanna* to judge for himself the accuracy and effectiveness of the two recently mounted 100-pounder Parrot guns.

At daybreak on the 8th, the ironclad *Galena* with the gunboat *Port Royal* as her consort headed up the James River. Within the hour firing was heard as the ships engaged enemy batteries at Day's Point. The sloop *Jamestown* sailed in at 8am and two hours later the *Susquehanna* was preparing for battle. With steam now up the side-wheeler, accompanied by the *San Jacinto*, *Seminole* and the *Monitor* headed for Sewell's Point, there to engage and attempt to silence the Rebel guns.

The Confederate position mounted 61 pieces of ordnance and was well supplied with some 200 rounds of shell ammunition. Bombproof shelters and magazines contained powder of British origin, and there were two rifled cannon sited in an iron casemated battery, their muzzles trained on the Union positions on the Rip Raps.

At noon the *Susquehanna's* drums beat to quarters and the ship was cleared for action. Half an hour's steaming brought the flotilla, now reinforced

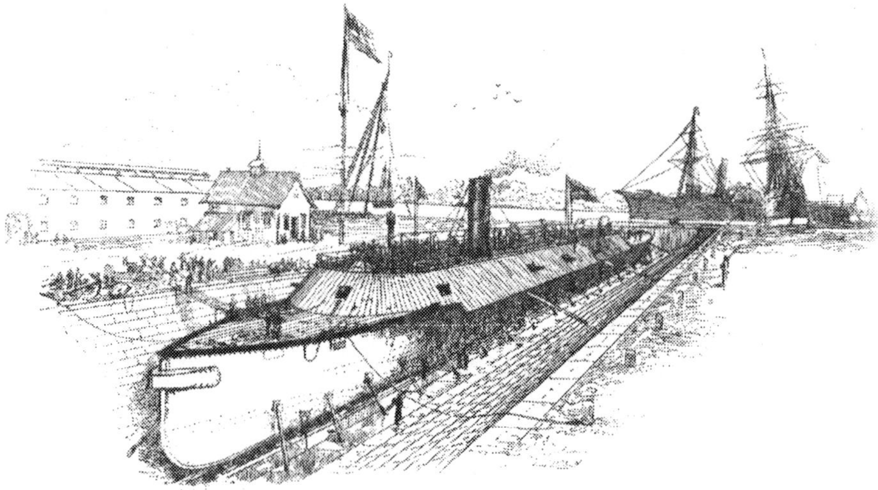

The *Virginia* under construction at the Gosport Navy Yard, Virginia.
Battles and Leaders

The Rebel ironclad *Virginia* steaming down to challenge Union warships, including the *Susquehanna* and the *Monitor*, engaging Confederate batteries on Craney Island.
US Naval Historical Center

by the *Dacotah* and the monitor *Naugatuck*, in range of their target, and the warships opened fire. Shells from the rifled and smoothbore guns of the Yankee vessels arrowed into the fort. The Rebels attempted to return the fire but most of their efforts fell short and at two o'clock their flag was shot away and their guns fell silent. The *Monitor* now moved in closer and fired two 'fluid' shells into the place, setting fire to a wooden building. Again the defenders opened fire and again Lardner's ship replied, a salvo of shells subduing the enemy gunners.

It was then that the *Virginia* was seen approaching from the Elizabeth River. Immediately the wooden warships took up a position by the Rip Raps and the two Union ironclads moved out to cover them and to give battle should the Rebel ram seek a confrontation. Scattered shots from the battered fort plunged into the water astern of the *Susquehanna* and for the third and final time devastating counter-battery fire thundered across the river pummeling the Rebel guns into final silence. Just before 3pm Lardner made the following signal to the ships under his command. "Enemy's fort appears to be abandoned."

While Lardner ordered his vessels to follow the *Susquehanna* down to Fortress Monroe the *Virginia* made her move; bearing slowly down on the Union squadron, she halted and took up a position near Craney Island. The Union guns on the Rip Raps opened fire on the Rebel ram as if to dare her to come further down and engage the Yankee ironclads, but just before 5pm she turned her back on the enemy and steamed sluggishly away up the Elizabeth River. The *Susquehanna*, obeying the flagship's signal to; "Resume your moorings", finished with engines and let go her starboard anchor into 15 fathoms of water

The *Susquehanna* made ready to resume the attack on the Rebel positions on the 9th but the expected orders failed to arrive. The day passed quietly for the crew with the only action emanating from the Union artillery on the Rip Raps sending the occasional shell into the Confederate lines. During the night of the 10th a large conflagration could be discerned in the direction of the Confederate-held navy yard at Norfolk, accompanied by sporadic explosions. One of these mighty detonations, timed at 4.45am, proved to be the end of the *Virginia*.

The advance of McClellan's army necessitated the evacuation by the Rebels of Norfolk, and because of her deep draft the ram was unable to retire to safety further upriver towards Richmond. Her officers set the ironclad ablaze rather than allow her to fall into Union hands. At 6am, preceded by the *Monitor, Naugatuck* and *Mount Vernon*, the *Susquehanna, San Jacinto, Seminole* and *Dacotah* slipped their cables and steamed cautiously upriver, ready for action. Approaching Sewell's Point the second cutter from the *Susquehanna* put ashore a small detachment of bluejackets under the command of acting master Churchill who found the enemy positions abandoned, the National colors were soon flying from the walls of the fort.

Approaching Craney Island, two Rebel banners were sighted. With the squadron forming line of battle, Lardner gave the command: "Man the starboard battery!" As the ships drew abreast of the works and with no sign of enemy activity a boat from the *Mount Vernon* rowed ashore to investigate. Shortly after, the secessionist flag was hauled down to be replaced by the Stars and Stripes the sight of which brought forth a wave of cheering from the flotilla.

Navigation was proving hazardous as the Confederates had removed the marker buoys and driven wooden piles into the riverbed to act as simple but effective obstructions. The *San Jacinto* was stopped but the *Susquehanna* would not be denied and Lardner's ship steamed full ahead passing safely over them. As the Yankee flotilla passed the old hulk *United States* and came up to Fort Pindan, a large casemated work sited on the right-hand bank of the river, pieces of wreckage were seen floating downstream and speculation was rife that they were the remains of the feared *Virginia*. Union soldiers crewing a passing tug confirmed that the *Virginia* was, indeed, no more and that the town of Norfolk and the navy yard had been abandoned by the enemy who, prior to departure, had set government buildings at the naval base afire. Passing Hospital Point the vessels came to a stop at Norfolk at 11am where the United States flag was already fluttering in the breeze above the Hospital and the Custom House.

With Norfolk and the nearby town of Portsmouth now under Union occupation, General Wool had appointed Brigadier-General E. L. Viele as military governor and martial law had been imposed on those citizens who chose to remain. Shortly after the *Susquehanna* had dropped anchor a special

Engraving of the *Susquehanna* riding out a gale.
US Naval Historical Center

steamer bearing President Lincoln, General Wool, Commodore Goldsborough and Captain Carse of the *Minnesota* arrived. While the flag officer repaired aboard the *Susquehanna*, the President and his following marched through the recaptured town with the Union troops, led by the marine drummers of the *Susquehanna*. On the evening of the 16th yet more distinguished dignitaries from Washington made their appearance including Secretary of the Navy Gideon Welles and his assistant, Gustavus Fox.

The decks of the frigate were crowded with extra passengers on May 17, as the entire complement of marines from the Union squadron were transferred aboard the *Susquehanna* in readiness for an attack on the remaining Rebel batteries on the James River. At 8am the ship headed down the Elizabeth River to Newport News where, with Goldsborough on board and in company with the *Dacotah, Wachusetts, Maratanza* and a tugboat, the *Susquehanna* stood up the James River. With the tug churning on ahead of the flotilla taking soundings, a Confederate banner was perceived on Battery Huger, atop

Hardings Bluff. The order to commence fire into the works and the surrounding woods was given but this action failed to elicit a response. Marines in tandem with a large party of bluejackets were rowed ashore to discover the fort, mounting 15 guns, to be deserted, the garrison having retired upon Richmond. Much of the interior had been destroyed the guns were spiked and their carriages burned. Yet another flag raising ceremony ended the operation before the sailors and marines re-embarked. By 6pm the *Susquehanna* was riding at anchor some two miles below Fort Huger.

The 18th was spent in mopping up operations with small landing parties destroying abandoned enemy fortifications; guns were spiked and their wooden carriages were left as smoldering timber; buildings and munitions were set ablaze and blown up. The party of marines and sailors put ashore at Rock Wharf Landing to neutralize Fort Boykin discovered the body of a bluejacket on the waters edge. Assumed to be a crewmember of either the *Cumberland* or *Congress*, it was a gruesome reminder of the late battle between those ships and the *Virginia.* After interring the body, the detachment set about demolishing the fort. Situated on a high bluff and surrounded by a 75-foot wide by 40-foot deep moat, Fort Boykin held a commanding view of the river and 14 guns were mounted in the earthwork embrasures. The interior held bombproof magazines and two citadels for the shelter of the garrison.

Much of the landing party's work had been done for them; the Confederates disabling the cannon and firing the carriages before departing. The seamen completed their task by setting fire to anything combustible inside the fort and blowing up the magazine. Their task completed they hauled themselves back on board the *Susquehann*a which returned to Hampton Roads, coming to her moorings at eight o'clock.

Having returned the marines from the *Minnesota* and *San Jacinto* to their respective ships, the *Susquehanna* steamed for Norfolk. It was here that the crew learned they were to lose their captain. No doubt prompted by the exemplary and efficient conduct displayed by Lardner in executing his duties while with the *Susquehanna*, the Navy Department had sent orders relieving him of command of the steamer. He was to repair aboard the sloop-of-war *San Jacinto* which would become his flagship and proceed with that vessel to take charge of the Eastern Gulf Blockading Squadron, reporting to, and subsequently relieving, Flag Officer William McKean.

At midday on May 20, all aboard the *Susquehanna* gathered aft to hear Lardner bid farewell to the assembled bluejackets. Amos Burton recorded the formalities. "At noon all hands were mustered aft, when Captain Lardner took leave of the ship's company, and spoke as follows. 'Men, I am going to leave you, and I am sorry for it. The officers and crew of the *Susquehanna* have gained a high reputation all over the country, and I am the only one as yet that has reaped any benefit from it. I hope you will be rewarded. Goodbye to you all.' His remarks were received with three hearty cheers. He then left the ship. As the *Susquehanna* shoved off, the band played 'Old Lang Syne' and 'Good-Bye' – the crew manned the rigging, giving three hearty cheers, feeling that we had lost a friend and an officer, cool, brave and kind to all, justly deserving the promotion bestowed on him." Along with command of the East Gulf Blockade Squadron came promotion to commodore.

Lardner's replacement was Commodore Robert B. Hitchcock, an extremely experienced officer in his early fifties. Appointed to the Naval College from the state of Connecticut on New Year's Day 1825 he served aboard the schooner *Shark* in the West India Squadron before transferring to the frigate *Delaware* for duty with the Mediterranean Squadron from 1829 to 1831. Receiving promotion to passed midshipman that same year; he next attained the rank of lieutenant on March 3, 1835. In 1837 he commenced two years of special duties before joining the frigate *Ohio*, sailing for the Mediterranean in 1840. His next ship, the frigate *Savannah*, on which he served for one year, showed the flag as part of the Pacific Squadron.

There followed spells on ordnance duty and as commander of the store ship *Relief* and on September 12, 1855 he was appointed to the rank of commander. In 1858 he captained the steam frigate *Merrimack*, part of the Pacific Squadron until returning to Washington in 1860, where he became Inspector of Ordnance, which post he was occupying when the war broke out in April 1861. Almost immediately he was relieved of that duty and promoted to captain.

Now as commodore, he was to take charge of the *Susquehanna*, and on May 21 his new command lay at Norfolk awaiting orders from Washington. These were delivered to Commodore Hitchcock the next day and detailed the ship to report for duty with David Glasgow Farragut's Western Gulf Blockading Squadron operating off the Confederate port of Mobile. Hitchcock was to make all sail for Mobile and upon arrival take charge of the Federal warships mounting blockade duties off the coast

MOBILE

With New Orleans under Union control Farragut had intended to mount an operation against Mobile, but events further up the Mississippi saw his plans forestalled. The hero of the battle for New Orleans, along with the majority of his fleet, was now absorbed in assisting Ulysses Grant's efforts to seize Vicksburg, thus wresting entire control of the Mississippi from the Confederacy and splitting the South asunder.

Armed Rebel steam vessels were reportedly preparing for the chance to come out and blast away the thin screen of Yankee vessels patrolling off Mobile Bay. The situation compelled Farragut to call for assistance and the *Susquehanna* was chosen for the task of aiding the hard-pressed flotilla. Her batteries being more than able to act not only as a deterrent, but if the Rebels ventured out to give battle, she carried sufficient firepower to engage the Confederate vessels in ship-to-ship combat.

On May 25 the frigate made sail for Hampton Roads, there to take on dispatches for Farragut. With repairs carried out on her machinery and the loading on board of shells and munitions for the fleet completed, the *Susquehanna* sailed at 9.30am on the 27th in cold, damp weather. A week spent battling against strong headwinds brought the *Susquehanna* in sight of Key West off the Florida coast and on June 5 the ship commenced to take on coal and provisions from the Union naval base.

Both port and starboard watches enjoyed spells of liberty ashore on Key West and on the 10th the steamer was declared ready for sea, sailing for Mobile Bay that afternoon after transferring the Gulf Squadron's mail to the *Kensington*, which had left for New Orleans at 10am. The following morning off the Tortugas Bank the *Susquehanna* came upon the schooner *Princeton*. She had left Havana on June 2 bound for Matamoras. Mistaking the Union sloop for a Spanish man-of-war the skipper, Captain D. Barnes, had made no effort to escape. An examination of her papers and cargo, plus the discovery of a Confederate flag was sufficient for Hitchcock to send her to Key West with a prize crew of three seamen with acting masters mate John Coffey in command. The schooner's manifest listed an assortment of items including drugs, dry goods and provisions together worth $5,663.

Hitchcock's ship arrived to take command of the flotilla off Mobile on June 14. He found only the sloop *Preble* and the gunboat *Kanawha*, the brig *Bohio* being some 14 miles westward near Petit Bois Island. Two elderly but formidable redbrick works, Forts Morgan and Gaines guarded either side of the entrance to the 2,000 yard-wide opening to the bay. Admiral Franklin Buchanan, once captain of the *Susquehanna* and lately skipper of the Rebel ironclad *Virginia*, commanded the defenses of Mobile and throughout August he had labored to strengthen both forts in terms of men and material.

Fort Morgan, a pentagonal work sited on the western tip of Mobile Point, and Fort Gaines opposite on Dauphine Island, now mounted impressive batteries of heavy guns; many of them rifled pieces, to keep the Yankees at bay. Augmenting these land-based defenses, Buchanan had wooden pilings driven deep into the seabed of the main channel, forming a narrow passage 500 yards wide, forcing incoming ships to pass under the guns of Fort Morgan. A minefield of explosive 'torpedoes' anchored just below the surface of the water completed the static defenses.

Bobbing gently at their moorings in the bay lay Commander Randolph's flotilla of three gunboats and the iron-plated ram *Baltic*. The gunboat *Morgan's* battery consisted of ten 32-pound rifled guns; the *Gaines* carried the same and the *Florida* four rifled pieces. As for the *Baltic* she mounted four guns; two Dahlgrens and two 32-pound rifles on her berth deck and two small brass pieces topside. Accounts from Confederate deserters verifying the strength of the forts and warships made disquieting news for Hitchcock. Mobile Bay would indeed be a tough nut to crack for any attacking force.

A flurry of activity kept the *Susquehanna* and her crew occupied over the coming days. On the night of the 19th, a pilot boat schooner loaded with cotton attempted to run out past the squadron under cover of a squall but was driven ashore, but she was refloated before the Union ships could get within range. The *Rhode Island* arrived on the 21st with mail, newspapers and two days' provisions, which included a consignment of beef, part of which was so rotten as to be completely inedible; the spoiled meat was soon heaved unceremoniously over the side. Later that day the *Bohio* sent in a small sloop, the *L Rebecca* captured off Biloxi.

Captain Febiger in the *Kanawha* ran a schooner aground on the 22nd, wrecking her completely. As sailors from the gunboat boarded the stranded blockade-runner a party of Rebel cavalry fired on them. The gunboat opened fire shelling a patch of woods where the Confederates were positioned. The exploding rounds soon flushed them out, forcing them to take flight at a gallop.

A Rebel steamer was seen to be fast aground under the guns of Fort Morgan early on the 29th and two smaller steamboats were observed to be alongside unloading her cargo. The shallow waters prevented the *Susquehanna* and the *Preble* closing with the stricken ship and Hitchcock ordered the sloop to find the light draft gunboat *Kanawha* – absent since the previous evening – and return with her. Upon the arrival of the gunboat the three Union vessels got under way and were soon on the receiving end of fire from Fort Morgan, the shots however falling short.

The warships returned the fire causing the two Rebel craft to haul off and the crew of the stranded steamer to jump ship. A towline was fixed to the abandoned blockade-runner by the *Kanawha* and she was hauled out to where the *Susquehanna* lay. Upon examination her engine room was found to be shipping water due to the cutting of the injection pipes and the opening of the stopcocks. Two boats crews were sent on board and two of the *Susquehanna's* engineers rigged emergency pumps to bale her out. A squad of marines was also dispatched to guard the cargo..

The craft was identified as the iron-built steam vessel *Ann*, constructed by Richard & Son of Hartlepool, England. At 350 tons and boasting three watertight compartments, her cargo consisted of muskets, 50 tons of powder, cartridge boxes, coffee, tea, paper and ale besides small quantities of luxury goods. The Rebels had succeeded in removing much of the shipment before the arrival of the *Kanawha*. Hitchcock took it upon himself to remove 39 gallons of oil and 10 pounds of citric acid for use aboard the *Susquehanna*. The *Ann* would be sent north for adjudication in a prize court.

In a dispatch to the Navy Department sent aboard the *Ann*, Hitchcock voiced his despair at the paucity of vessels with which to carry out effective blockading operations off Mobile. He warned of the increasing numbers of slight but swift schooners and brigs making use of the various inlets from the Swash Channel near Fort Morgan, round to the Pelican Channel off Fort Gaines, a distance of some 15 miles. The Confederates were in possession of gunboats powerful enough to engage and sink any of the craft Hitchcock chose to station in these areas. The commodore completed his report with the following request. "Captain Febiger of the *Kanawha*, is and has been most indefatigable in his efforts to prevent the passing in or out of vessels at this point; but I trust the Department will, as I have no access to the flag officer of this squadron, excuse me for urging an increase of gunboats or steamers of light draft to guard this portion of the coast. The signals from the fort show that they are expecting vessels to arrive, and we know they have them waiting to get out."

Hitchcock also sent a similar report to Farragut, pleading for an increase in superior ships to be assigned to the squadron. Although fully cognizant of the importance of Farragut's position at Vicksburg he stressed the point that all areas of Farragut's command should be efficient. Also, if intelligence passed on by the former commander of the *Susquehanna*, James Lardner, was to be relied upon several steamers, possibly armed, were gathered at Nassau in preparation for running through the blockade. Hitchcock stated that he was virtually powerless to stop them.

Independence Day, 1862 passed quietly with no celebrations aboard the *Susquehanna*. The prize ship *Ann* left for New York bearing Hitchcock's dispatches and the mail. The Rebel warships *Morgan, Florida* and *Gaines* ventured out as far as the Sand Island Light and threw a few shells at the flotilla before returning to the bay and safety.

The *Cayuga* arrived from New York that evening carrying mail for the Union ships. Hitchcock detained her until the *Kanawha* could make the journey to Ship Island to coal and provision, this task completed the *Cayuga* was released to continue her voyage to New Orleans. Reports continued to reach the *Susquehanna's* skipper of the build up of Confederate shore batteries around the bay and the arrival of reinforcements and guns for the forts. The storeship *Harvest Moon* sailed in on July 7 with fresh supplies for Hitchcock's ships.

Four days later the Royal Navy steamers *Rinaldo* and *Landrail* made their appearance having come from the Mississippi. Shortly after their arrival the unarmed Confederate steamship *Crescent* came out of the bay under a flag of truce. She requested permission to communicate with Captain Hawitt of the *Rinaldo* as the *Crescent* had on board the English consul from Mobile. Hitchcock agreed and after a brief meeting aboard the warship the consul re-

The formidable Fort Morgan, guardian of Mobile Bay.
Battles and Leaders

embarked on the Rebel steamer and the *Crescent* returned to Mobile. The two frigates departed for Pensacola that afternoon.

At noon on the 13th the *Rhode Island*, on her way north from New Orleans, passed mail and papers to the *Susquehanna*. Sailing for Boston that afternoon she took with her Paymaster Washington Irving Jnr, Acting Assistant Engineer F. E. Brown and a coal-heaver, one George Williams – all suffering from various maladies which necessitated sending them home. On the 15th the *Kanawha* hove in view towing a schooner suspected of trying to run in to Mobile. Her captain was ushered aboard the flagship where his papers were examined. Hitchcock, giving him the benefit of the doubt, had the relieved master rowed back to his ship where he made a present of some bottles of wine and several bunches of choice Havana cigars to the *Susquehanna's* officers. The day ended with the ship's crew assembled for a formal dress parade, an event that according to Amos Burton was none too successful. "At 6pm the entire ship's company fell in for dress parade; imperfect as it proved to be it was witnessed by officers from the *Preble* and *Kanawha*; I am sure they will often laugh over the grand parade they witnessed aboard the *Susquehanna*."

There was little excitement to spice the remaining days of July, but on the 25th just as dawn was breaking, the *Kanawha* signaled, reporting a steamship some eight miles distant closing fast with the coast. Permission was given for the *Kanawha* to pursue with the purpose of driving her towards the *Susquehanna*. Unfortunately by the time the frigate had weighed anchor the steamer, flying the Palmetto flag and believed to be the *Cuba*, reached the safety of Fort Morgan. The crew was mortified at missing this opportunity of securing a valuable prize.

Commodore Hitchcock could barely contain his anger as evidenced in his report addressed to Assistant Secretary of the Navy Gustavus Fox dated July 31. "My position is an awkward one and not at all pleasant. Your order to come here and stop, and the one in relation to Porter is all I have. Not the first word from Farragut. No communication with anyone." In relation to the escape of the blockade runner Hitchcock continued: "A fine steamer ran in on the 25th…either the *California* or the *Cuba*...they are both very fast. Captain Febiger, who has been a passenger in them, tells me they will go over 15 knots.

Do, in mercy, send some steam vessels here that we may look out for this place. Do all we can, it is impossible to keep steamers out if they wish to go in. It will not be long before you hear of some of our vessels being taken." Here, Hitchcock was making reference to the very real menace of Rebel steamers darting out from Mobile Bay and seizing unprotected Union merchant ships.

Of the three vessels on duty with Hitchcock he wrote: "I do not think the *Preble* and the *Bohio* are of the least use here, but in the way...I have no orders and am in the dark as to everything in relation to this squadron." A further problem plaguing the flag officer concerned the crew of the *Preble*. Many were one-year men and the enlistments were due to expire, what was to be done with them and how would they be replaced? However, Hitchcock's paramount concern was the *Susquehanna* herself. "We shall soon have to go to Ship Island or Pensacola for coal, which will take a week or ten days. The ship is not fitted to take in coal expeditiously; in fact is a dozen years behind the times, battery and all.

"The next two months will no doubt give us bad weather, and, if a heavy gale, we will stand a bad chance with our defective shaft. If I had been ordered to the ship and told to go to sea when she was ready, I should have made a statement of her defects, which embrace almost everything about her ...God grant we have no more bad luck, but I fear it without we get some more steam vessels soon."

Commodore Hitchcock addressed a similar dispatch to Secretary Welles, containing a plea for adequate vessels to be sent for duty with his command. Hitchcock closed his communication with the opinion that the Rebels were satisfied with their coastal defenses and were confident of repelling any assault mounted against them. Confirmation had also reached the commodore that the vessel that ran past him into Mobile was the *Cuba*. She had been carrying a full cargo of arms, ammunition, medicines and blankets.

On the 29th, a courts martial was convened on the *Susquehanna* and two seamen were tried for insubordination and disobedience to orders. The charges being proven resulted in the disrating of one of the bluejackets, a maintopman.

The night of the 31st was to be a trying one for the crew of the steamer. At 11pm mysterious blue and white lights accompanied by rockets sparkled in the heavens to seaward. Immediately the men went to general quarters and stood by their guns for three hours until the *Kanawha* came within hailing distance to pass the word that the strange vessel had been identified as the Union warship *Connecticut*. Already in a high state of alert, the attention of the crew switched to the shore when at 1am more rockets soared up into the night sky from the ramparts of Fort Morgan, they signaled an escape attempt by six soldiers from the garrison.

These desperate fellows, having been relieved from watch duty, had slipped away and lowered the commanding officer's gig into the dark waters of the bay. They then rowed for their lives, carrying with them their arms and accoutrements, knowing that discovery and capture would bring harsh punishment from their former comrades. When questioned by Hitchcock they swore they were Union men who had been pressed into service in the Confederate army and had served in the fort for 18 months awaiting an opportunity to abscond.

At 4am the weary gun crews again manned their battle stations as yet more signal rockets plus the report of a gun, this time from the direction of the *Bohio,* indicated that vessel's need for assistance. The *Susquehanna* immediately slipped her cable and was soon alongside the brig *Mechanic* of Harpwell, Maine. Her papers showed her to be making for New Orleans but the commodore suspected the ship's actual destination was Mobile. However, there being insufficient evidence to detain her, the brig's captain was warned off the blockade and sent on his way. Thus ended a fairly miserable night for the men of the Federal frigate.

Over the next four days the *Susquehanna* was involved in routine duties off the coast. On August 4, the sloop *Richmond* arrived from New Orleans, her crew in a pretty unhealthy and exhausted state from the rigors of duty at New Orleans and Vicksburg. She remained four days at Mobile before proceeding to Pensacola to rest her crew and recruit new hands.

If there was one thing that sailors on wooden vessels feared it was the outbreak of fire on board. Shortly after the *Susquehanna* got underway at 4am on the 8th the ardent clamoring of the fire alarm bell rang out. For some minutes all was pandemonium below as the source of the fire was sought. The cause was discovered to be a leaking boiler through which a great quantity of steam had escaped and frightened crew members, taking it for smoke had raised the alarm. The poor state of the *Susquehanna's* engines and boilers was now proving a danger to the firemen and engineers.

Late on the evening of the 11th unidentifiable signal lights were reported and Amos Burton wrote: "At 1 o'clock am., a steamer was seen coming in on the blockade, which created great excitement; beat to general quarters; slipped our cable; trained our guns on the steamer; opened fire on her, causing her to heave to; we moved up within hailing distance; when asked 'What steamer is that?' Captain Renshaw reported her, the US gunboat *Westfield*, from New Orleans, saying he had made his numbers twice; also showed other lights when coming in. She had a narrow escape from our shot; they were well intended but poorly aimed. This crew passed a sleepless night owing to the misunderstanding described above. Secured our anchor this forenoon this is the hottest day of the season." On the morning of the 14th the after starboard boiler sprung a severe leak causing hot water and steam to gush forth, severely scalding James Caswell, a fireman.

Friendly vessels appeared on a fairly regular basis, stopping only to pass mail and supplies before sailing on to New Orleans or Pensacola. On the morning of the 19th the *Hartford*, with Farragut aboard, accompanied by the sloop *Brooklyn* made a brief appearance, arriving off Mobile from New Orleans to a salute fired from the *Susquehanna*, which was returned by Farragut's flagship. Both warships sailed for Pensacola that afternoon. News was received of the death of former President Martin Van Buren the day following Farragut's visit and flags were lowered to half-mast and at midday 30 minute-guns were fired from the *Susquehanna*.

Hitchcock's concern over the capability of the scanty flotilla to mount a tight blockade off Mobile was lessened with the arrival of two gunboats to assist in the task. The *Pinola* sailed in on the 24th with the *Oneida* following in her wake the next day. Yet another vessel reported for duty with Hitchcock's squadron, the gunboat *Winona* arriving from Pensacola with dispatches for the commodore on the 28th.

Three Confederate runaways brought before Farragut on board the *Hartford* in New Orleans, claimed that the Rebels had evacuated Fort Gaines and transferred the heavy artillery to new defensive positions nearer to the city of Mobile itself. Anxious to prove or disprove this information Farragut instructed Hitchcock to take the *Susquehanna* close into the fort to determine whether the garrison had indeed departed. Consequently the sloop weighed anchor at 9am on August 29 and stood in for the fort. It was to be a short trip. As the ship came within range of the works the engine gave out and she was forced to lie off while repairs were carried out. Piloted close in by the *Kanawha*, the *Susquehanna* opened fire on Fort Gaines with one of her rifles.

The response was instant. Burton recorded later that day: "A small Rebel flag flying at the fort was hauled down, and a larger one run up. The ramparts were thick with men. A few more shots were fired from our pivots and rifles; our work was accomplished; on returning they fired a raking shot – the first and only one – which convinced us that they still lived. During the time we were under way, the Rebel flagship of Commodore Randolph and two other steamers, lay off Fort Morgan, watching our movements; returned to our anchorage at 5pm."

This brief action signaled the end of the *Susquehanna's* spell of duty off Mobile, and in the early hours of the morning she hauled up her anchor and laid a course for Pensacola.

PENSACOLA

Seven hours' sailing brought the *Susquehanna* in sight of her destination. She was joined by the *Rhode Island*, which arrived at Pensacola at noon. A quarantine pennant fluttered from a halyard on the latter's mizzen top, signaling an outbreak of Yellow Fever aboard. No contact with the vessel was permitted and she sailed for Boston early that evening.

Pensacola was an ideal anchorage, being capacious with adequate protection from the elements afforded by the Santa Rosa breakwater. Fort Pickens on Santa Rosa Island and Fort Barrancas on the mainland backed up by various earthwork batteries guarded the entrances to the harbor. The town of Pensacola itself lay seven miles up the coast to the northward and was the site of a rail terminus that connected the Atlantic coast with the Gulf.

When Florida seceded from the Union the small garrison of United States regulars withdrew to Fort Pickens on January 10, 1861, abandoning Pensacola and the navy yard to Florida state forces. Refusing all requests to surrender the tiny garrison held on, supplied by Union ships from the blockading squadron. The Confederates continued to occupy the shore opposite Fort Pickens until withdrawing on May 9, 1862. Federal troops took possession the following day. Before decamping, Confederate soldiers had put to the torch the Warrington Navy Yard, a government hospital and a newly constructed marine barracks.

Besides the *Susquehanna* Pensacola played host to Farragut's flagship *Hartford*, the frigate *Potomac* and the sloops *Brooklyn, Vincennes* and *Preble*. Also at their moorings rode the gunboats *Harriet Lane, Iroquois, Kanawah, Kennebec, Westfield* and *Jackson*. The 31st being a Sunday the usual ship's inspection followed by a church service took place aboard the vessels in the bay. The steamer *Kensington* nosed into Pensacola from New Orleans during these activities and off-loaded mail. The last day of the month ended with a heavy rainstorm.

September 1, 1862 would be a day of sorrow for many Union tars. The Navy in its infinite wisdom had decided to eliminate the spirit ration. From that day onward the American Navy would be a 'dry' navy. Amos Burton registered his disapproval. "This day will ever be remembered by all bluejackets and marines now serving in the United States Navy. The abolishing of the spirit ration act, which went into effect today, has called heavily the curses of Jack on the heads of those who were the instigators of it."

That afternoon the chief engineers from the *Hartford, Brooklyn, Harriet Lane* and *Cayuga* boarded the *Susquehanna* and descended 'tween decks to make a thorough examination of the ship's mechanical condition. Their report recommended the following course of action, that "...at the earliest possible moment the ship can be spared from the station, she be sent to some navy yard where the conveniences of a machine shop and the necessary facilities for repairing can be had." Their comments only endorsed Commodore Hitchcock's recommendations for a complete overhaul of both engines and boilers. The captain forwarded the engineers' report to Farragut.

Amos Burton also left a detailed account of their findings. "The starboard cylinder very much cut all around: the inboard starboard pillow-block badly broken: the center shaft cracked and otherwise defective in starboard inboard journal. In connection with the engines, the boilers were also examined: found the legs and the water bottoms very much corroded, needing much repair: the cutting of the cylinder was caused by improper adjusting of the packing in the first place; being compelled to use boiler iron plate in its rough state, instead of the proper packing rings. The breaking of the pillow-block was an accident to which all engines are exposed, and could not have been prevented. The crack in the shaft was known to the contractor when it was put into the ship, as patches were put in to cover the defect; from constant use it has partially developed its imperfections; the boilers have been in the ship six years; the corroding has been caused by long and constant use."

September passed slowly for the men of the *Susquehanna* with little excitement to break the routine of drills and inspections. Many vessels were logged entering and leaving Pensacola for destinations as far apart as Mobile, Galveston, New Orleans and New York. Reports of the successful infiltration of the blockade off Mobile by a Confederate gunboat in broad daylight were disclosed with the arrival of the *Winona* on the 5th. The Rebel warship had been flying the British ensign and pennants, and Captain Preble on the *Oneida* recognized the ruse too late. His error would result in dismissal from the service for dereliction of duty following a court of inquiry. Supported by letters from Admiral Farragut and Navy Secretary Welles to President Lincoln, he later lodged a successful appeal and was reinstated at his old rank on July 16, 1862.

Sunday the 7th and this particular Sabbath had an added touch of poignancy as the flagship *Hartford* buried one of her crew. On the evening of the 9th, Confederate guerrillas fired on Union pickets outside Pensacola, there were however no casualties from this minor fracas. Part of the starboard watch were given $5 and allowed 48 hours liberty in Pensacola on the 12th and it was a merry crowd of bluejackets who went ashore on the steamer *Rosalie*. The *Susquehanna* commenced coaling and powder was also taken on board and transferred below decks to the magazine. Assistant engineer Arnold returned from Ship Island on the *Jackson*, bringing with him material to make repairs to the engine. He also brought a mail delivery and the latest papers from New Orleans, which were eagerly scanned by the crew.

Towards the middle of September the weather turned cold and wet and a savage rain storm, beginning on the 15th and lasting three days, lashed the vessels in Pensacola harbor and delayed the sailing of the steamer *Connecticut* for New York, carrying the squadron's dispatches and mail. She also carried 11 of Amos Burton's shipmates, bound for new duties and new ships. Included in this group was third assistant engineer David Green,

Pensacola Harbor with Fort Pickens to the right and the *Powhatan,* sister ship of the *Susquehanna* in the foreground.
Battles and Leaders

ordered to report for duty at the temporary Naval Academy at Newport, Rhode Island. Burton referred to him as "...an officer highly esteemed by the officers and men."

The *Susquehanna's* plight so eloquently and forcefully chronicled in Hitchcock's dispatches to both Farragut and Washington solicited the following communication from Secretary Welles to the flag officer. Dated September 23, 1862, the communiqué terminated: "I believe the *Susquehanna* can with skilful management, be kept on her station until the 1st January next. Her condition is no worse now than it has been during the last three months. The machinery is in a very inefficient state and should be used as little as possible, but the vessel's services can be commanded with it for the time stated...a new shaft, pillow block etc. are ready at the New York Navy Yard, and have been for several months."

On the 25th, seaman Dennis Mansford fell from the spar deck into the forehold, a depth of some 20 feet, inflicting severe injury. This accident preceded the death five days later of one of Amos Burton's comrades. Edward Keefe, a hospital attendant, died from heart disease following a short illness. A native Irishman, he had been living in New York since emigrating from the old country. This was the first death from sickness aboard the *Susquehanna* for

19 months. Keefe's demise was duly recorded in the ship's log. Commodore Hitchcock had granted shore leave to the crew and the final party returned from Pensacola with the exception of an ordinary seaman named Percy, who had taken advantage of the liberty to desert.

The *Kennebec* limped into Pensacola on the 26th from Mobile, her smokestack, steam pipe, main topmast and main and head-stays carried away, together with loss of one cutter and her starboard anchor. She had been caught in the storm of the 15th while off Mobile Bay. The arrival of the *Honduras* on the 28th from New Orleans caused a stir for she carried 17 secessionist prisoners, mostly politicals, who were to be incarcerated in Fort Pickens. Among the captives was Dr Mackin, a notable Crescent City physician, arrested for selling drugs and medicines to Confederate forces; and a guerrilla leader, one Captain Rolla.

The warship *Tennessee* which had paid a brief visit to Pensacola set off for New Orleans at five o'clock in the morning of October 1, carrying mail and dispatches from the *Susquehanna*, but her voyage started badly for she went aground shortly after passing Fort Pickens. The *Susquehanna's* boats were lowered but try as they might they could not shift the stranded warship. The funeral party of the late Edward Keefe, led by Hitchcock, left the *Susquehanna* at 4pm. His coffin, draped with the Stars and Stripes, was first placed on the quarterdeck and then lowered over the ship's side to an accompanying funeral dirge from the band before being rowed ashore. Keefe's messmates bore the coffin to Warrington cemetery where Surgeon Joseph Beale read the burial service before the deceased was laid to rest. A board stating the name, age and date of death was placed at the head of the grave.

The *Tennessee*, finally freeing herself, sailed for New Orleans. Several barks and schooners arrived on the 3rd, among them the Rebel prize ship *Florida*, captured while flying English colors by the gunboat *Jackson* off Ship Island. The *Tennessee* returned from New Orleans at 7.30am on the 4th, and half an hour behind her the gunboat *Albatross* from Galveston dropped anchor in the harbor. She however, was sporting a quarantine pennant, signifying yet another outbreak of Yellow Fever aboard a Union vessel. Shortly after her arrival the expected signal forbidding contact with the *Albatross* broke from the mizzentop of the flagship.

At 10am Farragut, accompanied by the chief engineers of the flagship and the *Brooklyn* came on board for a run up the coast to test the condition of the renovated engine of the *Susquehanna*. Amos Burton's account of the sea trial is fairly detailed. "Weighed anchor, starting on a trial trip, gained but little headway when our engine gave out: made repairs and started up again: ran up as far as Pensacola, discovered steam escaping from the starboard cylinder; returned to our anchorage, examined the cylinder, and found a crack in it eight feet in length. The working of the engine may be set down as a failure."

Commodore Hitchcock's anxiety over his vessel's seaworthiness was confirmed on October 6 when a detailed survey held by chief engineers' Brooks, Kimball and Sewell condemned the starboard cylinder. With the *Brooklyn* preparing to sail for Mobile, one of the *Susquehanna's* rifled Parrots was transferred aboard the screw frigate. Farragut came aboard and following an inspection of the *Susquehanna*, dined with Hitchcock and his officers.

At 10am on the 8th, Farragut, along with officers from the *Hartford, Tennessee* and *Potomac* boarded Hitchcock's ship to witness a final test run for the steamer's machinery. The *Susquehanna's* engineers had disconnected the starboard connecting rod; the port engine only would be in action. With maximum steam pressure raised the warship went ahead very slowly and all attempts to 'back her' astern ended in failure. Farragut was now fully convinced that the *Susquehanna* should sail north immediately for refitting, and stated so in a report to Secretary Welles in Washington. "The *Susquehanna* is now completely broken down; her starboard cylinder is split from bottom to top in addition to other breaks; if she had only a less draft I would, when the Department thinks proper, take her into Mobile, but with such a heavy draught as 20 feet (which is as light as I can make her for practical operations) she would be very liable to get ashore, and with but one engine it would be almost impossible to go her off or manage her so that I fear I shall be compelled to send her home. But I must do her commander and officer's justice to say that they evince no anxiety of the kind, but on the contrary all appear to be anxious to do everything in their power to keep the ship out, in order to take their share in the next fight."

Warships and transports continued to slip in and out of harbor, some bringing welcome provisions and letters from home. The days passed for the most part uneventfully, General Butler arrived from New Orleans on the 9th for a brief tour of inspection, returning to New Orleans the same evening. On the 11th the *Rhode Island* came to anchor and passed on a box of hospital stores donated by the ladies of Boston for wounded seamen. There were none aboard the *Susquehanna* but presumably the stores found good homes anyway! The brig *Bohio* arrived from Galveston on the 13th bringing news of the bloodless occupation of that port by Union forces. As if to alleviate the boredom, at least for some, Farragut ordered ashore all the marines from the squadron. They assembled at Warrington Navy Yard where a full battalion drill and dress parade commanded by Captain Brown of the *Potomac,* was enjoyed by a large number of officers from the fleet.

On October 21, in accordance with orders from Farragut, a general courts martial was convened on the *Susquehanna* for trying several offenders from various ships of the fleet. The cases ranged from minor infractions of the rules and regulations to more serious crimes such as treason. At 10am on the 23rd the *Cayuga* fired off a signal gun announcing the commencement of the courts martial, presided over by Commodore Hitchcock. The first case was that of Thomas Roscommon, a seaman from the flagship *Hartford*. The accusation was one of treason. The case concluded the next day and next up before the court was Thomas Mopely. He was charged that, whilst serving aboard the mortar schooner *John Griffiths* he deserted to the enemy. Acting master's mate Leben Sellar of the same ship appeared on the somewhat lesser charge of neglect of duty and insubordination to a superior officer.

As October gave way to November, still more unfortunates were facing the court. The charges varied from drunkenness, abusive language, and treasonable utterances – usually while under the influence of alcohol – sleeping on watch and threatening to strike a superior officer. On November 5 the court was adjourned *sine die* after a session of 13 days. During the period of the hearings several officers and members of the crew left the ship. Some were transferred to other commands, others, their term of enlistment having expired, accompanied invalided seamen home. One of the officers relocating was Lieutenant Commander Weaver, the *Susquehanna's* executive officer. He was to take command of the gunboat *Winona* whose present skipper Captain Thornton, had been ordered to Washington. Weaver had been with the ship since the outset of her voyage to the Mediterranean and the officers and men of the *Susquehanna* regretted his going. His replacement was Lieutenant Commander Montgomery Sicord who joined the ship along with John Parkman of Boston, who was to serve as Commodore Hitchcock's private secretary.

On October 29 at six thirty in the morning, the gunboat *Mercury* steamed in from Mobile along with a prize taken off that port, the steamer *Caroline,* formerly the *Carlisle.* Captured after a seven-hour chase, she was reputed to be the most valuable prize so far taken in the Gulf. November blew in cold and wet. On the morning of the 3rd the steamer *Kensington* came alongside with fresh drinking water for the *Susquehanna.* Friday the 7th marked the first anniversary of the Battle of Port Royal, and with the departure for New Orleans of the *Hartford* with Farragut aboard, together with the sloops *Richmond* and *Tennessee,* Hitchcock became acting flag officer at Pensacola.

Fourteen landsmen from the frigate *Potomac* joined the *Susquehanna* on the 8th, filling the places made vacant by death, sickness and termination of service. The next day being a Sunday, ship's inspection was held, followed by the usual religious service. Barely had the devotions been completed when the crew learned of the death of a young Dublin-born Irishmen, Francis McOwen. Only 18 years old the youth had been suffering from a mystery illness for the past seven weeks, borne, according to Amos Burton "...with great patience. All that medical attendance and kind attention could be shown was done for him, but he sunk under the disease. Of him may be said, by his correct deportment and kind disposition, he won the esteem of all his shipmates. The deceased leaves a father in Boston to mourn his early death." He was interred the next day near to his former shipmate Edward Keefe in Warrington cemetery.

Wednesday the 12th and the *Brooklyn,* displaying Commodore Bell's pennant arrived to relieve Hitchcock as flag officer. Bell's ship had been commissioned in 1859 and her single, twin-bladed screw when hoisted out of the water, greatly added to the vessel's sailing qualities by reducing drag. Another unique feature was her telescopic funnel. On the evening of the 13th the *Susquehanna* received a 100-pounder rifled pivot gun, brought by the bark *Burnside.* Powder and fixed ammunition were taken on board the next day.

Although seemingly exempt from sea duty for the present, the crew of the *Susquehanna* was not to be found idle. Amos Burton set down in his journal: "Very little has occurred during the last week, either to interest or amuse. The crew, as usual, have plenty of work of different kinds; exercised at general and fire quarters, also drilled at broadside guns and small arms... Captain Hitchcock has kept our crew busy discharging vessels chartered by the government, also at different works about the Navy yard. Our firemen were employed in repairing engines on other steamers; also working in the machine shop. The Marines have had plenty of drill and target practice, while the odd hands about deck were scrubbing copper, or away in boats." The weather had also turned warm and pleasant and the health of the ship's company Burton recorded as being good.

On November 26 the *Brooklyn* sailed for blockade duty off Mobile, and the *Susquehanna* resumed her duty as flagship at Pensacola.

A seemingly trivial incident aboard a Federal steam transport bound for Fort Pickens from Pensacola had escalated into a near mutinous and murderous conclusion. Amos Burton set down the event. "The propeller *General Meigs* was the theatre of a bloody scene on her down trip from Pensacola to Fort Pickens. Quite a number of officers and men from Barrancas (Regulars), were on board. Four of the soldiers went into the engineer's room; ordered him out; a quarrel ensued; the men overpowered the engineer, when he cried for help. The crew and passengers went to his rescue; they were none too soon; having got the man down, they (the soldiers) had drawn knives, swearing they would cut his throat. The soldiers were secured by being tied. The leader was bucked and gagged. One of the party, using very abusive language, was approached by an Army officer who said that if he did not desist from the language used he would buck and gag him. The man replied, 'You have me now, I am tied; if I was loose you could do nothing with me.' The officer struck the man with a handspike, causing him to fall insensible on the deck, the blood gushing from his ears and nostrils. His skull being fractured it was thought he would not survive the blow. Upon reaching the fort the officer was put under arrest. Great excitement was felt among the soldiers, which grew to such a pitch that the officer had to be placed in close confinement."

December brought little respite from the mundane round of duties for the men of the *Susquehanna*. Sailing vessels and steamers appeared over the horizon bringing reinforcements for the Union troops at Pensacola and replacements for the vessels lying at anchor in the harbor. Occasionally they carried supplies – but no fresh beef – mail and newspapers; and tales such as that of the six Confederate deserters from Fort Morgan, found drifting by the Union warship *Montgomery* some 60 miles out to sea in a leaky cutter without oars. The *Susquehanna's* patched up machinery survived a trial run, no doubt much to the relief of her skipper.

In the days leading up to Christmas, the warships in the harbor left to take up their various blockade stations until by Christmas Day only the *Potomac,* the *Preble* and a handful of mortar schooners remained with the *Susquehanna.* Pleasing weather on Christmas Day brightened the bluejackets' spirits and many of the crew were allowed ashore on a liberty. They returned in a high state of jollity no doubt helped by a moderate intake of alcohol.

Three weeks previously, the crew of the *Potomac* had issued a challenge to the second cutter's crew of Hitchcock's ship. The trial was to be a race over a distance of three miles for a purse of almost $500. Then, on Christmas Eve, they surprisingly withdrew from the contest. The boys on the *Susquehanna* were somewhat disappointed as they were confident of victory, but they found solace in the form of an evening's entertainment afforded by the newly formed '*Susquehanna* Minstrels.'

A number of officers from other vessels were invited aboard and Burton depicted the ensuing festivities. "Negro melodies, music, burlesque and dancing filled the programme. The whole concluded with the laughable farce 'The Barber's Revenge.' Thus Christmas night passed merrily...The whole entertainment passed off pleasantly, and much to the credit of all concerned. They were received with great applause by the audience throughout the performance."

Unknown to the ship's company, it was destined to be the last Christmas celebrated aboard by the present crew of the *Susquehanna*. Despite the sloop's dire need for a major refit Hitchcock had received orders to run down to Mobile and assume command of the vessels operating off Fort Morgan.

MOBILE AND THE *FLORIDA*

Arriving off Fort Pickens on December 26, the *Susquehanna* lay up until high tide the following day. Crossing the bar at noon and making four knots, the steamer cruised southward and came in view of Rebel held Fort Morgan at 10pm and dropped anchor for the night. At daybreak the *Susquehanna* moved down to take position with the blockading vessels five miles off the enemy coast whereupon Hitchcock took command of the flotilla. His squadron consisted of 11 ships including the *Oneida, R R Cuyler, Kanawha, Aroostook* and *Pembina*. Hitchcock was almost immediately deprived of one ship, the *Oneida* sailing for Pensacola for repairs following an accidental collision with the storeship *Supply*.

On station only a few hours, the *Susquehanna's* complement was reduced by one with the death of a 42 year-old marine, Charles Connor, who succumbed to dysentery and was buried at sea the following day. Once again the task of conducting the committal service fell to the *Susquehanna's* Philadelphia-born physician Joseph Beale. Beale began his sea-going career as an assistant surgeon in September 1837 and his current status after 25 years' service was that of Medical Director, the equivalent commissioned rank was captain.

Confederate steamships and gunboats still hovered close under the protective guns of Fort Morgan "...on whose summit the flag of disunion floats daily," wrote Amos Burton. Hitchcock's final report to Farragut for 1862, dated December 31, made for gloomy reading. It incorporated details of the damage sustained by the *Oneida* in her brush with the *Supply* and Hitchcock took the opportunity to voice his concern regarding the state of the ships under his command. "The *Oneida* left here Sunday Nov 28th. Her forecastle is moved bodily over an inch or two, the spirketing is broken in at the forward port, the oakum started out of the seams under the port, the forward rifle gun cannot be worked. How long it will take to make the repairs I cannot say, but I directed all the force of the yard to be put on her. Referring to your remark 'that only such repairs shall be made as will keep the vessel going' – each day repairs are becoming more necessary, even upon those (ships) sent from the Northern yards, (the *Pocahontas* for instance). There is hardly a vessel here that, if you do not make repairs upon them, will soon break down."

Hitchcock also informed Farragut that at least two warships were off station at any one time, either taking on coal or for repairs, and that he saw many changes about the Rebel works since the *Susquehanna's* previous spell off Mobile in September. Concerning his own command, the commodore closed his dispatch with the heartfelt comment: "It is sad to write of this ship. We will do all we can."

New Year's Day 1863 opened quietly, the weather being agreeably mild. The *Circassian* from New York sailed in carrying mail, fresh provisions and a number of officers assigned to duty with various ships in the flotilla. The following afternoon Hitchcock's squadron was further reinforced with the arrival of the *Tennessee*, from Galveston. On the afternoon of the 3rd, the English six-gun sloop-of-war *Vesuvius* from New Orleans, approached the flotilla. The crew of the *Susquehanna* beat to quarters and stood by their guns as the Royal Navy ship drew alongside and her commander Captain Croke came on board, stating that he wished to communicate with the British consul in Mobile. Hitchcock at once agreed and the two officers exchanged the usual courtesies, concluding with the English captain returning to his vessel that moved a distance from the *Susquehanna* before letting go her anchor.

A severe gale howled down on the squadron overnight and

Hitchcock signaled his command to be ready to slip cables and run for deeper water if necessary but the tempest finally blew itself out just before dawn. Early the next morning a small gig rowed away from the *Vesuvius* towards the shore, tying up at the landing near Fort Morgan. Late in the evening of the 4th the *Pocahontas* came in from Ship Island, relieving the *Kennebec* which immediately made for that place to take on coal and supplies.

At two o'clock on the afternoon of the 5th the Confederate steamer *Crescent* was observed heading out from Mobile Bay towards the Union squadron. A white truce flag soon broke out from the *Susquehanna's* peak and the Rebel craft came alongside. Her captain requested permission to make for the *Vesuvius*, moored some 500 yards to the west of the Federal sloop, and informed Hitchcock that he carried on board the British consul who had dispatches for Captain Croke. Hitchcock immediately gave his assent. At approximately five o'clock, the *Crescent* had begun her return journey when a lookout on the *Susquehanna* reported the appearance of a Rebel gunboat, the *Gaines*. She passed the *Crescent* near the lighthouse on Sand Island and held a brief communication with her before continuing on her course, straight for the Union warships. Captain Croke, who was now on board the *Susquehanna*, witnessed the unfolding drama. Commodore Hitchcock ordered the cables slipped and beat to quarters. Signals were sent to the *Cuyler, Kennebec, Pocahontas* and *Pinola* to get underway and for the *Cuyler* to position herself inshore of the Confederate warship.

According to Hitchcock's report to Farragut, Captain Croke approached the commodore and asked: "What do you make of this?" Hitchcock replied: "Let her come on. At 500 yards I will give her our broadside." At this point the Royal Navy officer prepared to take his leave. Hitchcock then gave the order: "Stand by!" A split second later one of the pilots on board the *Susquehanna*, a man named Freeman, called to the commodore that he had glimpsed a small white flag at the gunboat's fore peak. The Rebel ship was soon within hailing distance but an attempted conversation proved impossible to comprehend. Finally, they lowered a cutter, which came alongside the Yankee flagship. A youthful Rebel naval officer climbed up the *Susquehanna's* tumblehome and explained that Admiral Buchanan had ordered their ship to take the British consul to the *Vesuvius* but

Commodore Robert B Hitchcock, who commanded the blockading squadron when the Rebel commerce raider *Florida* made her daring escape.
US Naval Historical Center

they then discovered that duty had been carried out by the *Crescent*. As his ship had come so far out his captain thought it polite to inform the Union commander of the circumstances. Hitchcock replied: "It was unnecessary: but please say to your commander, if he approaches us again with a flag of truce, a larger one may prevent the unpleasant occurrence of our firing upon a vessel with a white flag."

"We did not see you hoist a flag." the Confederate responded.

"That should have prevented you approaching us." This concluded the exchange and as soon as the launch returned to the *Gaines* the Rebel gunboat stood in for Fort Morgan. "I am truly thankful that I did not fire. Nothing but the pilot saved me from it", Hitchcock wrote. According to Amos Burton the Confederate officer was attired in a Royal Navy uniform and Captain Croke, who apparently was still on the *Susquehanna* afterwards stated somewhat indignantly: "This is a high handed affair, for the Rebels to take advantage of my ship being here. I will acquaint my admiral of this affair."

There is an unusual postscript to this episode. On January 23, Farragut wrote to Navy Secretary Gideon Welles regarding information, which had only recently come to light via a sworn deposition given to Captain John Clark, the provost marshal general for Farragut's department. If true, Jefferson Davis, President of the Confederacy, came within a whisker of being captured, or even worse becoming involved in a ship-to-ship engagement that could have had only one possible outcome. The deposition reads as follows:

"President Davis and many important personages came nigh being captured on New Years. Were on a trip visiting the fortifications and Fort's Morgan and Gaines; machinery of steamer becoming temporarily disabled, she drifted out to sea, and within hailing distance of the blockading squadron. You may remember hearing an account of a strange occurrence of a steamer about that time."

Farragut goes on: "Thus it will be seen that, if this report be true, Commodore Hitchcock had Jefferson Davis and his suite within his grasp, and was deprived of his prize by a scrupulous regard for the sacred respect due a flag of truce on the one side and by the prostitution of it on the other side." Documented records show that President Davis was in Mobile on an inspection tour at the end of December 1862.

The Confederate raider *Florida*, photographed at anchor in Brest, France circa August 1863, following her daring escape from Mobile. *Library of Congress*

The arrival of the *Nassau* from Ship Island on January 6 carrying dispatches from Admiral Farragut brought disquieting news. The Rebels had attacked the Texas port of Galveston and after a desperate, bloody fight two Union gunboats, the *Westfield* and *Harriet Lane*, had been lost. The former vessel, an 822-ton side-wheel steam ferryboat purchased by the Navy from Cornelius Vanderbilt in November 1861, had been aground when the Confederates appeared. Her commander, Captain W. B. Renshaw, quickly taking stock of the situation, gave orders to abandon the *Westfield* and, to save his vessel from falling into enemy hands prepared to destroy his ship. Having disembarked his men and set a trail of gunpowder to the magazine Renshaw also quit the doomed gunboat. When the expected explosion failed to materialize Renshaw returned with a boat's crew to add more combustible material. Just as the cutter was pulling away from the *Westfield's* side the magazine blew up, killing the skipper and the volunteers in the boat.

The 600-ton *Harriet Lane*, a two masted, wood-built side-wheeler had only been launched in 1857 and before transfer to the Navy had been the only steam powered vessel in service with the United States Revenue Service. Her skipper Captain Wainwright, having steam up, awaited the two oncoming Rebel vessels, the *Bayou City* and the *Neptune*. The decks of the secessionist steamships were protected by bales of cotton behind which stood sharpshooters who opened fire, picking off the gunners on the *Harriet Lane* as they stood by their pieces. Wainwright himself was hit, and realizing it was becoming impossible to man the guns gave the order to run the Rebel ships down. It was a courageous and desperate gamble that ended in failure as the two Confederate vessels closed on the *Harriet Lane*. After ramming her twice, boarding parties from the Confederate steamers poured on to her blood-streaked decks. In the brief but desperate hand-to-hand combat that followed a number of her plucky crew were killed or wounded, including the injured Captain Wainwright who had his brains blown out by a Rebel officer. The surviving members of the *Harriet Lane* were taken prisoner and the Confederates took possession of the gunboat.

Morale was lifted somewhat on the evening of the 8th with the arrival of the captured English steamer *Antona*. She had cleared from Liverpool two months previously, bound for the Cuban port of Havana. Early on the morning of the 6th the *R R Cuyler*, stationed on the eastern wing of the blockading flotilla signaled that she had sighted a ship. The seamen on her consort *Pocahontas* set all available sail and the warship set off in pursuit. The chase lasted most of the day before the *Antona* hove to and surrendered.

She was an iron built screw-powered vessel with a speed of eight knots and weighing some 246 tons. She carried a crew of 22 and, so her captain claimed, had tried unsuccessfully to run in to Charleston before making for Mobile. Her cargo was made up of medical supplies, ammunition, opium, brandy and a complete battery of rifled cannon. Captain and crew were transferred aboard the *Susquehanna* and a prize crew of 19 men was placed aboard the *Antona*, which sailed for Philadelphia via Pensacola.

Sunday January 11 found the crews on the ships off Mobile enjoying the continuing mild winter weather. The Sabbath passed quietly, the only arrival being the *Circassian.* She tarried briefly to unload supplies into launches sent by the *Susquehanna* before heading out of the bay for New York at midnight taking with her paroled prisoners, parts of the crews, lately exchanged, of the two captured Union ships *Westfield* and *Harriet Lane* and invalids from the fleet. This scene of apparent calm and tranquillity was soon to change. A combination of bad weather and ill fortune would result in an ignominious chapter being entered into the records of the blockading squadron off Mobile. In particular, Hitchcock would be subjected to an official inquiry into his conduct while senior officer at the time of the incident.

On June 4, 1861, James Bullock stepped ashore at the quayside in Liverpool, England. An ex-US Navy officer, his mission was to acquire warships for the Confederate Navy and send them forth to attack and destroy Union merchant vessels wherever found, on the seas and oceans of the world. They were to be purchased and built in Britain and France with funds transferred from Richmond to the Southern-owned Liverpudlian firm of Fraser, Trenholm & Company and Bullock's first port of call was to their dockside offices and an appointment with Charles Prioleau, the Confederacy's fiscal representative in Liverpool. The first of these commerce raiders was the *Florida,* known as the *Oreto* while on the stocks of ship builders William Miller & Sons, of Liverpool. This company, accustomed to building wooden warships for the Royal Navy, laid her keel the same month and proceeded with the work in hand. Constructed on the lines of a British naval dispatch boat, she was a three masted barkentine rigged ship with twin smokestacks, capable of nine and a half-knots, increasing to 12 under sail. Her engines were made and fitted by another Liverpool company, Fawcett and Preston & Company.

Alerted to the Confederate agent's mission, the United States authorities in Liverpool watched his every move. Bullock had the story spread that the *Oreto* was destined for an Italian shipping company. With US consular officials exerting daily pressure on the British government to ignore this unlikely tale and impound the *Oreto*, Bullock decided to take no chances and plans to put to sea were set in motion. Flying British colors and with a British captain at the helm, the raider slipped quietly from her berth on March 22 carrying a handful of civilian passengers for a so-called trial run. She cruised round the harbor for a while before offloading all but one of these 'guests' into lighters, which rowed for the shore. The one passenger who remained on board was a Confederate naval officer, John Low. Now under his command, the steamer made for the open sea and the five-week journey to Nassau where she rendezvoused with the supply ship *Bahama,* which had carried the *Florida's* weapons and munitions from Scotland.

On board the *Bahama* was Captain John Newland Maffitt, a North Carolinian who had served in the antebellum US Navy for 29 years; he was to take command of the *Florida*. He had spent 14 of those years surveying and charting America's Atlantic coast. Maffitt was an acknowledged expert on the currents, tides and treacherously shifting sandbanks of the Carolinas. From day one he encountered nothing but ill fortune with his new command. Delayed by unforeseen circumstances in Nassau she lost most of her crew, but Maffitt managed to replace them with local seamen. Sailing to Green Key, the raider took on board her guns, shells and powder that had been transferred from the *Bahama* onto a small schooner chartered for the mission. Her main armament consisted of two 7-inch and two six 6-inch Blakely rifles, and one 12-pound howitzer. The transfer and fitting out consumed a week's valuable time before Maffitt finally commissioned the *Florida* into the Confederate service on August 17, 1862.

As if to further mock Maffitt's efforts an outbreak of the dreaded Yellow Fever forced the *Florida* to head for the Cuban port of Cardenas where medical help was sought. As the epidemic worsened Maffitt's next port of call was Havana where he secured the services of a pilot who promised to guide Maffitt into Mobile. The Rebel captain was now himself seriously ill. Five seamen along with Maffitt's stepson had perished; all were buried at sea as the ship headed towards Mobile. By now word of the privateer's presence in Gulf waters had reached the Union ships patrolling the area and consequently the blockading vessels were keeping a sharp eye out for the *Florida*.

Weighing up the risks, Maffitt still determined to make for Mobile and the first week of September found the *Florida* off the Southern coast. Although there were several Union warships standing watch outside the channel entrance the raider ran past them at high speed sustaining some damage from the guns of the Federal ships before reaching safety. The *Florida's* deep draft prevented her moving upriver nearer to the city of Mobile, therefore all supplies and repair materials had to be brought down to her. These logistical problems combined with unsettled winter weather ensured that almost four months were to elapse before the *Florida* was ready to go to sea in search of her quarry.

Command of the blockading squadron outside Mobile had by then devolved on Commodore Hitchcock. He and his subordinate commanders were well aware of the situation and full instructions together with a special code of signals for use at night had been arranged to raise the alarm if, and when, the *Florida* sought to make her escape to the open waters of the Gulf.

Hitchcock had placed his vessels in a semi-circle off the coast and with the weather worsening to gale force on the evening of January 12, 1863, it was felt that the Rebel warship may attempt to take advantage and break through the cordon of Union vessels. The bad weather showed no signs of letting up, but on the afternoon of the 15th with conditions improving briefly, the *Florida* was sighted a little to the east of Fort Morgan, having all the appearances of making ready to run out.

Fearing an escape attempt that night Hitchcock made a telegraphic signal to all ships. "*Oreto* (*Florida*) expected out; keep full steam." He also ordered his captains to close the distances between each vessel and sent the *Pembina* to make verbal contact to confirm these instructions to the *Pinola* and *R R Cuyler* stationed to the north-east of the *Susquehanna*, and the *Oneida* positioned to the north-west of the flagship. The *Cuyler* and *Oneida* being the fastest ships in the squadron were instructed to pursue the enemy should the *Florida* slip past the blockading flotilla.

At 3am on January 16, Maffit seized his opportunity. A heavy squall had descended on the area and this, combined with the pitch-blackness, decided Maffitt's course of action. The Confederate commander weighed anchor and the *Florida* headed towards the waiting Yankee warships. The gunboat *Pembina* reported: 'A sail running into this pass.' A further signal, this time from the *R R Cuyler* read: 'Steamer running out of this pass.' Almost simultaneously the shadowy outline of a vessel passing to the eastward and to starboard of the *Susquehanna* was spotted. At the time it was assumed this was the *Pembina,* it was in fact the *Florida.* She had eased between Hitchcock's ship and the *R R Cuyler* before sparks from her smokestacks gave her position away. A flurry of alarm signals flashed among the surprised Federal warships. Hitchcock beat to quarters and prepared to slip cables, he at once instructed the general 'Chase' signal telegraphed.

The gunboat *Oneida* had been designated to pursue the *Florida* should she slip through the ring of Union warships. Her commanding officer Captain S. Hazard had posted extra lookouts and at 3.25am they reported sighting the white and red signal 'Vessel running out of this pass' from the *Susquehanna.* This was swiftly followed by the white and green 'Steamer running out' from the *Pembina.* Hazard beat to quarters and made ready to slip his cable and give chase but stated in his written statement later that he saw no sign of the *Florida* and did not sight the 'Chase' signal made by the flagship. Hearing no gunfire and mistakenly assuming the *R R Cuyler* to be still in her berth, when in fact she, along with the *Pembina* was hot in pursuit of Maffitt's ship, he concluded that it was a false alarm and remained at anchor.

The fleeing raider, utilizing every stitch of canvas and making full steam easily outdistanced the *Pembina* which could not maintain the pace and gradually fell behind, but as first light brightened the horizon, the *R R Cuyler* was only three miles astern of the *Florida* and steadily gaining. Maffit now pulled off an unusual stroke of improvisation; he stopped engines and took in all sail. The low silhouette of the *Florida's* hull was partially hidden by the huge green ocean swells. The Yankee warship, unprepared for such a unique maneuver, failed to spot her prey stopped dead in the water and sailed straight past.

The escape of the *Florida* was to prove costly for the Union merchant marine. In a two-year rampage across the high seas she sank 57 American ships causing losses amounting to over $4 million. Her career was finally ended by the sloop *Wachusett* which illegally rammed and boarded the commerce raider on October 4, 1864 while she was coaling in the neutral Brazilian port of Bahia. Towed back to the United States she became the center of a fierce diplomatic row between the Brazilian and American governments. The South American's had international law on their side and as in the *Trent* affair the Federal authorities backed down. There was however a twist in the tail. As the *Florida* was preparing to leave harbor at Newport News to return to Brazil on November 28, 1864, she was mysteriously rammed and sunk by the Union army transport *Alliance*.

HOME

The *Tennessee* arrived from New Orleans at midday on the 17th bearing reports of a sea fight off the port of Galveston, Texas. The sloop *Brooklyn*, commanding the Union squadron off Galveston ordered the gunboat *Hatteras*, a pre-war side-wheel excursion streamer, to investigate a strange sail making out to sea. The Federal warship soon came within hailing distance and in reply to her challenge as to the identity of the steamship, received the answer: "This is Her Majesty's steamer *Petrel*." A boat was lowered from the *Hatteras* and had covered barely half the distance between the two ships when a voice cried out from the blackness: "This is the Confederate States steamer *Alabama*. Fire!" A volley of musketry flared out from the 'English' warship. This was followed by a devastating broadside upon the unsuspecting gunboat.

As the acrid fog of burned powder partially cleared, the dazed sailors aboard the *Hatteras* glimpsed a Confederate naval ensign break from the mizzen top as the mysterious craft revealed her true colors. A general action was now underway and although the Yankee steamer put up a spirited fight she never recovered from that stunning opening salvo. Captain Raphael Semmes' Confederate gunners, many of whom were Liverpool seamen, poured round after round of short-fused shells into the *Hatteras* until the boilers were shot to pieces and her hull glowed dark red from the several fires started below decks. In less than 15 minutes the Union gunboat was put out of action and her captain struck his flag. Two Union sailors were killed and five wounded. All the survivors were taken on board the *Alabama* as the *Hatteras* began to sink beneath the waves. She was the only warship to fall victim to the guns of the *Alabama*, destined to become the most famous of the Confederate commerce raiders.

For two days Hitchcock's flotilla endured a savage battering from a storm that eventually died down on the morning of January 19. Amos Burton detailed the damage in his journal. "Although no accident happened to any of the crew, the wood work about the guards and bow of the ship was carried away; even our good commodore's dinner was washed away by the dashing waves, upsetting stoves and very nearly cleaning out the contents of the galley, cook and all! The ship was at times nearly on her beam ends. Two Mobile pilots on board pronounced this to have been the severest storm experienced in this coast for the last twelve years."

For several weeks relatively few incidents of any consequence disturbed the shipboard routine of the crews of Hitchcock's flotilla. On January 26 a rainstorm set in which blew itself out by the following morning, revealing a Confederate steamer the *Metagordo*, beached near to Fort Morgan. She had obviously planned to break out during the night using the darkness and rough weather to disguise her endeavor but had been seen by the *Kennebec* which opened fired, forcing the steamship back inshore where she ran aground. In a report to Farragut, Hitchcock detailed the incident stating that he later went aboard the *Kanawha* to take the Rebel's bearings to ascertain if any of the Union vessels could approach near enough to have a crack at finishing her off but concluded it was unsafe to do so. Within two days the Confederates had lightened the ship sufficiently to allow her to be refloated and taken back inside the bay.

Hitchcock included a plea for a supply of spyglasses for his flotilla and finished with the subject closest to his heart. "We will have to return to Pensacola by the last of February (if we hold out so long). The weather has been heavy for a crippled ship like this. I hope it will be no worse. I do not wish to complain, for things are bad enough without saying so." A slight flurry of snow fell on the decks of the *Susquehanna* on the evening of the 27th.

The commodore also confided in his close friend Captain Thornton Jenkins, former commander of the gunboat *Oneida* and now Fleet Captain stationed in New Orleans. In a letter dated February 3, he again stated his concern over the *Susquehanna's* deteriorating condition. "Will not the admiral (obviously referring to Farragut) make some arrangement for a vessel to take the place of this one? We may be done up at any moment. It is no fun, but sad reality. I am ready and willing to stay here, but this ship is helpless. Since you left we have had a smart blow from the eastward; the sea distressed us very much; we took in a large amount of water. The ship does not ride well in a heavy sea at anchor. If we have a gale she must be lost. To me it seems very wrong to expose a ship in the condition of this one to an anchorage like this. I do not know that there is any ship to relieve us, but I do know we must go to Pensacola in a short time (if we do not become too disabled to get there)."

Hitchcock also recounted to Thornton an incident during the night of January 22 involving the Confederate runner *Rocky Hill*. Although visibility was hampered by bad weather and darkness a strange sail was made out and the crew manned their guns. A swiftly fired round from the *Susquehanna's* sternpiece achieved little apart from shattering all the aft cabin windows and stoving in the gig suspended from the sloop's stern. Hitchcock detached two vessels from the flotilla to chase the enemy craft but she eluded her pursuers in the Stygian blackness.

The commodore's situation was worsening day by day. He closed his letter to Captain Jenkins with the following lament: "I have not had more than 4 of the gunboats here at one time since you left. They are breaking down faster and faster; 2 are now at Pensacola, *Kanawha* for her IX-inch gun and Kennebec for coals and repairs. *Pocahontas* will have to go the moment one returns. The *Pinola* is waiting for a chance. There is not one but requires some repairs."

On February 10, a schooner arrived from New York bringing fresh supplies, long overdue, for the tars on the blockading ships. At midday the supply ship *Union*, along with more provisions for the flotilla, brought two officers for duty with Hitchcock's squadron. Lieutenant Commander Jonathan

Young (late of the *Susquehanna*) was to succeed Captain Temple of the gunboat *Pembina* and Lieutenant Commander Mayo, who was to relieve Captain Febiger on the *Kanawha.* Temple and Febiger availed themselves of Hitchcock's hospitality aboard the *Susquehanna* while awaiting passage on a northbound vessel.

Throughout the war one of the Navy's greatest ongoing problems was the acute shortage of manpower. This was partially solved by the recruiting of runaway slaves. These 'contrabands', ranked as landsmen, integrated fully into the ships' companies despite certain prejudice from some quarters. Due to incidents of physical and verbal abuse aboard the *Susquehanna* involving black crew members, Commodore Hitchcock issued the following orders to the marine guard on February 11. They were: "Not to allow any one to strike or abuse any contraband on board this ship." On the 14th the first punishment for an infraction of this new ruling saw a boy seaman named Jeffries put in the brig under guard on bread and water for striking colored seamen who had insulted him. Amos Burton commented: "The Emancipation Act is carried out to its fullest extent by its many admirers on board this ship. Comment is wholly unnecessary." Burton's viewpoint appears similar to that held by many fighting for the Union. Whilst bearing little or no animosity towards Negroes, either freemen or those held in bondage, the volunteers' principal reason for enlisting had been to preserve the Union, not to free the slaves. Although recruitment was encouraged and their presence on board Union warships tolerated, few seamen considered them to be their equals.

At daylight on February 15, a schooner ran through the blockade and into Mobile. She was not spotted until safely under the guns of Fort Morgan. It is hard to apportion blame to the lookouts on the Union flotilla as thick fog banks descended daily over the area and visibility was at times less than a ship's length. At eight in the morning, the English sloop-of-war *Styx* arrived from Havana, Cuba. The crew beat to quarters and stood by their guns in salute until the sloop's captain came on board; bringing with him New York newspapers dated January 2. He dined with Hitchcock that evening along with Surgeon Joseph Beale and Captain's Temple and Febiger before being rowed back to his vessel, the band of the *Susquehanna* playing 'God Save the

Queen' on his departure. After dispatching a small cutter ashore with dispatches for the British consul in Mobile the next morning, the *Styx* departed for New Orleans under cloudy skies with a strong gale blowing at 5pm that evening, carrying with her dispatches for Farragut together with the squadron's mail.

Near midday on the 20th the *Crescent* was seen putting out from Fort Morgan. Flying French and Confederate colors she approached the gunboat *Kennebec.* A cutter was lowered and ran alongside the Rebel ship. The French consul from Mobile climbed down into the small boat and was rowed to the *Susquehanna* where he presented a request for several French families residing in Mobile to be allowed to travel to New Orleans. Hitchcock promised to pass on his petition to Admiral Farragut. The consul took his leave and returned to the *Kennebec* and from that ship transferred to the *Crescent*, which headed back into Mobile Bay.

At 7am the following morning the topsails of a strange vessel were sighted approaching the blockade. The *Susquehanna* made the recognition signals, which were returned but not understood. Understandably unwilling to take any chances Hitchcock beat to quarters and the frigate's gun crews manned their stations. All to no avail as the newcomer revealed herself to be the brand new sloop *Lackawanna*, under the command of Captain Marchand. Her cruise had shown up several minor mechanical defects and Hitchcock ordered her to Pensacola for coaling and repairs to her machinery and she sailed that afternoon.

Sunday February 22 broke clear and sunny, a fitting climate for celebrating George Washington's birthday, which the Confederates chose to mark with a midday salute fired from Fort Morgan. However, it being the Sabbath, celebrations on board the Yankee warships were held over to the Monday when all the vessels displayed their National banners from tops and peaks, and at noon a salute was fired accompanied by the playing of patriotic airs by the *Susquehanna's* musicians.

Towards the close of the forenoon watch on the 24th the gunboat *Clifton*, from Ship Island, neared the *Susquehanna*. She reported having picked up three Rebel deserters off Mobile. These seamen had received permission to take a small boat to fish for oysters. Concealing the boat on the beach the men had hidden themselves for two days before making their escape. Fortunately for them the *Clifton* sighted them. Under questioning from Union officers they claimed the Confederate flotilla had planned an attack against the Union ships outside the bay, but several of their vessels grounded and the attack was abandoned. They insisted that Admiral Buchanan, undeterred by this setback, was still waiting a favorable opportunity to make a sortie against Hitchcock's ships.

The deserters also imparted detailed descriptions of the condition of the Confederate vessels in Mobile Bay and the batteries in the forts. Morale appeared to be a distinct problem. On the *Gaines*, eight men were clapped in irons for drawing their cutlasses on an officer and for mutinous conduct and the defectors claimed that half the crew was just waiting for a chance to mutiny and take over the ship. The Rebel seamen were on half rations and although discipline was slack, several had been flogged. Two more rams were reportedly on their way downriver from Selma. Upon arrival at Mobile they are to be fitted out with guns and sent out to challenge the squadron. As to the Rebel works, Fort Morgan mounted between 120 and 125 pieces of ordnance in two tiers; Fort Gaines' batteries consisted of 27 guns.

On February 28, Hitchcock bade farewell to his two guests as Captain's Febiger and Temple departed for Pensacola on the gunboat *Pocahontas*. The frigate *Colorado* had been detailed to relieve Commodore Hitchcock of command of the Mobile blockade and the commodore penned a communication to Thomas Jenkins in New Orleans, detailing the precautions to be taken and giving advice to be passed on to the *Colorado's* master. Following the successful Confederate foray at Galveston which cost the Union two ships, vigilance must never be relaxed. Hitchcock constantly feared an attack by Buchanan's gunboats and advised that guns must be kept loaded with solid shot ready for ironclads. Presuming the onslaught would be after nightfall, the flag officer advised that all ships should keep steam up and be ready to slip their cables at a moment's notice. No vessels should be caught at anchor. If a strange sail were sighted the incumbent commodore was to treat the approaching ship as hostile until identified and to always send two ships to investigate, these vessels should take up a position inshore of the suspect craft.

The first day of March was clear and cool and in the early morning light two Rebel schooners were sighted some distance from Fort Morgan, having passed undetected through the weakened ring of blockading ships during the night. Around noon, two steamers nosed out from beyond the fort and began towing the schooners inside the bay, unmolested by the Yankee warships. Amos Burton summed up the feelings of all the officers and crew on the *Susquehanna* when he wrote: "The crew felt a deep mortification at this occurrence, hoping that we should soon be relieved from duty on this blockade,"

At eight in the morning of the 2nd, the gunboat *Pembina* approached Fort Morgan under a flag of truce. She was carrying dispatches for the French consul in Mobile. As the warship came abreast of the Rebel works she was hailed by a small boat and told to come no further. The excuse given was that there were hidden obstructions nearby but in all probability the Confederates were none too keen on the sharp-eyed Yankee officers noting details of their defensive capabilities.

On March 3, in what was to prove Hitchcock's final letter from Mobile written to his confidant Captain Jenkins in New Orleans, he mentions among other matters the pending official investigation into his conduct regarding the events concerning the escape of the *Florida*. "As to the court of inquiry, it is all right; you will be my principal witness. If it will only take me out of this ship before something still worse occurs I shall be thankful." he continued: "One thing must be kept in mind. This ship will be of no use after we get to Pensacola. (Has she been of any use for the last year?). Our repairs will take us weeks and weeks." The ever-present danger of attack from the Confederate squadron in Mobile Bay and the lack of suitable vessels to combat the menace prompted Hitchcock to comment: "I think that Admiral Buchanan will use his ironclads against us before long. I am keeping the best lookout I can. Two gunboats are close in to the bar, and each sends in a boat at night when circumstances will permit. You shall have a copy of the memoranda that I gave to Marchand (Captain Marchand of the *Lackawanna*), so that the admiral and you may judge if we are doing all that must be done."

An amusing episode brightened Burton's journal on March 5, which coincidentally proved to be the *Susquehanna's* last day on the Mobile blockade.

The *Union* came in from New Orleans northbound for Pensacola, bringing mail and newspapers. Also on board were a large number of passengers consisting of invalids and seamen whose term of service had expired. Hitchcock transferred the three Confederate deserters picked up by the *Clifton* and as Burton recorded "...on going on board the steamer, they found three of their former comrades, who had been sent to look after the other three. They forgot to return themselves!"

Also sent home sick aboard the *Union* were two of Burton's comrades, Peter Brown and George Shea and their condition prompted Burton to write: "Our pity is much excited when we see how little is provided for the sick. Poor fellows, they suffer under painful circumstances until an opportunity of being sent home. It is really affecting to see the once healthy shipmate reduced to a skeleton – carried on his cot which, with himself, is lowered over the ship's side into a boat which conveys him to the homeward bound vessel, which takes him to home and friends, where he hopes to be restored to health and fitted for duty once more."

Hitchcock's immediate problems were solved as the dispatches carried by the *Union* included orders for the *Susquehanna* to sail for Pensacola. The commodore's worn out vessel was relieved from the Mobile blockade after more than eight weeks' arduous duty and the ship prepared for the run to Pensacola. However, her final day was not without incident and mishap. At first light the *Pembina* signaled the *Susquehanna* that one of her cutters, which had been rowing guard during the night, was missing. However, as preparations for a search got under way, the boat was sighted and the relieved sailors were picked up by the mother ship. Strong winds had driven the little craft out to sea and for seven hours her crew had fought manfully to regain their vessel.

Finally getting underway at 7am, those on watch were going about their allotted tasks aboard ship. They included one John Lamb, ordinary seaman, who almost became another fatality to be entered into the ship's log. Amos Burton takes up the story. "During the forenoon, while working on the port bow, John Lamb (ordinary) fell overboard. His presence of mind, also being an expert swimmer, cleared him from the wheel. The dashing waves carried him some distance from the ship. The lifebuoy was cut adrift, also the

3rd cutter manned and sent to his rescue. Our boat's crew with great alacrity reached him, hauled him inboard, and returned him in safety aboard this ship."

Coming to her moorings in Pensacola Bay at four thirty that afternoon the *Susquehanna's* skipper found a fairly crowded anchorage. Union warships anchored in the bay included the frigate *Potomac*, the sloop *Preble*, the steamships *Union* and *Tennessee* and the barks *Anderson* and *Coon*. Within three days of arrival a tragic accident claimed 11 lives. A group of soldiers from the 15th Maine regiment accompanied by sailors from the *Preble* had been sent on an expedition in an elderly schooner. Obviously unseaworthy, the centerboard gave way and she rapidly filled with water, taking her unfortunate crew down with her.

Dispatches and mail for the squadron arrived on board the *Owasco* from New Orleans in the afternoon of March 9. Having discharged her duty she sailed for the blockade at Mobile the next day while the *Susquehanna* commenced taking on coal from the bark *Sierra Nevada*. Pensacola and its environs were facing up to the increasing threat from Confederate forces and a short sharp fight flared up when Federal outposts were attacked during the night of the 10th, the Rebels being driven off after a brief skirmish.

Reports of the worsening situation at Pensacola had reached Washington, and a decision was taken to evacuate the town. Consequently on the 17th the transport *Star of the South*, eight days out of New York, dropped anchor in the bay carrying orders for the immediate withdrawal of Federal forces. Those civilians with Union sympathies were offered shelter in the relative safety of the navy yard. At nine in the morning the *Susquehanna* raised her anchor and headed towards Pensacola, lying just off the town until 4pm whereupon she returned to her moorings. Several buildings had been set ablaze during the night and a female refugee who had taken passage aboard the transport *Rosalie* had fallen overboard and drowned. Her body was not recovered.

The Union garrison was carried to safety aboard the transports *Eastern Queen* and *Star of the South*, a portion being landed at Fort Barrancas with the remainder traveling on to New Orleans. With the successful embarkation of the soldiers only the gunboat *Preble* and the bark *Bohio* remained, anchored within gunshot of the town. On the 22nd news of Admiral Farragut's run past the Rebel batteries at Port Hudson on the Mississippi reached the *Susquehanna*. This welcome news being somewhat marred by the loss of the *Susquehanna's* prototype the *Mississippi,* which had run aground during the fight. A destructive fire from the shore-based Confederate artillery had caused extensive damage and many casualties, and it had proved impossible to refloat the ship. Ablaze from stem to stern with 54 of her complement dead and with the roaring flames flaring along her tarred rigging and wooden spars, her intrepid crew finally abandoned her. The doomed and deserted vessel, the oldest steamer in the service, then slid off the sandbank and drifted downriver, before exploding as the fire engulfed her magazine.

As March drew to a close there was little to disturb the mundane routine aboard ship, and although his thoughts must have been concentrated on the approaching court of inquiry to be held on board the *Susquehanna,* Hitchcock still found time to write a lengthy report regarding the predicament facing the West Gulf Blockading Squadron. In a communiqué to Secretary Gideon Welles dated March 25 he detailed the urgent need for men and vessels:

USS *Susquehanna,* Pensacola Bay, March 25, 1863

"Sir; The condition of affairs in this squadron forces upon me the necessity of retaining men on board this ship whose times have expired. I have reported the circumstance to Admiral Farragut, but as communication with him is now cut off, can not receive a reply; even our communication with New Orleans is rare and uncertain.

"Accompanying this is a statement of the expiration of times of the crew for the next three months. You will see by it that nearly all of the petty officers of this ship will be entitled to return home. Their places can not be filled. We have not received a man aboard this ship since I had the command above the rate of landsman. Three of our guns have to be manned by the marine guard.

"Every vessel in this division of the squadron, except the two last arrived, are short of men. There are now in this port seven vessels, not any of them fully manned; one of them (the *Anderson*) has been here for four months, not able to go to sea for want of men. *Potomac* only able to man five or six guns. The town of Pensacola has just been evacuated by the Army. Under all these circumstances I trust that the Navy Department will approve of my retaining the men whose time has expired.

"More vessels are required in this division of the squadron. The gunboats off Mobile have been on such constant service that the repairs have been only such as were imperatively necessary. The number has been too small to spare any from Mobile. Shortly a number of them will have to be taken off for repairs, if they do not break down entirely.

"The *Pocahontas* has just come in with almost the whole bottom of her boilers gone. She also leaks badly at her bow near the garboard strake (22 inches per hour when underway). She is not fit for the service of blockade.

"There is strong evidence that an attack will be made by the Rebel force at Mobile when they get their ironclads down from Selma and Montgomery. That our force should be strengthened is to me very evident. Some of our gunboats can not make 7 knots and all of them require repairs, which, as I have said, can not be given them from the force not being adequate to the duty required of them.

"This ship I have reported as inefficient again and again. We have done all that is possible to do with the means in our power, but her defects are beyond our means to remedy. She is almost useless, still counting for her number of guns."

Very respectfully, your obedient servant. R. B. Hitchcock
Commodore, Comdg. Division West Gulf Blockading Squadron.

Saturday April 4 and the official inquiry into the escape of the *Florida* convened aboard the *Susquehanna* with Commodore Smith presiding over events. Sitting alongside him were Commodore's Brasher and Gibson. In preparing his defense Hitchcock had circulated a questionnaire on March 22 to the commanding officers of those vessels attached to his squadron at the time of the affair inviting their comments as to the measures taken by himself to effect a secure blockade off Fort Morgan and his preparedness for the

Hitchcock's friend and confidant, Captain (later Admiral) Thornton Jenkins
Fleet Commander in New Orleans.
Battles and Leaders

prevention of the flight of the *Florida*. The questions invited these officers' opinions as to his competence while in command. Had they noted a lack of zeal or enthusiasm on his part? Had they detected any major deficiencies aboard the *Susquehanna,* or indeed among the rest of the squadron? He included questions as to whether the blockading ships were correctly positioned; could better tactical arrangements have been made to prevent the escape of the *Florida*? And finally, were there any other instances of inefficiency, which could be laid at Hitchcock's feet which aided the escape of Maffitt's ship?

Only Lieutenant-Commander Franklin of the *Aroostook,* failed to give Hitchcock adequate backing. In reply to the questions posed by Hitchcock, there were veiled suggestions as to whether the siting of the commodore's vessels off Mobile that night was all that it could have been. One comment being the practicability of placing a ship inside the bar to give early warning of the movements of the Confederate warship. Franklin, in a private addendum to the flag officer, which accompanied his testimony, assured Hitchcock of his personal regards. It cut no ice with his commanding officer, Hitchcock was livid. In a letter to Captain Jenkins in New Orleans dated April 3, 1863, his pent up emotions boiled over. "With these answers he (Franklin) sends me a letter marked 'private' in which he expressed the greatest regard for me. Well! He has a right to answer as he thinks is right, but it is somewhat strange, I think, to say it would have been a better arrangement to have had a vessel inside the bar, and yet he would not have put one there. No! I will promise he would not, if he had to go in her. He has at all times expressed more anxiety about going in there than any other commander."

Hitchcock continued: "You may show the admiral (or anyone else) his testimony. I think it rich even if it hangs me. I do not expect to get out of the scrape any better than Preble; (here Hitchcock is referring to the escape of the Rebel warship *Winona* from Mobile and the subsequent court martial of Captain Preble, commanding officer of the *Oneida*). Still it does not trouble me very much. I think it is hard to have been kept here for a year in this ship, but if I can get home and out of the service it will be enough for me. God grant you are safe; truly you have all my best wishes and prayers that you may come well out of it, with glory and all its profits."

The court convened daily for the next week, but due to the absence of witnesses and ongoing ship's duties adjourned indefinitely on April 12. The saga was to drag on until August, long after Hitchcock had left the *Susquehanna.* Captain Thornton's testimony aided by the many dispatches sent by Commodore Hitchcock to both Washington and Farragut detailing the weakness of his squadron prior to the *Florida* incident went a fair way to exonerating the commodore of all blame. Replying to the question regarding the efficiency of the placement of ships off Mobile to prevent the breakout of the enemy raider, Captain Thornton, who had been on deck with Hitchcock that fateful night having been relieved of command of the *Oneida*, answered: "No better arrangement could have been made, but the orders of Commodore Hitchcock were not carried out on board the *Oneida*, Captain Hazard." Although no doubt the clearing of his friend's name and reputation was Thornton's uppermost objective, there was little doubt the facts as presented pointed to a deficiency almost amounting to negligence, in Hazard's lack of action.

For nearly two weeks the *Susquehanna* lay idle at her moorings in the pleasant spring sunshine. Various transports and warships came in to Pensacola, the former discharging supplies while the latter, once replenished, sailing for their allotted destinations and duties on the blockade. The *Susquehanna's* final task before sailing for home was to make once more for Mobile, carrying supplies for the frigate *Colorado*, which vessel held command of the blockading squadron off Fort Morgan. Consequently, on April 14 all spare shells, shot and fixed ammunition were transferred aboard the storeship *Nightingale* and at 7am on the 16th after seven weeks at Pensacola, Hitchcock's ship crossed the bar steering a north-westerly course for Mobile. Six hours sailing brought the *Susquehanna* in view of the Union flotilla and she was soon occupied in provisioning the flagship with the stores brought from Pensacola. Besides the *Colorado* there were seven other vessels on station; the sloop *Lackawanna*, the gunboats *Pocahontas, Kanawha, Cuyler, Kennebec, Aroostook* and *Pinola*. Extra stores were sent aboard the *Lackawanna* and surplus ammunition was distributed among some of the other ships. The commanding officers from the squadron were invited to dine with Hitchcock aboard the *Susquehanna.*

The *Tennessee* had appeared early on the 16th and paused long enough to transfer mail accompanied by dispatches ordering the *Susquehanna* to proceed north to New York. The *Susquehanna* took her leave of the Western Gulf Blockading Squadron the next evening and Burton transcribed the following in his journal: "Sailed from off the blockade on the 17th, cheered by the crews of the ships lying close by our anchorage."

Knowledge of her departure when discovered by the Confederates ashore probably brought a minor twinge of disappointment to Confederate admiral Franklin Buchanan. In a letter to Commodore Jones CSN, Hitchcock's opposite number enthuses over the possibility of taking positive action against the squadron of Federal warships off the bar, and the *Susquehanna* in particular "...it would please me not a little to sink my old ship the *Susquehanna* now off this harbor." Fortunately, he was never to be given the opportunity.

The ship had one final stroke of good fortune. Making a southeasterly course a strange sail was sighted running ahead but on a parallel heading at daylight on the 18th. The crew went to battle stations and after a pursuit lasting seven hours, entirely due to the state of the *Susquehanna's* machinery, the schooner *Alabama* was finally overhauled. She flew no colors but hove to following a single warning shot from the *Susquehanna's* signal gun. The schooner's six-man crew was taken aboard the warship and her Canadian-born captain Alexander Newton, was taken before Hitchcock. When asked to produce his papers he declared; "I carry no papers and fly no flag; I am one week out from Havana, bound for Mobile, which place I ran out of four weeks ago today; if I had a little more wind, you would not have caught me." In fact, acting under instructions from the owners, he had jettisoned overboard all papers and flags as the *Susquehanna* gained on his fleeing craft.

In conversation with Hitchcock, Captain Newton revealed that he had been a United States citizen for the past 18 years and had in fact served in the United States Navy on the frigate *Columbia*. Upon inspection the schooner's manifest listed her cargo as claret, casks of brandy, coffee, cheese, sweet oil, soap, soda, dry goods and cigars. Securing the schooner by a stern line to the *Susquehanna*, she was taken under tow manned by a prize crew consisting of five seamen and two marines, commanded by master's mate E. B. Pratt. The *Alabama* had the somewhat dubious honor of being the last blockade-runner to fall victim to the *Susquehanna.*

On her three day voyage to Key West the *Susquehanna* stopped three vessels. Only one, the *Clarita,* aroused suspicion but she was allowed to continue her journey. The other ships were carrying stores and supplies for government use. On April 22 the sloop arrived at the Florida naval base coming to anchor off Fort Taylor. A salute from the *Susquehanna* was returned by Acting-admiral Bailey's flagship, the frigate *St Lawrence.* The prize schooner *Alabama* was moored under the batteries of Fort Taylor. The rigors of the trip had told on the weakened machinery of the warship and Hitchcock calculated that at least a week to 10 days' work would be needed on the engines and boilers before the ship could proceed northwards on the final leg of her cruise.

The next morning the sum of $5 was issued to the starboard watch who were granted 24-hour shore leave. For those left aboard there was little to do except witness the daily activities among the flotilla. Five marines from Hitchcock's ship were transferred for duty aboard the *St Lawrence,* and the *Alabama* was turned over to the prize court. Two of the *Susquehanna's* officers, Captain Fendall of the marines and Lieutenant Kempff were ordered on board the flagship for courts martial duties.

The 24th being the first anniversary of the taking of New Orleans the warships lying at Key West were adorned with colored bunting from stem to stern. At noon salutes were fired from the *Susquehanna* and the flagship. The festivities continued into the early hours with a general ball, held in the government storehouse ashore, the band of the *Susquehanna* providing the music. It was the turn of the port watch to sample the delights of Key West the next morning as they were rowed ashore with the princely sum of $5 burning holes in their pockets.

Admiral Bailey paid a visit to the ship on the 25th, and two days later the gunboat *De Sota* arrived accompanied by eight prize vessels, one of which was the *Clarita,* taken while attempting to enter Mobile Bay. That evening it was the turn of the *Susquehanna* to host a grand party. The quarterdeck was, in the words of Amos Burton "...beautifully decorated with flags, and festooned

The most famous Rebel cruiser, the CSS *Alabama*.
Battles and Leaders

with the native flowers of the islands. Weapons of warfare were so arranged as to render it a novelty, and yet a pretty adornment. In fact the entire decoration reflected great credit upon our Quartermasters, who had control of these matters." Many high ranking officers, from both the Army and the Navy plus several important civilians, male and female, enjoyed themselves into the small hours dancing to the *Susquehanna's* band, the party finally breaking up around one in the morning. With the departure of the last guests peace again descended on the warship, disturbed only by the steady tread on deck of the anchor watch coupled with the sentinels' regular shouts of "All's well!"

A heavily laden troopship, the *Henry Clinton*, 28 days out of New York, had put into Key West earlier that afternoon to replenish her water supply. She carried a Massachusetts artillery battalion consisting of 350 men and 500 horses, their final destination being New Orleans. The following morning, heading in the opposite direction, came the steamer *McClellan*. One of her passengers was a Captain Griffin who offered to transfer to the *Susquehanna* to aid with the navigation of the homeward passage of the steamer. Those crewmembers still ashore returned to the ship and

Wartime engraving of the Washington Navy Yard.
Battles and Leaders

preparations for getting underway were put in hand. At four thirty on the afternoon of the 29th the *Susquehanna* quit Key West, passing the *Circassian* from New Orleans, on her way into the anchorage.

The first day of May 1863, the weather cool and agreeable. During the day the warship overtook and boarded two schooners, only to find their papers to be in order. The Bermudas were sighted and passed that evening. A further two days' sailing brought the ship off Cape Hatteras and with a fair wind in the offing, the billowing canvas soon caught the breeze and sped the *Susquehanna* onwards. Amos Burton took time to sum up his time on the *Susquehanna* and recorded some pertinent facts. "We are homeward bound after a cruise of thirty-three months duration. During that time we have traversed 33,000 miles."

He remembered the feelings of unease among the officers and men while in the Mediterranean, conflicting loyalties brought to a head following the confirmation of the election of Abraham Lincoln to the Presidency. Then came the shock news of the fall of Fort Sumter. "The blow had been given; states had seceded; and secesh feelings rankled in the breasts of our leading officers." Receiving orders to sail for home Burton noted: "The order was promptly obeyed by our captain, as he together with other officers, were anxious to take part with the South. On our arrival in Boston the Confederacy gained some of our most able and efficient officers."

As to the *Susquehanna's* part in the conflict so far, a justifiably proud Burton wrote: "Scarcely had we reached the first blockaded port, when we were ordered to Hatteras. Arriving at that place we entered at once into the first naval engagement after the breaking out of the rebellion, which proved a signal victory. We have been on the blockade twenty-one months, during which time we have been attached to three different squadrons...between Hampton Roads and Mobile Bay."

Referring to the deaths of shipmates during the cruise he noted that "...eleven of our number have died. Four died at sea, and were committed to the deep; the remains of two were left in foreign lands; and five have been buried in Southern soil. We have been fortunate in battle and storm. Having been in three engagements we have lost but two of our crew, and they received their death blows while in the discharge of their duty."

Doubling Cape Hatteras at noon on the 4th the *Susquehanna's* progress was impeded by the closing in of a dense fog around nine o'clock on the 5th and she was forced to lay to, the shrill notes of her steam whistle and the occasional burning of signal lights warning off possible approaching vessels. The mists finally lifted around midnight and under a full moon the warship got under way. The morning blew in wet with a strong northeast wind. The Highlands were sighted at 9am and a pilot was taken aboard. Passing through the Narrows the *Susquehanna* dropped anchor in the Quarantine grounds to await an inspection by the health officer.

The ship's company was certified as being passed fit and healthy and this last official act brought down the curtain on the cruise of the *Susquehanna.* All that remained was the discharge or transfer of officers and seamen and the placing of the *Susquehanna* at the disposal of the waiting authorities at the New York Navy Yard. On leaving the ship, Amos Burton made a final entry in his journal. "The anchor is dropped; the cruise is now up... the crew have done all they have been called upon to do; and if anything has been left undone it is no fault of theirs. They have been tried, and have not been found wanting...

let our compass be true, that we may escape shipwreck from the evils of which attend our passage through life; and when "all hands" shall be called, may we look well to it that we do not miss our muster."

The *Susquehanna* was decommissioned on May 14, 1863 at the New York Navy Yard. Although no records exist detailing her refit it is safe to assume that new engines and boilers were fitted, yards, standing and running rigging replaced. Also, extensive shipworm infestation may have been discovered, a common occurrence with wooden sailing vessels of the period. This condition may have been exacerbated because of the duration of her time at sea, especially in Southern waters.

The sloop was laid up for 14 months. Although this appears to be an excessive period even for a major overhaul, it may well be that the shipyard was concentrating its efforts on turning out more modern screw-powered vessels. Whatever the reasons behind the delay, the warship would resume her blockading career in July 1864 and would be present for the deciding operations against the Confederacy.

TO SEA ONCE MORE

On July 20, 1864 the *Susquehanna* was taken over from the Navy yard and formally recommissioned into the service. Lieutenant Commander J. B. Blake, Chief Engineer John Johnson and Lieutenant J. R. Bartlett were among those officers officiating at the handover. Several weeks of hard work still lay ahead before the ship would be ready for sea and capable of resuming her role in the blockading squadrons. Her batteries now comprised two 100-pound rifles, twelve 9-inch smoothbores, one 12-pound and one 30-pound rifle.

While time had stood still for the *Susquehanna*, the conflict at sea and on land had grown in intensity. Sweeping north on a tide of victory in late June of 1863, Robert E. Lee's seemingly invincible veterans had been fought to a standstill by the Army of the Potomac during three days of continual bloodletting at Gettysburg. On July 4, as Lee's beaten army prepared to retire back across the Potomac into Virginia, came further disaster for the Confederate administration. Vicksburg's surrounded and starving garrison had been brought to the end of its tether and General Pemberton, commanding the Rebel forces in the city, had met with Ulysses Grant to seek surrender terms. With the river fortress's capitulation on Independence Day, the Union now controlled the entire length of the Mississippi; the South was torn in two.

It was now a fight for survival for the Confederacy, with its armies fighting on several fronts stretching its military and economic capacity to the limit. As the blockade tightened its grip, the pressure on the Confederacy was intensifying. The inevitability of defeat was staring the Confederate people and their leaders in the face, and the tide of final victory was slowly but inexorably shifting towards the North.

The reinforcement of the blockading squadrons by more modern and speedier warships was making life increasingly hazardous for the flying blockade-runners and their daring crews. Ship after ship fell victim to the Federal cruisers, prowling the waters off the coasts of Bermuda and the Bahamas. Others were driven ashore and destroyed as they ventured in to, or out of, the handful of Southern harbors still open to them. Regardless of the risks involved, there appeared to be no shortage of Southern entrepreneurs willing to stake their capital in outfitting a runner and investing in a lucrative cargo from Europe. Undaunted by the odds stacked against them, devil-may-care skippers continually imperiled their ships and their lives for the huge financial rewards to be gained by a successful run into Wilmington or Mobile, where the cargoes would be auctioned off and the profits shared by the investors and the captains and their crews.

Both North and South were now feeling the pressure that total war brings. By 1864 the Federal government had to rely on conscription and bounties to find replacements for the volunteers that had originally manned its ships. These new men tended to be of inferior quality and the *Susquehanna* received her share of undesirables. On July 21, while the crew was occupied in loading fresh supplies and generally making the ship ready for sea, seaman Henry Harris was caught attempting to desert and put in double irons. If this was intended as a deterrent, it proved ineffective; by evening muster, 18 of his compatriots had jumped ship.

Having taken a supply of powder on board, the vessel was hauled off the quayside and on the 27th towed by a tug out into the main channel and made fast by her starboard anchor chain to a buoy. Men reported aboard daily and were inducted into their respective watches and divisions and their stations on the warship. On the 28th shells were transferred from a lighter and taken below to the magazines.

On the penultimate day of July fires were lit under the boilers and just after midday the ship's engineers began preparing the engines for the shakedown cruise. On the first day of August fresh beef for the crew was received and two days later the *Susquehanna*'s new master, Commodore Sylvanus W. Godon stepped onto the quarterdeck of his new charge. A new command indeed but the 55 year-old Godon was no stranger to the *Susquehanna,* having served previously as her executive officer on the East India Squadron from 1851 to 1853. Born in Philadelphia on June 18, 1809 he became a midshipman at the tender age of 10 years, rising to passed midshipman in 1827.

Until 1836, less one year spent at the national school in Norfolk, Virginia, Godon saw service at different times with the Brazilian, Mediterranean and Pacific Squadrons. He was commissioned lieutenant on December 17, 1836. As an officer aboard the bomb ketch *Vesuvius* in 1847 during the war with Mexico, he was present at the siege and capture of Vera Cruz. Made commander in September 1855 Godon skippered the *Mohican* of the Pacific Squadron until 1860. In 1861, now a captain, he was ordered to take command of the sloop *Powhatan,* sister ship of the *Susquehanna,* and sailed with Du Pont's expedition to Port Royal where "...he was conspicuous for his skill and gallantry." His reward came in the shape of elevation to the rank of commodore on January 2 1863 and the taking up of special duties, which occupied him until his present transfer to the *Susquehanna.*

On the morning of August 3, the men of the frigate were mustered aft where they were addressed by their new captain who officially assumed command from Lieutenant Commander Sicord who had been in charge of the *Susquehanna* during her refit at the navy yard. Activity aboard ship grew as final preparations were made to get underway. On the morning of the 7th, Godon read the Articles of War to the assembled crew, and on the 8th they began the filthy task of coaling ship, taking on 22 tons in one day. Civilian workers from the navy yard came to assist the ship's carpenters and the engineers below decks. For one it was to be a short stay. Four bottles of liquor were found concealed on his person, which the sly fellow most likely intended

Sylvanus Godon - shown in this portrait as an eager young officer - took command of the *Susquehanna* following her extensive refit and led one of Porter's divisions in the attack on Fort Fisher; he was to be her last wartime commander.
US Naval Academy Museum

The CSS *Tallahassee*. The *Susquehanna* scoured the seas in search of the raider. *Illustrated London News*

to sell on, at a hefty profit, to thirsty sailors. No doubt to the disappointment of many on the *Susquehanna* he was swiftly returned to shore under the escort of a ship's officer. Coaling resumed the following day and those not employed on this wearisome task were set other chores such as washing clothing, scrubbing the decks, hauling rigging taught and squaring away the yards.

At last came the orders Godon had been awaiting. Admiral Hiram Paulding at the New York Navy Yard instructed him to be ready to sail at a moment's notice and for the ship to be stationed accordingly. In obedience to Paulding's request, at 3.30am on August 11, the weather being overcast and foggy and with a light breeze, the *Susquehanna* moved ponderously down the East River and by early afternoon had passed Governor's Island in the North River before letting go her port anchor into six fathoms off the Battery.

Godon's mission was to track down and sink or capture the Confederate privateer *Tallahassee*. The Rebel raider, sailing from Wilmington six days previously and armed with two 100-pound pivot guns and two 12-pound howitzers had been reported off Sandy Hook, seizing and burning

Yankee merchantmen. Together with the *Pontoosuc* and *Eolus* the *Susquehanna* was to set sail and run the Rebel down. The workers from the navy yard were still below assisting the engineering department but at 6.30am on the morning of the 12th a tug came alongside with fresh dispatches for Commodore Godon. Shortly after receipt of these orders, fires were started under the boilers and a pilot came aboard. Unable to put to sea because some of his officers were still ashore, a delay that lost Godon 12 vital hours, the remainder of the day was spent methodically securing the ship for sea.

At 2.30am on the morning of the 13th, the call: "All hands up anchor" was piped followed quickly by the pounding of feet on the wooden decks as the crew rushed to their stations. Within half an hour the *Susquehanna* was underway and standing down the bay. In the hazy pre-dawn light with hardly a breath of wind she cleared the harbor bar just before 6.30am. Twenty minutes later steering southeast by south, the sloop passed the Sandy Hook lightship. Still within view of land she stopped and boarded the bark *Juno* whose master reported sighting a small steamer to the east just before daylight. The *Susquehanna* proceeded on course making six knots. Sighting the bark *Suliote* some 20 miles off Fire Island the *Susquehanna* hove to in order to communicate with her captain.

On board the small vessel were the passengers and crew of the ship *Adriatic* and the pilot of pilot boat *No.24*. Both vessels had been captured and burned by the *Tallahassee* the previous day whilst some 40 miles to the southeast of Montauk. The shaken travelers had also witnessed the subsequent destruction of pilot boat *No.22* following which the raider sheared off in a southeasterly direction. In the first two weeks of August while prowling off the New England shoreline, the *Tallahassee* had accounted for some 30 Yankee ships. Armed with this information, Godon intended making for Bermuda in an attempt to head her off. The ship's engines now began to cause problems and Godon recorded in the log: "The first two days the engines did not work as well as could be desired, the journals and guides heating. The buckets in the wheel became loose; one of which we lost, with a number of bolts; were compelled to stop not less than six times, and could not make great speed. The fire crew, too, were very new to the work. We have done better since, but I regret to find thus far no satisfactory speed obtainable.

I hope for better things in this respect."

The 14th being a Sunday, divine services were held as the *Susquehanna* maintained her course for the northwest Atlantic port of Bermuda. To make up time the maximum amount of canvas was set including the foresail, jib and spanker. The crew on the 6pm to 8pm watch was exercised at shortening sail by scampering aloft and reefing the fore and main topsails. On the 16th the *Susquehanna* made Bermudan waters. Coinciding with the sloop's arrival was the demise of seaman Charles Sage who succumbed to pneumonia and whose body, stitched in his hammock and weighted down was slipped over the side that evening. The next day Godon proceeded to sail around the island in search of the *Tallahassee* but his only contact with another vessel was the English warship *Spitfire* whose captain passed on news of an outbreak of Yellow Fever on Bermuda but reported seeing no sign of the Rebel privateer. It was the same story with each vessel the frigate came across.

Stymied in his mission, and having burned up almost 400 tons of coal Godon decided to set course back to New York. Following a line in from the Cape Fear River to within 120 miles of the coast steering along the edge of the Gulf Stream the *Susquehanna* passed Hatteras with Godon stopping and boarding every vessel that he encountered including the British steamer *Nymph* bound for Liverpool on August 18. It took a shot from the howitzer to bring her to but the captain's papers were in order. Indeed, only the sighting of considerable numbers of cotton bales floating in the sea, presumably thrown overboard by a fleeing blockade-runner, relieved Godon's frustration. At two in the morning on August 24 the *Susquehanna* crossed the bar off Sandy Hook and passed through the Narrows, coming to a stop at the Quarantine station where she was boarded by the health officer. Her crew cleared of any contagion, the side-wheeler moved ahead before coming to anchor in the East River an hour later. She immediately began hauling on board more coal ready for a quick return to the South Atlantic.

Filling the ship's bunkers continued apace but for one of the *Susquehanna's* complement, seaman Lewis Eldridge, the hustle and bustle of shipboard procedure held little importance. He was near death's door, a victim of 'congestion of the lungs'; his struggle for life ended that afternoon. Coaling was completed late in the evening. The grimy, coal dust covered crew had heaved aboard 102 tons.

Godon received orders the next morning from the Navy Department to put to sea as soon as was practicable and cruise the latitudes from New York to Cape Cod and toward Cape Sable, Nova Scotia. His primary duty was the protection of Union merchant vessels from the ravenous attentions of the *Tallahassee,* and the resumption of the search for the elusive corsair. The commodore was to run in to the nearest port at least every two days to report his position and also to telegraph any news of the whereabouts of the Rebel warship. Godon was requested to use sail power whenever possible to conserve the precious coal his men had labored so hard to stow aboard. There was also a rumor circulating that there could be another Confederate raider on the prowl, the *Edith,* either at sea or in readiness to sail.

On the 24th the late Lewis Eldridge was lowered over the side of the *Susquehanna* in a coffin to begin his final journey ashore for burial. Unfortunately, he was not alone in bidding farewell to the ship. At 8.30 that evening three marines and a seaman lowered themselves into a launch and rowed for shore. Although a marine on sentry duty fired off one round from his musket it failed to deter the absconders. The boat was recovered later. Two of the deserters obviously reconsidered their actions and later returned to the ship; they were immediately clapped in double irons. Requested to hold his position and not to set sail until fresh orders were delivered, Godon took this opportunity to request mechanics from the navy yard to check over the engines in an effort to prevent a recurrence of the problems encountered on the trip to Bermuda. The never-ending job of coaling continued and fresh provisions were swung aboard from a small schooner. On August 30, 11 men were sent ashore to the hospital suffering from various maladies.

On the first day of September orders to proceed to sea finally arrived. These new instructions deviated little from those of August 25. Godon was now to make for Cape Cod then on to Cape Sable, Nova Scotia and as far east as Halifax. His principal role was still to safeguard northern cargo ships but his secondary objective was the interception of blockade-runners. With Yellow Fever raging in both Nassau and Bermuda the Navy Department's assumption that these craft would now be running between Wilmington and Halifax led to a strategic reappraisal regarding the placement of the blockading ships in the North Atlantic. Godon's directive also enclosed details of those vessels believed by the Navy Department to be actively engaged in running contraband. The communication closed with another reminder to be sparse with the use of coal. Forty replacements – seamen, ordinary seamen, landsmen and firemen, reported on board on September 2.

The weather had deteriorated over the past 72 hours with heavy squalls and gale force winds making life fairly miserable for all on the rolling, pitching decks of the sloop. By 5.30am on the 3rd the boilers were operational and the *Susquehanna* got up steam. With a pilot to guide her downriver she left the bay and came to anchor off Sandy Hook. There the frigate lingered, riding at anchor in the East River for the remainder of September. Godon's orders for sea duty had been rescinded and he was to await further instructions. With little to occupy the hands other than the daily round of exercises, inspections and drills, broken only by swinging the ship to check compass deviations, it is no surprise that certain tars decided they had had enough of Uncle Sam's navy. On the 7th as the *Susquehanna* made her way back towards New York several of these fellows dived overboard into the waters of the East River. A volley of musketry halted their flight and, dripping wet, they were dragged back on board and clapped in irons. Additional replacements were received on the 26th, both seamen and landsmen.

The chaplain conducted religious services on Sunday October 2 and late that afternoon a tug bearing dispatches for Commodore Godon came alongside. The *Susquehanna* was now to become part of the North Atlantic Blockading Squadron and Godon's orders were to proceed to Hampton Roads. Boilers and engines were made ready and with a light breeze in the offing, the ship up anchored the next morning. Godon indulged the gun crews with some target practice and three rounds of shell were fired from each of the pivot guns at a stationary target at 1,400 yards range with telling effect.

Reaching Sandy Hook the pilot was discharged and, making a south-south-westerly course her jib pointed the way to Fortress Monroe. Old Point Comfort was sighted on the 5th and the ship hove to in order to take on a pilot to navigate the sloop into Hampton Roads which place was reached the following day. Disembarking a party of indisposed sailors to the hospital ashore the *Susquehanna* began taking on coal and fresh beef.

Admiral David Porter took up command of the ships in the roadstead, flying his pennant in the *Wabash.* The remainder of October was spent in Hampton Roads. The traffic in the bay increased daily, not only warships but also supply and transport vessels came in and let go their anchor chains in the dark tidewaters opposite Fortress Monroe. It was fairly obvious to even the most naive of webfeet that preparations for a major operation were underway. On the 11th the *Susquehanna's* sails were loosed to dry in the breeze for two hours before being furled. The following day the marine detachment exercised with small arms while the remainder of the crew was engaged in cladding the outer hull with sheet iron chains, the work consumed several days. The ammunition and powder magazines were replenished on the 15th; fifty 9-inch shrapnel shells, thirteen 150-pound rifle shells and further assorted solid shot and shells were hoisted off the supply schooner and taken below decks.

Gun drill was stepped up and target practice using live rounds was carried out on more than one occasion. Launches were lowered and the boat's crews exercised with howitzers mounted in the bows of the cutters. On the morning of the 20th the mizzen topmast, fore and main topgallant masts were taken down and sent with spare spars on a tug to the Norfolk Navy Yard. Several of the *Susquehanna's* complement assisted the tug's crew, including one Thomas Murphy, seaman. He failed to return to the ship with the rest of the work party. Murphy had embarked on a drinking spree and showed up the next day, still the worse for wear to face the wrath of the officer of the deck. Charged with drunkenness and leaving the ship without permission, he nursed his hangover with 12 hours' solitary confinement on bread and water.

In the early hours of the 25th while fresh provisions were being swung aboard, the sloops *Vandalia, Kensington* and the gunboat *Monticello* steamed into the roads accompanied by a transport, the *Governor Buckingham,* thus adding to the powerful armada assembling at Norfolk.

As November blew in with gales and savage squalls Commodore Godon received orders from Admiral Porter to escort the ironclad *Monadnock* to New York for repairs. At 8.30am on the 6th the flagship *Wabash* signaled Godon to: "Prepare for sea." After taking on a further supply of ordnance a pilot was taken aboard the *Susquehanna* and the launches and cutters were hoisted inboard and secured. The frigate got underway and stood out of Hampton Roads with the *Monadnock* following in her wake, a towing hawser attached to assist her laboring engines. Making a steady seven knots the ships made Cape Henry that evening. On the second day of the journey the ironclad's engines failed. Signaling her to heave to, the *Susquehanna* stopped engines and dropped anchor in 15 fathoms. By 3.30pm repairs had been made and the hawser was cast off, all hands were piped to raise anchor and both vessels got underway. Nearing Sandy Hook light at daybreak on the 8th, the ships were enveloped by a dense fog. A slight breeze failed to shift the heavy pea-souper and Godon decided to anchor for the night.

Able to proceed safely at 10am on the 9th, within a few hours the *Susquehanna* let go her port anchor in the North River while the *Monadnock* steamed on into the navy yard. Godon's ship partially refilled her bunkers over the next two days and was ready for sea on the morning of the 11th when the *Monadnock* reappeared, the repairs to her engines completed. Both vessels steamed slowly out of the harbor and anchored off the Quarantine grounds, Staten Island until 6.30pm when they stood down for the harbor bar and passed the Highland Light. Heading out to open water, the course was set for a return to Hampton Roads. Making six knots Cape Henry Light was passed at 1.30am on November 14 and within a matter of hours the *Susquehanna* was riding at her port anchor in the Virginia roadstead, canvas loosed to dry in the moderate breeze.

With most of the crew engaged for several days in painting the outer hull of the ship, the howitzer crews were taken ashore for a day's drill on the 18th. Winter had now set in and the weather turned foul, with strong to gale force conditions and frequent heavy squalls. On November 26 fresh supplies were received and those not engaged in hauling them aboard were exercised aloft loosing and furling the sails.

Coaling resumed on the 30th and new clothing was issued to the men on December 3. Four of the ship's company were discharged the same day, their time in the service completed. A particularly strong wind sprang up on the night of the 7th, sufficient to cause the flagship *Malvern* to drag her anchor. The steamer drifted to within a quarter of a mile of the shore when she finally 'brought up' with both anchors down, a similar experience to that encountered by the *Susquehanna* while with the Mediterranean Squadron.

On December 13 Porter's imposing fleet departed from Hampton Roads. The *Susquehanna* had attempted to weigh anchor at 10am in preparation for getting underway only to find the chain fouled. The anchor finally broke the surface along with 43 fathoms of twisted forged iron chain. The steamer left the bay in company with the rest of the expedition at 11am. Three days sailing would bring them to their goal – Fort Fisher, the most formidable stronghold in Dixie, and guardian of the port of Wilmington, North Carolina.

STALEMATE AT FORT FISHER

The Chase

Freed from the lingering chase, in devious ways
Upon the swelling tides
Swiftly the *Lilian* glides
Through hostile shells and eager foemen past;
The lynx-eyed pilot gazing through the haze,
And engines straining, "far hope dawns at last."

Now falls in billows deep the welcome night
Upon white sands below;
While signal lamps aglow
Seek out Fort Fisher's distant gleams,
The blockade runners' keen supreme delight, –
Dear Dixie Land, the haven of our dreams!

James Sprunt, *Tales of the Cape Fear Blockade*

When Colonel William Lamb assumed command of Fort Fisher, North Carolina on July 4, 1862, the defenses consisted of several detached earthworks and a casemated battery of sand and palmetto tree logs mounting four guns, only one of which was of a heavy caliber. Lamb, a former newspaper editor in Norfolk, Virginia before the war, lost no time in procuring 500 Negro laborers to assist the garrison in strengthening the place. Allowed the best part of two years to complete the task, by the winter of 1864 Confederate engineers had turned the fort into the largest earthwork in the Southern Confederacy. Located on the peninsula formed by Onslow Bay and the Cape Fear River, known as Federal Point – renamed Confederate Point during the war – the 'L' shaped fortification named for Charles F Fisher, a North Carolinian killed at First Bull Run, shielded the northeast access to the river mouth, while the older brick and masonry construction of Fort Caswell protected the approaches to the southwest channel. These two inlets gave ingress into the Cape Fear River and on up to the city of Wilmington.

Lamb based the design on the Russian Malakoff redoubt at Sevastopol which had proved virtually impregnable against British and French artillery in the Crimean War. The ramparts of the fort were constructed from earth and bolstered by heavy timbers overlaid with tons of sand, topped off with a covering of sodded marsh grass. The stronghold boasted 169 cannon, 44 of which were large caliber pieces; 10-inch and 8-inch Columbiads, 7-inch Brooke rifles, 8-inch Blakely rifles plus a fair sprinkling of 6.5-inch rifles, all mounted on Columbiad carriages. These mighty pieces of ordnance were positioned on wooden platforms in between 30 huge earthen traverses 25 feet thick and between 12 and 15 feet higher than the parapet. The conical traverses were designed to minimize damage and casualties from enfilading fire. If one of the batteries received a hit, the neighboring gun and its crew were likely to remain unscathed. Several of these colossal mounds were hollowed out to serve as bombproofs, magazines and officer's quarters.

The overland works, beginning approximately 100 yards in from the Cape Fear River extended for half a mile across the neck of the peninsula to the northeast bastion. The open ground in front of this landward face had been planted with lethal, electrically controlled 'mines' to check infantry assaults. If the attacking troops forced a pathway around these perilous objects, they would then have to fight their way over a wooden palisade. These outer defenses supported the main line, consisting of 20 heavy guns and rifles sectioned in pairs.

From the north-east bastion the parapet made a sharp right angled turn to the east, running parallel to the sea shore in an irregular contour for three quarters of a mile, accommodating further batteries comprising 24 rifled pieces and Columbiads in self-contained batteries, their menacing black muzzles thrusting out of the embrasures covering the approaches to the bar from the Atlantic Ocean.

At the southern end of the beach anchoring the end of the line was the Mound Battery. A truly formidable piece of engineering rising 60 feet above the sand, its 10 inch Columbiad and 6.5-inch rifle zeroed in to send a plunging fire onto targets in the New Inlet, where the channel ran close to the beach inside the bar. The final link in the chain of this mighty bastion was Battery Buchanan, sited a mile from the Mound Battery on the west bank of Cape Fear River. Elliptical in design, its four guns, two of which were 11-inch rifles, were manned by a detachment from the Confederate Navy.

There were vulnerable areas in the fort. No moat, scarp or counterscarp could be built as the shifting sands made their construction impossible, and in order to fire on storming parties of Union troops the defenders would be forced to stand atop the walls and traverses, thus exposing themselves to enemy artillery and musketry. Apart from infantry rifle pits zigzagging from the Mound Battery to the river, the rear of Fort Fisher was unprotected. When Admiral David Porter's fleet appeared off the fort to join the transports packed with General Benjamin Butler's troops just before Christmas of 1864, the garrison of Fort Fisher numbered 1,400 men, of whom two thirds were militia who had never fired a shot in anger, there were also 60 sailors and marines. Colonel Lamb's orders, telegraphed direct from Robert E. Lee were clear and unequivocal; Fort Fisher must be held at all costs.

Wilmington. The very name was almost guaranteed to bring Gideon Welles to a state of apoplexy. The one remaining Rebel harbor open to the outside world was a thorn in the side of the Union Navy. Not only were hundreds of tons of vital war materiel slipping in through the Union blockade, the port also played host to commerce raiders such as the *Tallahassee*. Admiral S.

A carte de visite taken at Gurney & Sons Gallery, New York, shows Commodore Godon as he appeared when in command of the *Susquehanna*.
Courtesy of Picture History

P. Lee first proposed a plan to attack the place in May 1863. A substantial infantry force would be required, for the fort could not be reduced purely by naval action, the narrow and dangerous channels and bars prevented the Yankee warships from closing with the place as had been done so successfully earlier in the war at Hatteras Inlet and Port Royal. The Northern high command was keen to bring the plan to life but sufficient troops could not be spared at the time, so the operation was shelved.

In the summer of 1864 as Ulysses Grant's soldiers slogged it out with Lee's hard-bitten veterans in Virginia in the final push towards Richmond, Welles and Secretary of War Stanton appealed to Grant, now commander-in-chief of all Union forces, to release enough troops to enable the expedition to finally get underway. If Wilmington could be closed, he was told, not only would Lee's remaining source of supply for his army disappear, but also the last surviving bolt hole for Confederate commerce raiders and blockade runners would be closed. Initially lukewarm to the idea and with his mind concentrated on driving Lee from the Petersburg trenches, Grant grudgingly agreed to supply approximately 5,000 troops for a combined operation by the beginning of October. If the enterprise were a success – fine, if not it would not be a calamity.

Admiral David Farragut was offered command of the expedition but declined, pleading mental and physical exhaustion following the hard fought battle of Mobile Bay. He also harbored doubts as to the outcome of the operation and had no wish to close a distinguished naval career with an embarrassing defeat if the attempt ended in failure. So, the responsibility devolved on the brash, self-assured and somewhat boastful David Dixon Porter. Relieved of duty with the Mississippi Squadron he took control of the North Atlantic Squadron on October 1, 1864.

Eventually 6,500 Union troops were provided for the land assault. These men, drawn from the Army of the James, were to be led by the infamous and egotistical Major-General Benjamin Butler. Fort Fisher came under the military district Butler was responsible for and he took upon himself, as was technically his right, the control of the land forces committed to the operation. Arriving at Hampton Roads on October 12, Porter began to assemble a mighty armada of warships, the most numerous and formidable fleet of the war, 150 vessels mounting 600 guns.

Desperate to get underway before bad weather set in Porter was frustrated by several delays, not the least of which were continuous newspaper reports detailing the expedition's planned attack on Fort Fisher, which of course gave the Confederates ample warning of his coming. The flotilla of transports carrying Butler's soldiers sailed from Beaufort, North Carolina arriving off the enemy held peninsula on December 15. There was no sign of Porter's ships. The vanguard of the fleet eventually appeared on the horizon three days later.

The *Susquehanna* made out the waiting fleet of transports at first light through a rainsquall, and in company with the *Ticonderoga, Colorado* and *Powhattan* came to anchor within sight of Fort Fisher. The fore and main topsail gaffs were taken down and the ship was cleared for battle. The 17th brought thick fog and subsequently no action. Admiral Porter arrived in the flagship *Malvern* the following afternoon, but the weather deteriorated to such an extent that Porter advised Butler to take his transports back to Beaufort, some 75 miles distant, to await more favorable conditions. It was sound judgment on Porter's part as the weather worsened. The gales and high winds abated after five days and Butler sent word his ships would be arriving off Fort Fisher late on Christmas Eve.

Porter decided not to wait for Butler and instead put into action a fantastic plan cooked up by Assistant Secretary of the Navy Gustavus Fox and eagerly endorsed by General Butler. An elderly, flat-bottomed former blockade-runner, the *Louisiana*, had been packed with 215 tons of powder, shells and other combustibles. The scheme called for the ship to be towed through the shallows and grounded within 500 yards of the fort and detonated using a new but complicated clockwork timing mechanism. Porter was confident that the resulting cataclysm would so affect the Rebels that "...houses in Wilmington will tumble to the ground and much demoralize the people, and I think if the Rebels fight after the explosion they have more in them than I give them credit for."

Concerned for the safety of his own ships, Porter planned to move his force 12 miles out to sea and await the big bang. The responsibility for maneuvering the *Louisiana* into position rested with Commander Alexander Rhind of the *Wilderness*. In pitch-blackness the *Wilderness*, manned by a small volunteer crew, towed the *Louisiana* in toward the shore. With little idea of his proximity to Fort Fisher, Rhind dropped anchor upon hearing the surf breaking on nearby rocks and his men set the clockwork detonators before rowing back to their ship. Far from being 400 yards from the fort, the *Louisiana* now lay 500 yards off the beach. Shortly before abandoning the vessel, he ordered fires started in the ships stern as a secondary measure should the timers fail to do their job. In the ensuing two hours before detonation, the ship drifted even further from the shore and was some 1,100 yards distant from the fort when she at last blew apart.

At 1.40am the crew of the *Susquehanna* heard several low, rumbling detonations as the *Louisiana* erupted. The result was dismal failure. The fires started in the stern of the vessel had reached the powder before the timing detonators had time to work, and instead of one colossal blast a series of smaller explosions destroyed the ship. Much of the powder proved defective and although a brilliant orange and red flash lit the sky and the tremors from the explosion were felt in the fort, the sturdy works were completely unshaken.

As a dirty black sulphurous cloud drifted out to sea, covering the fleet, Porter signaled his ships to get underway. At 6am on Christmas Eve, the crew of the *Susquehanna* sprang into action as she prepared for combat and smoke belched forth from her tall smokestack as the fleet closed in line of battle with the fort. By midday she was within extreme range of the Mound Battery and at 2pm, the sloop's starboard battery of eight 9-inch guns together with her two 150-pound rifles opened fire. Porter's fleet positioned in a vast semi-circle confronting the fort's sea face poured in over 10,000 rounds of solid shot and shell in five hours of mayhem.

Colonel Lamb stated that the bombardment was "...the most terrific from the fleet which war ever witnessed. Ship after ship discharged its broadsides, every description of deadly missile, from a 3-inch rifle bolt to a 15-inch shell flying widely into and over the fort until the garrison flag-staff was shattered...the wooden quarters of the garrison were set on fire by the bursting shells and more than half of them consumed." Because of the hydrographic conditions the fleet could not close with the fort and were firing at long range, consequently this affected the accuracy of the bombardment and the immense earthworks and traverses remained largely unscathed by the incoming rounds. Colonel Lamb's guns answered the Union fleet's fire sporadically. At 5.30pm the *Susquehanna* received a signal from the Malvern to break off the action and the

Major General Benjamin Butler who commanded the Union troops in the initial unsuccessful attack on Fort Fisher.
Battles and Leaders

fleet withdrew for the night.

In his report of the day's happenings Godon stated that: "The firing from Fort Fisher was not sustained and was often silenced for a considerable time. The distance, however, seemed too great, although the practice was good and kept the fire of the enemy down."

Butler and a portion of his transports arrived on the scene at dusk on the 24th and during a meeting with Porter he informed the admiral that the remainder of his force would be arriving the following morning. Porter was confident that the bombardment had shaken up the Confederates to such an extent that when Butler landed his troops they would face little opposition from the fort's defenders. However, Porter agreed to throw in a few shells to cover the landings, and launches and cutters scuttled back and forth among the supply ships on Christmas morning replenishing the fleets' empty magazines, exhausted in the previous day's action. The *Susquehanna* received hundreds of rounds of solid shot, fused shell and rifled ammunition.

In a light breeze the sloop up-anchored and took position in the battle line and steamed ahead for Fort Fisher. By the time the warship reached her station part of the fleet was already engaged. At 1.20pm the *Susquehanna*'s drums beat to general quarters and the ship was cleared for action. Half an hour later the side-wheeler stopped engines and cast down her stern anchor on the port quarter in six fathoms of water within half a ship's length on the starboard bow of the Colorado. An entry in the ship's log recorded, "Ship in fine position inside the line of large ships with Fort Fisher bearing abeam distant about 1,700 yards." Once again the guns of the *Susquehanna*, firing by division, roared out across the water in unison with those of the fleet. In reply Fort Fisher's batteries opened a slow, desultory fire and a solid shot went completely through the *Susquehanna*'s smokestack. Another round tore away the port main lift.

A little after 1.30pm 2,000 Yankee soldiers under Major-General Godfrey Weitzel scrambled ashore above the fort and formed for an assault. Far from being demoralized and ready to capitulate, the Rebel garrison emerged from their bombproofs and manned their batteries. Infantry swarmed up the parapets and traverses to face the advancing blue lines. A reconnaissance in force started across the open ground towards the fort but soon came under a steady fire of musketry and artillery and consequently was not pressed home with any real enthusiasm. The Federal losses amounted to only 16 casualties. Both Weitzel and Butler were of the opinion that the place could only be taken by instigating siege tactics, and they had neither the necessary force nor equipment. Then Butler received reports from Rebel prisoners that Confederate General Hoke with 6,000 men was moving down from Wilmington on his rear. This was enough to convince Butler he had outstayed his welcome and he ordered Weitzel to call off the attack. As dusk fell the Federal troops clambered back into the flat-bottomed surfboats and returned to their transports, minus 700 soldiers left behind on the beach.

The Rebels were jubilant. Despite receiving 20,000 rounds spread into and around the fort, the damage inflicted was minimal. Some wooden buildings were burned and three guns on the land face dismounted from their carriages, and these were replaced with little difficulty. Concerned with conserving precious ammunition Lamb's gunners had expended but 672 rounds in reply to the Union fleet's cannonade. One Confederate had been killed and 22 wounded during the two-day bombardment. Porter's losses were almost double. Several 100-pounder rifles, firing too rapidly, exploded at the breech killing and injuring their crews. Colonel Lamb wired Richmond. "This morning, December 27, the foiled and frightened enemy left our shore."

Other than the shot which pierced the smokestack, the *Susquehanna* received few hits from the Rebel guns and came through almost unscathed. One shell exploded outside the wheelhouse, a piece of which struck a shot rack and deck of the engine room hatch on the starboard side. Boatswain Whitmarsh reported both main topmast stays and foretop bowlines shot away. All other damage to the ship was in fact self-inflicted, the first cutter and barge were battered by the concussion of the guns so as to be beyond repair and the gig was torn apart by a snapped hawser leading astern.

In his official report to Porter on the two-day fight, a proud and satisfied Commodore Godon singled out several individuals for special mention. "From my position on the wheelhouse overlooking my entire battery, I had every officer and man under my observation, and I have sincere pleasure in testifying to the fine bearing, zeal and gallantry of the divisional officers. Lieutenant Commander Blake, my executive officer is all I can desire in battle – cool and collected, calm and intelligent. He is my right-hand man.

Commodore Godon (sixth from right), and the officers and crew of the *Susquehanna* pose proudly on the deck of their ship (one of her giant paddle wheels can be seen behind the standing rigging). Photograph taken in 1864.
Library of Congress

"I also beg to call special attention to Ensign Preble, the master of this ship, who, whether under fire or any other circumstances, has proved himself without a superior in intelligence or ability aboard the vessel. My aid, Master's Mate Cooper, was prompt in answering signals and in his spare moments used the 12-pounder howitzer on the hurricane deck with effect.

"Thanks to the officers of the powder division Acting Ensign Bernbum, Gunner Waugh and Sailmaker Holbrook, the ammunition was promptly supplied throughout the engagement. The engines, under the control of Chief Engineer Johnson and his able assistants, were at all times ready for duty. The subordinate officers of the divisions, the captain's of the guns and their spirited crews have my thanks for their labours those two days. In short, I have every reason to believe that in action this ship will always be found efficient, wherever she may be placed."

The next morning as the frustrateed Porter's fleet departed, his gunboats covered the withdrawal of the 700 marooned bluecoats. Porter was beside himself with anger at Butler's inept performance and his eagerness to quit and return to Hampton Roads. He dashed off communiqués to Grant lambasting Butler and requesting the return of the Army, reinforced and under a new commander.

The Union commander-in-chief acquiesced and advised the admiral to remain on station off Fort Fisher to await the arrival of General Alfred Terry, Butler's replacement. Porter however decided to make for Beaufort to refit, re-provision and take on more coal. Over the next three days while awaiting orders to make for Beaufort, the *Susquehanna* replenished her magazines with ammunition. The 2nd and 3rd cutters were lowered and employed in transporting the deadly cargo from the supply ships back to the *Susquehanna* for transfer into the magazines below decks.

On the 28th in obedience to signals from the *Malvern*, the sloop got underway, arriving off Beaufort the following morning. On the 31st the crew was mustered and received clean hammocks and the men were allowed to wash their clothes and air their bedding. At 2pm Godon's tars weighed anchor and the sloop moved five miles offshore before letting go her port anchor in 10 fathoms.

The new year of 1865 found the *Susquehanna* preparing to coal ship. The dirty chore began on the 2nd but only 48 tons had been heaved aboard before worsening weather forced the abandonment of the work. Attempts to recommence the next evening again had to be aborted and heavy seas almost extinguished the boiler fires in the engine room. Despite the conditions, 63 rifle shells were transferred from the schooner *Little Ada*. The *Susquehanna's* small launch was sent to bring back more ammunition from the schooner on the afternoon of the 4th, and at last coaling was completed, 123 tons were now piled in the bunkers below. Costain lights and further powder and shells were taken on board the next day.

Three days later General Alfred Terry's transports, carrying 8,000 troops sailed into Beaufort and he immediately reported to Porter on board the *Malvern*. Terry was a veteran of Army–Navy combined operations, and he and the capricious Porter worked well together and co-operated closely in the planning of the second attack on Fort Fisher.

Foul weather descended on the anchorage and for several days strong gales and squalls buffeted the fleet. As the barometer rose heralding clearer weather, Porter's squadrons made ready to depart, and on January 12 at 8.30am the *Susquehanna* steamed away from Beaufort heading southward in company with the fleet, set for a final head on encounter with Fort Fisher.

"AWAY ALL BOATS!"

In the first dull light of January 13, 1865, officers in Fort Fisher lifted field glasses to tired eyes and took in the imposing sight of Porter's returning armada. The long roll brought the fort's defenders to their posts and the gun crews swarmed around their pieces preparing the giant Columbiads for action. For the past fortnight Colonel Lamb, left with only 800 soldiers to man the works, had pleaded for reinforcements from Hoke's division but General Braxton Bragg, Lamb's superior, refused his request. Bragg informed the fort's commander that he did not believe another assault would be mounted so soon after the first. Besides, he felt that the defense of Wilmington itself took priority and Hoke's men could not be spared. Lamb did however receive additional troops and on the eve of battle the garrison numbered around 1,500 men.

General W H Chase Whiting, the district commander, decided to throw in his lot with Colonel Lamb. Born in Biloxi, Mississippi he finished top of his class at West Point and proved to be an excellent engineer. His *ante bellum* career was spent in overseeing fortifications along America's eastern seaboard. With the coming of the war he resigned his commission and joined the Confederate army and saw action at Bull Run and fought with Jackson

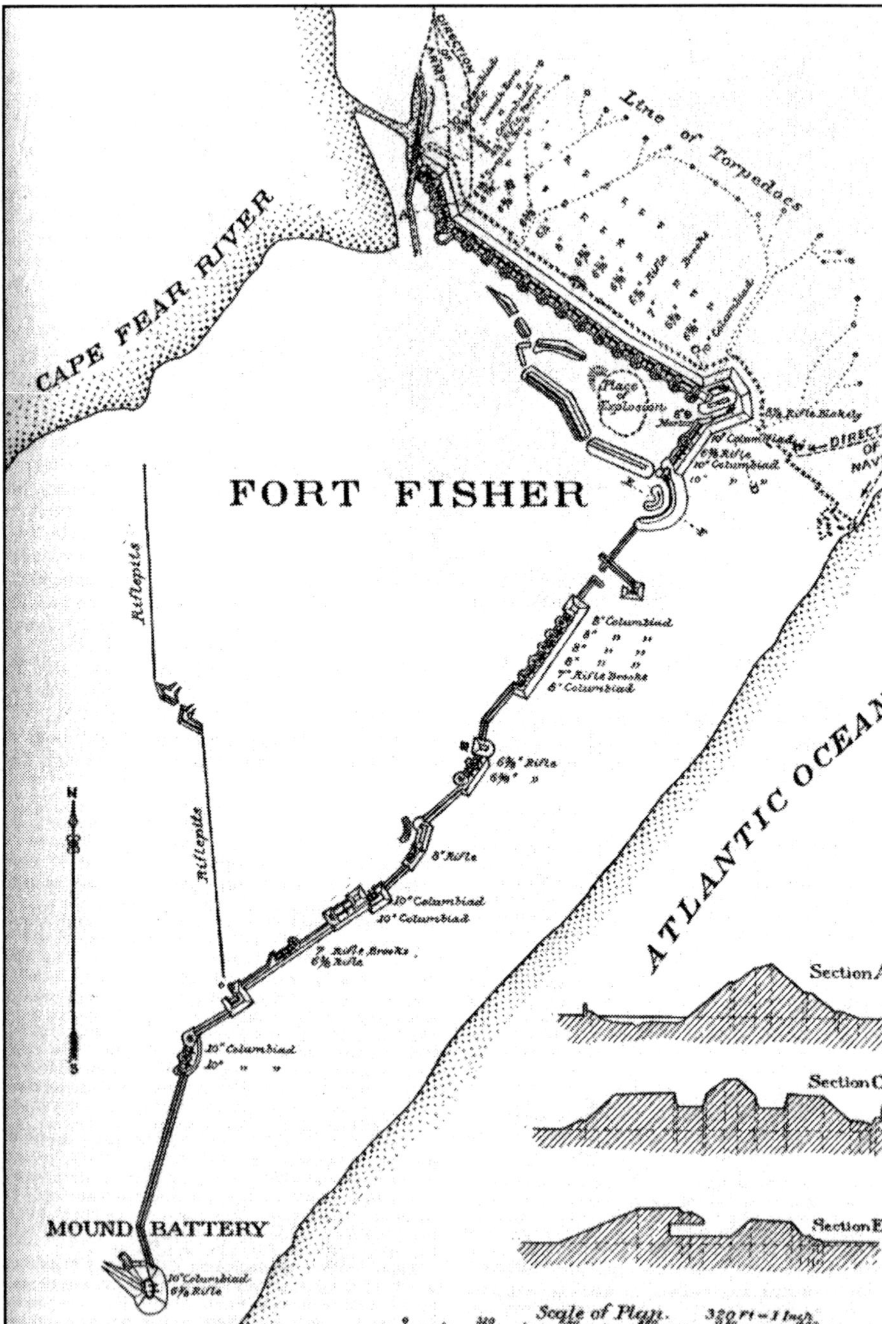

Sectional plan of Fort Fisher showing the formidable strength of her batteries.
Battles and Leaders

during the Seven Days campaign in Virginia. His 5′ 2″ stature had earned the 48 year-old the sobriquet 'Little Billy' among his men. He had assisted greatly in the two years it had taken to plan and build Fort Fisher.

On greeting the 29 year-old commander Whiting said: "Lamb my boy, I have come to share your fate. You and your garrison are to be sacrificed." Understandably taken aback by this statement, Lamb replied: "Don't say so General; we shall certainly whip the enemy again!"

Aboard the *Susquehanna* long before daybreak the crew had readied the ship for action. With additional percussion shells and rounds for the batteries safely stowed in the shot lockers and in the magazines below, the frigate moved to take position in the main battle line of large warships. Porter had 44 vessels, including five ironclads, and in a change of tactics from the Christmas cannonade when fire from the fleet had 'blanketed' the fort with little effect. He instructed his captains to concentrate their fire on individual gun emplacements, taking out each battery in turn before switching to fresh targets. At dawn, the signal flags broke out from the flagship *Malvern*, and the bombardment commenced.

Godon had been assigned command of the 4th Division, consisting of 11 warships including the *Wabash, Colorado, Powhatan* and *Ticonderoga* and upon reaching her assigned location, nearly 1,500 yards distant from the north-east bastion just before 9am, the *Susquehanna* let go her anchor. At Godon's command, the gunports were lowered and the starboard battery belched forth flame, smoke and 11-inch shells. All that day and through the night the massed batteries of the fleet poured their deadly fire into the fort. A never-ending deluge of shells pummeled the earthworks. Colonel Lamb recorded his predicament. "All day and night on the 13th and 14th January the Navy continued its ceaseless torment; it was impossible to repair damages at night on the land face. The *Ironsides* and monitors bowled their 11 and 15-inch shells along the parapet, scattering shrapnel in the darkness. We could scarcely gather up and bury our dead without fresh casualties. At least 200 had been killed and wounded in the two days since the fight began. Only three or four of my land guns were of any service."

At 8am on the 13th, General Terry's regiments had begun landing on the beach, five miles north of the fort. Altogether 8,000 troops had been conveyed to the landing spot in 200 small cutters and launches, towed by naval tugs. Each man carried 40 rounds of ball cartridge and food for three days. It took time for the brigades to wade through the surf and deploy on the beach. They would begin the assault on the landward face at 2pm on the 15th, aided by the guns of the fleet.

The Confederate garrison enjoyed a brief respite on the 14th as bad weather forced the Union armada to seek deeper water, but the warships returned to the attack the next morning and at 10.45am the *Susquehanna's* starboard batteries opened fire. In reply, the Mound Battery sent irregular salvos of shells scudding across the water, some striking home, while others fell short sending giant geysers of water high into the air.

To support the infantry's advance Admiral Porter put together a landing force of 1,600 sailors and 400 marines led by Lieutenant-Commander K. Breese, the Fleet Captain. The naval force splashed ashore on the morning of the 15th, their objective was the sea face of the northeast bastion of the fort. The garrison were sheltering in the bombproofs, so the landing went undetected and therefore, initially unopposed. Among the naval contingent were 75 sailors and marines from the *Susquehanna* under Lieutenant-Commander Blake. Assisting him were Lieutenant John Bartlett, acting ensign William Rhoades and acting masters mate Cooper. Lieutenant William Wallace led the marine detachment. Blake reported to the Fleet Captain who instructed him to send 10 of the *Susquehanna's* seamen to assist with digging rifle pits, the remainder were assigned to the first battalion of sailors commanded by Lieutenant-Commander Cushman. Wallace and his men made their way to the marine battalion. The bluejackets were armed with nothing more than cutlasses and pistols, the marines carried rifle muskets with which to give covering fire as the sailors charged across the sandy beach.

The webfeet helped dig trenches in the soft sand and awaited the order to advance. Shells from the fleet roared overhead smashing into the fort. After several hours cowering in their shallow works the men were becoming jumpy and their officers were battling to keep them in check. Breese's instructions were to attack in three columns in concert with General Terry's advance on the land face, the minute Porter lifted the bombardment. But as the allotted time for the attack came and went and with his men becoming increasingly jittery he was on the verge of advancing independently of Terry.

Until just after midday the *Susquehanna,* in concert with the fleet, kept up a steady and deliberate fire on the works, then orders were received from the *Malvern* to speed up the bombardment. The toiling gunners aboard the *Susquehanna* worked feverishly, sending in a brisk and hot fire. It was too hot for the forward pivot-mounted 150-pounder Parrott rifle. After 88 rounds had been expended the barrel burst, cracking the breech completely in half and carrying away the upper portion of the gun and right trunnion extending a distance of five and a half feet towards the muzzle. Jagged fragments of iron whizzed around the deck felling four seamen, William Taylor, Dennis Walsh, William Lewis and Thomas Arnold, a landsman, who suffered a severe contusion of the thorax caused by the blast.

On the beach some of the incoming rounds from the more distantly placed warships were landing uncomfortably close to the Yankee sailors, adding to their discomfort. Then, just before 3pm, the guns of the fleet at last fell silent. An officer leapt to his feet and screamed, "Charge! Charge!" With a cheer the sailors ran towards the fort. A Confederate sentinel raised the alarm and the parapet was soon packed with Rebel soldiers who opened a devastating fusillade on the onrushing seamen. Lieutenant-Commander Blake recalled later that "...as soon as we commenced to move the garrison opened with musketry; feebly at first, but more vigorously as we advanced until the fire became severe." The heads of the attacking columns were soon broken up by rapid volleys of rifle fire and the sailors hurled themselves at the palisade in one confused mass.

Men were falling in crumpled heaps as bullets, spherical case shot and canister bursts cut swathes through the advancing ranks. Despite the hurricane of fire, hundreds of sailors, including Blake and his men, succeeded in reaching the smashed palisade in front of the walls of the fort. However, until the unruly mob of bluejackets could climb the parapet and get to grips with the enemy, their pistols and cutlasses were next to useless. The defenders on top of the works fired down into the sailors, bunched under the dubious cover of the wooden walls, unable to advance further. A Federal soldier saw a Confederate officer atop the wall "...standing there clapping his hands, singing out to his men to kill the Yankee sons of bitches." Blake graphically described the position his men found themselves in. "They were packed like sheep in a pen, while the enemy were crowding the ramparts not 40 yards away and shooting into them as fast as they could." It was becoming obvious to their officers that the sailors could not stand this punishment indefinitely.

It was now the turn of the marines to move forward to give covering fire with their muskets while the sailors stormed the walls. However, the pinned down marines had suffered enough and broke under the concerted fire from the fort, flying back towards the waters edge leaving 300 of their number lying dead or injured in the sand. In these desperate minutes, one of the *Susquehanna's* crew performed a selfless act of bravery that would earn him the Medal of Honour. Landsman Henry S Webster from Stockholm, New York had enlisted in June 1864. The 20 year-old came upon one of the *Susquehanna's* officers, Lieutenant Wallace, lying badly wounded and unable to move. Despite bullets kicking up the sand around the pair, he refused to leave his stricken comrade until eventually help arrived from the rear and Wallace was carried from the field. Of the *Susquehanna's* detachment, besides Wallace, two marine privates, Thomas Brennan and Theo Minkoff and seaman Thomas Scott had perished in front of the palisade. Two marines and eight sailors were wounded. Besides Webster's gallant conduct, there were numerous other acts of heroism during the assault. Acting Ensign William Rhoades and seaman James Shannon managed to clamber up the earthen bank and plant a flag on the works – both received wounds in performing this gallant act. The exhausted and fought-out sailors were posted in the trenches to relieve the troops and passed the night manning the hastily thrown up breastworks; they took no further part in the fighting.

The Confederates had little time to celebrate their triumph. The Union troops attacking the western salient had scaled the walls and broken into the fort. In the savage hand-to-hand fighting that followed, the Rebels defended each traverse until flushed out by the gleaming bayonets of the Yankee infantry, twinned with accurate fire from the ironclad *New Ironsides* and several smaller gunboats.

In the hectic and bloody fighting, Chase Whiting was surrounded by 20 Yankees who demanded his surrender. Ignoring the Federals' threat he attempted to pull down a Union flag rammed into the ramparts. The resultant

Colonel William Lamb, the courageous commander of Fort Fisher.
Battles and Leaders

volley dropped him on the spot. Pierced by at least two bullets, the stricken Rebel was carried off as a prisoner to Governor's Island, New York where he died from his wounds on March 10 1865. Colonel Lamb, Fort Fisher's gallant commander, also fell, shot through the hip whilst leading a desperate counterattack.

The fierce fighting continued well into the night with the defiant Rebels putting up a brave resistance, but with the land face now in Union hands it was only a matter of time before the fort fell. The last redoubt was Battery Buchanan but when Lamb's second-in-command Major James Reilly of the 10th North Carolina Volunteers reached the post he discovered it abandoned and with its guns spiked. Realizing the position was hopeless, he walked towards the advancing Federal soldiers on the beach holding a white flag. A Union officer approached the fatigued and battle-weary Confederate. Reilly said tersely: "We surrender." The battle for Fort Fisher had ended. Now the way to Wilmington was open for the Union, and closed forever to the blockade-runners and commerce raiders of the Confederacy.

When news of the capitulation of the Rebel garrison reached the fleet the night sky was illuminated by rockets, battle lanterns, blue and white lights and fireworks. Even among the grotesque scenes of death and destruction in the fort the Union troops celebrated. With the break of day it was time to count the cost of one of the most vicious small combats of the Civil War. The Confederates had lost 500 killed and wounded along with 1,000 prisoners. The Federal casualties amounted to 1,338 of whom 383 were sailors or marines. As Colonel Lamb was carried through the ruins of the fort he witnessed the grim aftermath of combat. "The scene was indescribably horrible, great cannon broken in two, their carriages wrecked, and among the ruins the mutilated bodies of my dead and dying comrades."

As the dawn crept over the eastern horizon, a massive explosion rocked the captured fort. Two inebriated seamen had, unknowingly, bedded down for the night on top of one of Fort Fisher's magazines. Upon waking, they decided to search for souvenirs. The men lit torches to explore the inside of the hollowed out traverse. Minutes later the tons of powder stored inside ignited, sending hundreds of tons of earth into the air, blowing the two trophy hunters to smithereens and leaving 104 Federal troops dead or injured.

On the 16th the crew of the *Susquehanna* went about the task of securing the ship from battle. Two launches loaned to the Army to land artillery from the transports had been badly damaged. The starboard battery of 9-inch guns had been engaged in the bombardment and had fired a total of 1,286 shells. The two 150-pounder rifles had each expended 215 rounds. Concussion from the guns had caused damage to most of the carriages and the upperworks fore and aft on the starboard afterguard. Portions of the deck and hull planking had worked loose and were leaking badly. A section of the starboard fore yardarm had been smashed when the Parrott rifle exploded, but ship's carpenter Joseph Miller reported that although general repairs were required the ship had suffered no serious injury. Surgeon John Barclay reported a total of 18 casualties, two of which were fatalities.

Godon set down in his official report to Admiral Porter the role the *Susquehanna* and her crew played in the fight. After detailing the positioning and movements of his vessel Godon praised the brave but forlorn attack by the naval force. "We all witnessed the bold and daring attempt of the tars to assault in front, and if it failed and resulted disastrously to us in killed and wounded, it at all events most effectually aided the main storming party of the gallant army by diverting the attention of the garrison and enabled them to gain a footing and finally to accomplish perhaps one of the most daring deeds of this war, the capture of Fort Fisher."

He then proceeded to catalogue individual acts of bravery and steadfastness under fire of officers and men of the *Susquehanna*. "I again desire to renew my warm thanks to the division officers, Lieutenant's Bartlett and Brown, Acting Master Porter, and Acting Ensign Laycock for their zeal and spirit, and to the crew for their hearty efforts and good conduct... I would also call you special attention to Ensign Preble, of whose efficiency too much can not be said...Lieutenant-Commander Blake, at the head of his men on shore, proved himself there, as he always shows himself on board, brave, zealous and useful. Lieutenant Wallace was wounded severely in the charge on the fort. I particularly regret the injury to this officer, as he can not well be replaced by his corps in the affections of this ship.

"I would recommend for favorable mention to the Department Ordinary Seaman James Shannon and Henry Webster, landsman, who by their good conduct and bravery at the assault, are deserving of medals." Godon closed his missive with his own salute to Admiral Porter's success. "I congratulate you sir, on this our new victory, and if it was delayed from the 25th December to the 15th January, the country, I feel sure, will not attribute it to any failure of the Navy, for we have demonstrated the truth of the remark in your former report that had the attempt been made the capture of the fort would have been easier than the then commanding general believed."

Following his adventures ashore, Lieutenant John Bartlett set pen to paper and wrote his sister of the dramatic events he had been a part of and of his own experiences while under fire. Bartlett's vivid description of the Navy's somewhat chaotic attempt to storm the sea face of the fort follows:

USS Susquehanna, at sea January 18, 1865

I will write this letter to both of you together, as you will expect a very long one, giving a full account of our doings at Wilmington.

Hurrah for our admiral! He said Fort Fisher could be taken and he was right. This is the first time since the day of the fight that I have had a chance to write. Is not the taking of Fort Fisher glorious news? It is a great loss to the Rebels. The papers will be full of detailed accounts of the fight. These you will most likely read before you get this letter, so I think my letter will be more interesting to you if I just write the part I took in the affair.

You will read in the papers how the troops were landed and fire opened the first day. The Rebels were not able to fire a single shot at us. We began the fire at about half past 4 in the afternoon, and continued until dark. At sunset it was a most beautiful sight. The sun set directly behind the fort. I think I never saw a more beautiful one. The smoke of bursting shell against the bright red sky and half the fort in full blaze made the most magnificent picture ever seen.

On the second day it blew a gale of wind so that nothing could be done with the fleet, still the *Ironsides*, monitors, and several of the small gunboats kept up a hasty fire all day.

On the morning of the 15th, Sunday, we were underway at 5 o'clock. It promised to be a beautiful day. At daylight the fleet was formed in line of battle and began to move toward the fort. We did not move into action however until after 10. At about 10 the admiral made the signal to "arm and away all boats" and to assemble on the beach. In a few moments the whole place was alive with hundreds of boats pulling for the shore. We landed and were formed into line. We had two boats from our ship containing 50 bluejackets and 18 marines. Lieutenant Commander Blake had charge of one boat and myself the other. When we were landed on the beach Jack was for making a run right for the fort, but it was hardly time yet. I should think there must have been over 2,000 ashore from the fleet. Each boat had five men armed with spades; these were immediately sent to the front to throw up rifle pits for our marines. As soon as the sailors were formed we marched up to within about a mile and a half from the fort, and drew up in three lines to wait for the Army. They were to be ready at 2 o'clock, when we were to make the assault together.

While here the Rebels fired a few shells, wounding several marines that were not in the rifle pits, but drawn up in front of the sailors. We all laid down in the sand to make as small a mark as possible, and waited patiently for the time to come for the assault. While we were here the fleet was hard at work, keeping up a terrific bombardment of the fort. We had a grand chance to see it. It was a most magnificent sight. We lay at this place till 2 o'clock. We were getting very hungry as we had taken our breakfast at daylight. I was anxious to get into the fort to try some Rebel provisions. At 2 o'clock we learned that the army would not be ready till 3 o'clock. At about this time we filed down on the beach and marched toward the fort at the double quick; when within half a mile we lay down on the beach, the rise from the water protecting us from the musketry. We also threw up sand in front of us with our hands. I had command of the second company of the first division. This division was to lead the assault so I was near the head. The division was divided into three companies. While here the fleet was firing directly over our heads, which was far from pleasant, as some of them fell short among us, wounding several. All the time we lay here the Rebels kept up a heavy fire of musketry but fired much too high.

At 3 o'clock we made the charge for the fort on the double quick. We were to charge the fort on its front, or sea face, while the soldiers charged the eastern or land face. From the front of the fort there is a line of palisades running down to within a short distance of the water. When we started on the charge the fleet ceased its fire, but the Rebels opened on us a most murderous fire of musketry with now and then a round of grape and canister. There was a halt at the foot of the palisades till the sailors in the rear should come up. I stopped close to the end of them. Oh, such a fire as we were under. Sailors and officers were dropping all around me. Lieutenant Porter, a classmate of mine, was shot dead close by me, and Lieutenant Preston a few yards ahead. Both of these officers had just been released from Columbia jail, South Carolina.The sailors were coming up rapidly, so I jumped up and ran toward the fort with several other officers shouting for the men to follow. A few followed, but many fell. We reached the next angle of the stockade. Here I got a rifle from a marine and settled a few Rebels. They were standing right up on the top of the fort firing right down on us. The sailors were ahead and the marines in the rear. I was just aiming at a Rebel when I heard a shout behind. I looked around.

The sailors were all on the run down the beach. The marines broke and ran, the sailors following. Poor Jack. He could not stand the fire of bullets

Rebel gunners return the fire of the Federal fleet from the Mound Battery.
Battles and Leaders

Bluejackets and marines from the fleet, including men from the *Susquehanna*, assault the North-East salient of Fort Fisher.
Battles and Leaders

A view of the land front of Fort Fisher, North Carolina, the last Confederate sea port to fall to the Federals in 1865.This photograph, taken by Timothy O'Sullivan, shows a wrecked gun carriage in the second traverse.
Library of Congress

Another O'Sullivan view of the interior of Fort Fisher, showing one of her heavy pieces of ordnance smashed by fire from the Union fleet.
Library of Congress

and with nothing to fire back, as they were armed with cutlasses and revolvers. We tried to call the marines up to the front with their rifles to fire through the palisades, but they would not come.

I shouted and waved my sword for the sailors to come back, but no, off they went down the beach. About a dozen officers and 20 men remained at the palisades. I had made up my mind to go into that fort, and could not run. I could have cried when the bluejackets retreated, but it was high time for me to look out for myself. I began to dig a hole with my hands. You would have laughed to have seen me. It did not take me long to get a pile of sand in front of me high enough to screen me from fire. This was about half past 3. I kept on digging until I had a hole I could stand up in. The sand was very soft and dry, so that it was easily thrown up. Every time I threw up a handful of sand on the edge of my pit, a dozen bullets would skip over my head. It was rather unpleasant as it would knock the sand all down on me.

The Rebels had about one-third of their forces at this angle, and the rest where the soldiers were expected to charge, but when they saw us coming up the beach they thought it must be the main attack, and called "all hands" over to our angle; this gave the soldiers a chance to gain a footing at the other angle. But when the sailors retreated, most of them went back to meet the soldiers. Our soldiers fought like tigers, and the Rebels were not far behind them. I will send you a sketch of the fort. The soldiers gained the first mound or traverse, and then fought hand to hand with the Rebels for each mound. After the fight, between each mound, the killed were piled up a dozen deep. It was a terrible sight that day. Too horrible to describe.

We remained under the palisades until we could escape under cover of darkness. At a little after 6 we began to run the gauntlet, a few at a time the Rebels keeping up a good shower of balls. Soon after the sailors retreated the fleet opened fire again on the forts. We were now in a rather tight place, as some of the shell burst close to us, and we began to think of a surrender, but intended to hold out until a shell did land directly among us. They landed everywhere but just where we lay. I will end you a piece of the palisades, knocked down by a bullet above my head, also a piece of the Rebel flagstaff. It was a very long afternoon to spend in such a place. I wished myself most everywhere else.

When the sailors started to run they were shot down like sheep; over fifty lay dead at the foot of the palisades. Now and then a wounded man would raise his head; A dozen bullets would fly toward him in an instant. It was low tide when we made the charge and a few fell close to the water. Before dark the tide rose and the waves washed up on the poor fellows, some only wounded. It was hard to look on and not be able to give them any help. I wished to see if my friend Porter was still alive, so I waited till near the last. He was lying on the beach about a hundred yards from the palisades. I ran to him and dropped beside him. I found him dead, a shot having passed through his body. I took his sword, belt, and glove, and then, oh! how I did run for a little way. The Rebels fired about twenty shots at me. I had only got a few hundred yards when I met a poor fellow, a master's mate from the *Tuscarora*. He was wounded in the back and leg. I helped him down the beach about 2 miles, when I came to a camp fire where our surgeons were attending the wounded. While I lay in my hole under the fort I could hear our soldiers fighting, their cheering when they gained another mound, and the Rebels with their battle yell.

The Rebels fired grape several times at the party under the palisades. I don't like them at all. The soldiers took over two thousand prisoners. There were 2,300 Rebels in the fort and 2,500 of our soldiers in the assault. About 600 fell in the assault and 200 more were killed by an explosion the next morning. The cause is not known; supposed to have been caused through carelessness of some of our soldiers with a naked light going into a magazine.

The North-East salient of the fort, showing the ground over which the *Susquehanna's* contingent of sailors and marines made their doomed attack.
Battles and Leaders

There were 52 guns in the fort, all very heavy ones, besides a great many small fieldpieces. Of these heavy guns 35 were dismounted or rendered unfit for service by the fire of the fleet. The general shape of the fort is about the same as before the hammering, but there is hardly a square foot of the fort that has not been struck by our shell, each making a deep hole. The bombproofs of the fort were full of wounded men and the dead were lying in every direction, some terribly torn by shell. There was one magnificent gun in a battery just below Fort Fisher – 150-pounder Armstrong. It was presented to Jeff Davis by Sir W J Armstrong. It was kept bright and mounted on a mahogany carriage, beautifully mounted with brass. General Beauregard visited this fort a few days before our attack and said that it could not be taken; that it was the strongest work in America. Immediately after Mr Butler ran away on his mule captured here. The ladies of Wilmington held a grand picnic in honour of having driven the Yankees away. I saw some of the remains – champagne bottles lying about the ground. Now is our turn to have a picnic there.

After arriving at the hospital I busied myself till near 10 trying to get boats to carry off the wounded. At last one of the boats from our ship coming inshore, I filled it with wounded men and came off to the ship. They were indeed surprised to see me, as a few of the man who had returned aboard all said they had seen me fall at the palisades. I fell over men several times in

The final assault by the Union fleet on Fort Fisher.
Battles and Leaders

front of me, but soon got up again. The commodore would hardly believe it was I.

At half past 10 signal was made to the fleet that the fort was ours. The whole fleet gave three rousing cheers, threw up rockets, burned blue lights, and blew their whistles. I took charge of our whistle and made it express my sentiments in many a loud blast. I have visited the fort and will tell you all about it myself. I dated at sea; we are now on our way north – first to Norfolk and then to New York. I hope to be with you very soon. I am too tired to write any more tonight. Good night.

Your loving brother, Johnnie.

Even as Commodore Godon was in his day cabin composing his report to Porter, the admiral had already penned the following letter to his trusted subordinate. In part it contained orders for the *Susquehanna* to sail immediately in company with the badly disabled *New Ironsides*, and make for the navy yard at Norfolk, there Godon was to communicate with the Navy Department and await further orders. The bulk of the letter contained a warm commendation for Godon's performance over the past several days.

US Flagship *MALVERN off* Fort Fisher, January 17, 1865

I take this opportunity to express to you how much I appreciate the services you have rendered to me officially, and the kind, good feeling you have shown personally. I shall part with you and you ship with extreme regret, and as it is not likely that we shall be associated together again in the present war, I can only hope we may meet once more opposed to our outside enemies, where, fighting ship against ship, instead of against sand hills, you will, I am sure, be successful as you have hitherto been.

I do not say it to flatter you, but you vessel has been one of the best conducted in this squadron, and in going into action, or preparing for service, I never gave myself any thought about you, for I knew you would be ready at the right time and be in the proper place in action. You have rendered me the most essential service, and have conducted your ship not only with zeal, but with the right kind of intelligence, showing that you possess the highest attributes of a commander. You will have the satisfaction of knowing that your name will be associated with, I think, the most important event of the war, and the most damaging one to the enemy. We all know the part the Navy has taken in the capture of this stronghold. Every man who has done his duty, as you have, may rest satisfied that he will not be forgotten by his country when the time comes to reward those who have done the hard work and the fighting.

As I am now writing, the death knell of another fort is booming in the distance. Fort Caswell with its powerful batteries is in flames and being blown up, and thus is sealed the door through which this rebellion is fed. With my warmest wishes for your safe return home, and hoping this is not our last association on duty.

I remain, yours, sincerely and respectfully,
David D. Porter, Rear Admiral

At 6.15am on January 17, with the *New Ironsides* creeping along in their wakes the *Powhatan* and the *Susquehanna* got underway, their helmsman steering east by north. Making a steady six knots the vessels headed for Norfolk. The Cape Henry Light was sighted at 9.30pm the following evening and on the 19th, with the ship in charge of a pilot, the little flotilla stood in towards Cape Henry, coming to anchor in 10 fathoms at 5.30pm. In cold and overcast conditions the *Susquehanna* weighed anchor at 10am the next morning, only to run aground in 17 feet of water half an hour later. Godon ordered the ship's engines to be put into reverse but she refused to budge.

An Army steamer came alongside and a hawser was attached in the hope that she would pull the stranded sloop off, but the attempt ended in failure and Godon had to wait till high water before his ship was finally hauled clear in the early hours of January 21. The steamer got underway with a pilot aboard, her paddlewheels churning the water as she proceeded up the Elizabeth River, finally coming to her moorings at 10am. There she remained for the next seven days until Godon received orders to sail for New York.

The side-wheeler arrived off Sandy Hook early on January 30 on a clear cold morning with a moderate northwesterly breeze in the offing. At 9.30am her batteries roared out a 15-gun salute as she let go her port anchor into 30 fathoms off the Brooklyn Navy Yard and furled her canvas.

WINTER IN BROOKLYN, SPRING IN HAVANA

At midday on January 31, 1865, the sloop came to her moorings, linking her chains to a buoy. The first task was to replenish the ship's food supplies and fresh provisions were taken on board during the morning. That afternoon those wounded in the Fort Fisher fight were gently lowered over the side into waiting small boats and transferred to the naval hospital ashore. It would be sometime before the *Susquehanna* ventured out to sea again. Repairs, revictualling and refitting would mean a winter spent at her moorage in the Brooklyn Navy Yard.

The month of February saw much activity as workers from the navy yard descended on the ship. The residue of the *Susquehanna's* powder was discharged on the 2nd and the crew was kept busy on various duties. Shells were taken ashore, rigging was blacked, and provisions were loaded including 300 pounds of fresh beef, 300 pounds of vegetables, 210 blankets, along with boots and items of uniform. The crew was allowed liberty and small parties departed the *Susquehanna* daily to visit their friends and families or the dockside taverns and bawdyhouses surrounding the navy yard. On the

10th, in a heavy snowstorm the ship was made fast to the quayside. The boats and davits were unshipped and sent to the boat builders in the navy yard for refurbishing and the broadside 9-inch guns were dismounted to allow the damaged carriages to be repaired. Two sailors, William Diamond and Frank West, deserted from the ship.

On March 6 the city of New York held celebrations presumably to mark the swearing in of Abraham Lincoln for a second term in the White House. All work aboard the *Susquehanna* and in the navy yard was suspended and 29 marines were sent ashore to represent the ship. Unfortunately several returned the worse for drink and ended up in irons!

Almost every day seamen managed to get themselves into trouble. Whether it was smuggling whiskey on board, overstaying their liberty ashore, fighting, neglect of duty or disobeying orders, the end result was usually the same. The offender would be confined in single or double irons on bread and water for periods ranging from four hours to four days or more, depending on his crime.

Mid-month found more mechanics and laborers from the navy yard busy aboard rectifying boilers and engines and renewing the copper plating under the bows of the ship. Twelve marines reported for duty on the 14th whilst several of the *Susquehanna's* crew were transferred to other vessels. The frigate's bunkers were topped up with coal and civilian painters slapped a new coat of paint on the hurricane deck. A steady stream of provisions and supplies were hoisted aboard including soap, candles, wood and water.

On the 28th Godon received a communiqué from the Navy Department apprising him of his promotion to acting rear admiral, together with orders appointing him commander of the Brazilian Squadron. His flagship was to be the *Hartford*, which would be sent on, but in the meantime he was to proceed to sea in the *Susquehanna* as soon as she was ready. His elevation to higher office was well deserved, and no doubt the following commendation from Admiral Porter regarding Godon's conduct at Fort Fisher went a long way to influencing the Navy Department's decision to so honor the *Susquehanna's* skipper.

"Commander Godon commanding the *Susquehanna* is an unusually intelligent officer and who does not need to be told a second time where to go in time of action. This is the second important affair in which he has been engaged during this war, in both of which he has acquitted himself in the most handsome manner. His ship was beautifully handled, and impressed me with her good discipline and accurate firing. To me personally he has given his warmest support and I should fail in my duty if I did not give him the full credit he deserved. His conduct throughout this harassing affair has met my warmest approbation and I think he is one of those who merit promotion when the government thinks proper to reward those who have borne the brunt of battle."

Godon wrote two letters to Gideon Welles on April 1. In the first he tendered his thanks to Welles for the promotion bestowed upon him, and for the opportunity of independent command of the Brazilian Squadron. "I beg leave to return my sincere thanks for the honour you have done me. I trust, sir that my conduct in my command will justify the confidence the Department has seen fit to repose in me." In the second letter the admiral detailed his planned route to take up his station. He proposed standing well to the eastward so that he could avail himself of the trade winds, thereby saving coal; he also stood more chance of contacting American merchant vessels returning from China and the Pacific. His proposed course would carry him close to the island of Madeira and he sought Welles' permission to touch briefly at the island, and also at Tenerife and the Cape Verde Islands to seek information on the whereabouts of still active Confederate commerce raiders.

Work on the ship went on apace and the bluejackets were variously employed blacking down and setting up the topgallant rigging, scraping spars and loading 125 rounds of 30-pounder rifle and shrapnel shells. The first day of April, and the remounting of the 9-inch broadside guns onto their repaired carriages together with the hoisting aboard of a new supply of powder ensured little respite for the crew. Two new 11-inch rifles and a 30-pound Parrott together with carriages completed the *Susquehanna's* potent battery. On the 6th and 7th, 47 replacement seamen and landsmen reported on board from the receiving ships *North Carolina* and *Vermont.*

A brisk squall lashed the decks of the *Susquehanna* as she raised her anchor and cast off her lines from the dockside at 7.30am on April 8. An hour and a half later she let go her starboard anchor off the Battery. The quartermaster ordered her sails let loose to dry while the deck officer arranged for the dockyard mechanics and workers to be taken back to shore.

April 9, 1865. Palm Sunday. A light breeze ruffled the masthead colors as the chaplain held divine services on the berth deck of the *Susquehanna*. The only duty for the crew that day was the stowing below decks of 3,653 pounds of powder. They had no idea of the extraordinary events about to transpire in a little-known community in the war-torn state of Virginia.

Outside the sleepy hamlet of Appomattox Courthouse, General Robert E. Lee slowly mounted his horse 'Traveler'. He had agreed to a meeting with his hard fighting opponent Ulysses S. Grant to discuss terms for surrendering his ragged, half starved and surrounded army. The Federal commander finally emerged from Wilmer McLean's home with a paper signed by Lee agreeing to the capitulation of the Army of Northern Virginia. The news of Lee's surrender swept like wildfire through the waiting Union army. Richmond had already fallen and Jeff Davis and his government were on the run. Now, with Lee's agreement to lay down his arms, to all intents and purposes the war was over.

The North responded joyously to the news from Virginia. On the morning of the 11th the gun crews on the *Susquehanna* exercised at their stations in preparation for a 21-gun salute, which roared forth at 1pm. The next day Captain Donaldson, the *Susquehanna's* new master, presented himself to Rear-Admiral Godon. A coal barge came alongside on the morning of the 15th and coaling ship commenced. When the work was completed that evening, 53 tons had been crammed below decks.

Now came dreadful tidings from Washington. President Lincoln had been assassinated by John Wilkes Booth, one of the country's most popular actors, whilst attending a performance of the play 'Our American Cousin' in Fords Theater, Washington on the evening of April 14. Booth, a fanatical Southerner and a member of a famous thespian family, had crept into the President's private box and shot him in the back of the head with a small derringer.

On the 16th a navy tug came alongside the *Susquehanna* with dispatches for Admiral Godon. The missive detailed procedures to be implemented for mourning the late President. Commencing at 5am the next morning, the guns of the sloop began firing at half hourly intervals. With the departure of the coal barge at 6.30am, the *Susquehanna* was now in readiness for sea duty, and Admiral Godon so informed the Navy Department on April 18. "I have the honour to report the *Susquehanna* will be ready for sea by Saturday morning. I make this communication this early that the Department may furnish me with any further instructions if desirable. I propose stopping at St. Thomas and Barbados to keep my coal up."

At 9.30am on the 19th, the crew was mustered for inspection at quarters and the broadside guns of the side-wheeler commenced firing a salute to the deceased President at minute intervals, while the marine guard stood with reversed arms and the ship's band played the 'Dead March'. At 4 o'clock that afternoon a final 21-gun salute boomed out across the harbor. Death claimed not only the famous. In the late evening of the 20th, Albert Pratt, landsman, passed away aboard ship. His remains were transferred to the naval hospital ashore for burial the next day.

In clear and pleasant weather, Abraham Lincoln's funeral cortege traveled from New Jersey into New York on the morning of the 24th, and the *Susquehanna* saluted his passing with a salvo of 21minute-guns. The next morning a tug came alongside and conveyed a marine guard to the Navy Yard to attend the funeral procession. At 8am the colors were dipped to half-mast and the yardarms were crossed in salute. Just before midday all officers not on watch were rowed ashore to pay their respects. At 1.30pm the guns were fired at half hourly intervals, finally falling silent four hours later following the mustering of the ship's crew on the berth deck and the squaring away of the yardarms.

Three days later Captain Donaldson received orders detaching him from service with the *Susquehanna* and left the ship. Dispatches for Godon's attention were received from a tug on the April 29; he was to proceed to Hampton Roads and there take command of vessels then assembling, which would form his Brazilian Squadron. In response, the ship's guns were loaded with heavy charges and the boilers were fired up, and by 3.30pm the vessel had steam up and the engines were tested.

At 5pm on May 2, 1865 Captain A. W. Taylor exchanged salutes with Admiral Godon on the quarterdeck of the *Susquehanna*; he was to be the

The *Susquehanna* berthed at the New York Navy Yard, photographed just after the war. Note the US Marine officer in the foreground.
US Naval Historical Center

The Rebel ram *Stonewall*, photographed at Ferrol, Spain in March 1865, about a month before the end of the war.
US Naval Historical Center

sloop's new commanding officer. On the 4th while taking on coal and fresh water, one of the heroes of the engagement at Wilmington, acting master Laycock, left the ship, detailed by the Navy Department for other duties. A further 10 days passed before the *Susquehanna* at last made ready and secured for sea. The whaleboat and gig were hoisted inboard on the evening of May 14 and the sloop up-anchored and stood out for the open waters of the Atlantic. Within two hours she sighted the Sandy Hook Light and at 10.30pm passed the Highland Light.

Arriving at Hampton Roads two days later, Admiral Godon obtained new instructions telegraphed from Washington, to proceed to Havana at once with his whole force. The Confederate ram *Stonewall,* Captain Page in command, had been reported at the Cuban port on the 11th, but had apparently sailed two days later. Godon set out with his flotilla of four vessels, the *Monadnock, Monticello, Chippewa* and *Emma Henry* on the May 17 and steamed for Port Royal. Learning that Admiral Dahlgren was at Charleston, Godon boarded the *Emma Henry* and set off to request reinforcements from Dahlgren's squadron. Godon ordered his flotilla to maintain course for Port Royal where he would rendezvous with them as soon as he had completed his business in Charleston. To the rear admiral's disappointment, only one of Dahlgren's monitors, the *Canonicus,* was in a fit state for deep-water service. Godon arrived in Port Royal Sound in tandem with the ironclad and made ready for the journey to Havana. The *Fahkee,* released by Admiral Dahlgren, arrived in the roads and joined the remainder of Godon's ships in taking on coal. The small flotilla sailed at midday on the 23rd.

Godon intended to make directly for Havana to seek information on the whereabouts of the Rebel warship. He reasoned that as the Texas port of Galveston was the only Southern harbor still under enemy control, it was a likely destination for the *Stonewall.* Godon feared the powerful ram would scatter the wooden blockading ships outside the port and open the way to bring in supplies for the dying Confederacy, thus prolonging the agony a little longer. It would be a last, desperate gamble by Captain Page. If the Rebel ship found herself confronted by ironclads in overwhelming numbers, Godon felt that there could only be one outcome. In all probability her captain would destroy his own ship rather than surrender.

The trip was not without incident. The admiral was extremely satisfied by the performance of the *Monadnock*, but the *Canonicus* was very slow and even when under tow by the *Fahkee* did not exceed five knots. Off Cape Canaveral the *Susquehanna* took both vessels under tow, increasing their speed to around seven knots. The evening of May 28 found the Union fleet at their moorings outside the harbor of Havana, they had arrived too late to enter the port itself. By 10am the next morning however, they were at anchor inside the roadstead and to Godon's relief he saw the *Stonewall* moored higher up the harbor. She would pose no danger to any American vessel, for her the war was over without ever firing a shot in anger.

In an informal meeting with the Spanish Captain-General, Godon was informed of the details of the handing over of the *Stonewall* to the Spanish authorities. Captain Page had stipulated that his ship was not to be given into the hands of the American government, but the Spaniards refused his request, stating that once his vessel was under their control they would dispose of it as they saw fit, there could be no negotiation of terms. It was made reasonably clear to Godon that the Cuban authorities, following diplomatic negotiations, would eventually release the *Stonewall* to the Federal government. Godon needed to ascertain the condition of the ram and although he did not board her, he was rowed around the ship in a small boat and detailed his observations in a letter to Secretary Welles in Washington. "I am not very much impressed with her power. I think the *Canonicus* would have crushed her, and the *Monadnock* could have taken her beyond a doubt. Her rapid turning seems to be spoken of as her greatest merit, but in doing so she must lose her way, and her ram is reduced in power as her speed decreases. I do not consider that she would have lasted long under the treatment she would have received by this command."

The American flotilla had caused quite an impression among the local populace and was surrounded by dozens of small craft carrying hundreds of sightseers. Godon felt it proper to extend his squadron's sojourn in Havana and stated his intention to extend his stay when reporting to Acting Rear-Admiral Stribling. At the same time he requested 200 tons of coal and fresh supplies for his ships.

While the diplomatic wrangling over the fate of the *Stonewall* continued, Godon at last got to board the ship for a more detailed inspection. He thought her forward armament impressive, she carried a brand new Armstrong 10-inch rifle, but on finding her turrets protected by less than four inches of iron plate, he was even more convinced that if it had come to a fight between the ram and his squadron the monitor *Monadnock* would have proved her equal.

An invitation was extended to Admiral Godon and the *Susquehanna's* officers to dine with the Spanish governor-general on the evening of June 3. Dinner was to be followed by a ball, which was also attended by senior officers from Godon's squadron. Resplendent in their full dress uniforms the American naval officers were the center of attraction for every dignitary in attendance. In a departure from normal formalities, the Governor General proposed a toast to "...that great and good man, Mr Lincoln, late President of the United States."

Three days later dispatches arrived from Acting Secretary Gustavus Fox requesting Admiral Godon to send the *Monadnock* together with the remainder of his special squadron to Hampton Roads. The admiral himself was now to proceed with the *Susquehanna* to take up his station off the coast of Brazil, but before he could comply with these instructions, fresh orders called for the steamers to make a return trip to Norfolk, which place she finally left for South American waters on June 21. On the 28th the ship stopped at the island of St. Thomas where Godon went ashore for a brief visit with the governor. The next port of call was Guadeloupe where the *Susquehanna* dropped anchor on the evening of July 3 off Basse Terre, the seat of government on the island. Taking on 250 tons of coal from the American depot at Pointe a Pitre, the steamer next called in at St. Pierre on the French island of Martinique on August 8. Godon called on the governor and invited him on board the *Susquehanna* for a reciprocal visit.

On August 12, 1865, the side-wheeler's anchor plunged to the sandy bottom of Bahia Harbor, Brazil, and it is here in the sunny climes of the Southern Hemisphere that we must close this account of the voyages of the USS *Susquehanna.* From the foam-flecked rollers of the stormy North Atlantic to the blue waters and stifling heat of the Gulf of Mexico, the ship and her crew had endured many privations in almost three years of constant sea duty off the Southern coast whilst maintaining a seemingly never-ending watch for the audacious blockade runners, of whom six fell victim to the side-wheeler.

The warship had been tested too in the white heat of battle; at Hatteras Inlet, Port Royal and Fort Fisher. Even when her boilers and engines were falling apart she maintained her station, and like the officers and men who sailed in her, the *Susquehanna* was never found wanting.

CLOSING THE LOG

The *Susquehanna* completed her tour of duty operating along the Atlantic coastline of South America, returning home to be decommissioned on June 30, 1866. Barely four months later she was once again at sea as flagship of the North Atlantic Squadron. The side-wheeler's active service life ended upon her return to the New York Navy Yard where she was removed from the active list for the last time on January 14, 1868. As with all wars, when the smoke of battle clears and the victory parades are concluded, the inevitable cut backs in military spending follow swiftly, and the Civil War was no exception. For several years the *Susquehanna* lay idle in her berth, and then her machinery was removed as plans to convert her to a screw steamer began, but the work was never completed and the project was finally abandoned. The end came on September 27, 1883 when the *Susquehanna* was sold out of service for scrap for the sum of $13,143 to the New York shipbreakers E. Stannard and Company.

Although by no means the most up-to-date of warships sporting the Stars and Stripes in 1861, it was to the *Susquehanna* and vessels like her that the Union turned to in its hour of need. These ships battled against strongly constructed Rebel shore-based forts and redoubts. Gales and hurricanes battered their wooden walls; their crews endured long periods of tedious inactivity, bad rations, outbreaks of fever, frequent mechanical breakdowns and often fruitless pursuits of Confederate blockade runners. To their credit the men and their ships stuck doggedly to the task and played a vital role in bringing the war to a successful conclusion.

And what of her commanders? Those men who paced the quarterdeck during the War of the Rebellion, each of whom assumed the awesome responsibility for the safety of their ship and the conduct of the men under their command.

Where one wrong decision or a minor judgmental error could place their vessel and those aboard in peril. Charges of negligence or incompetency would often result in a court of inquiry where their capability to command would be questioned with the attendant risk to their reputation and standing in the Navy.

We must begin with George Hollins. This extremely competent officer, held in high esteem by the Navy Department and the *Susquehanna's* company, had served his country for many years. One can only imagine his inner turmoil as the *Susquehanna* sailed for home that fateful spring of 1861. The prospect of resigning his commission to take up arms with the South came ever nearer with each turn of the sloop's mighty paddle wheels. In May, fully convinced that Maryland was on the brink of seceding, Hollins tendered his resignation. Dismissed from the Navy on June 6, 1861, he was soon a Captain in the fledgling Confederate Navy. His was to be an eventful war. It began with a daring act committed early in the conflict. On June 29 1861, disguised as a woman and accompanied by a picked group of men, he seized the Union steamship *St. Nicholas* on Chesapeake Bay. He was then assigned to command the naval defenses along the James River in July before being ordered to New Orleans, there to mount operations designed to thwart the Union blockade and keep the port open for trade.

On October 12, commanding a small fleet of Rebel warships including the ram *Manassas*, Hollins attacked the Union squadron stationed at the passes of the Mississippi. The resulting action saw damage inflicted on the USS *Richmond* and another Union vessel was driven ashore. In recognition of this gallant action Hollins was appointed Flag Officer for New Orleans. However, when Farragut's squadron ran past the guns of Fort St Philip and Fort Jackson in April 1862, the city fell into Union hands. Hollins spent the majority of the war sitting on numerous boards and courts of inquiry, including that investigating the loss of the *Virginia,* destroyed by her crew during McClellan's Peninsula campaign. He chose a post war career in public office becoming a court officer in Baltimore, Maryland. He died on January 18, 1878.

And so to the *Susquehanna's* first wartime skipper, the competent but much disliked John Chauncey. That he was something of a martinet and certainly a strict disciplinarian is a matter of record. Recalled to Washington from the *Susquehanna* he was promoted to the rank of commodore on July 16, 1862. He was appointed Inspector of Ordnance at Reading, Pennsylvania in 1863 and served on special courts martial duties from 1864 to the close of the war. For a year he was stationed at the New York Navy Yard before retiring in 1868, he died six years later.

Chauncey's replacement was of a different ilk. Cool and brave under fire, James Lardner was an inspirational captain and very popular with the men. During his tenure of command the ship had seized or assisted in the taking of five blockade-runners. Promoted to commodore and appointed flag officer of the East Gulf Blockading Squadron, Lardner's distinguished career continued, albeit with a close call only weeks after taking control of his new command. Stationed off Key West Florida, an outbreak of the dreaded Yellow Fever ravaged the crew of the *San Jacinto,* carrying off 40 officers and men. Lardner himself fell ill and was invalided home in December. He returned to duty and from May 1863 to October the following year he led the West India Squadron until his retirement in November of 1864. Appointed rear admiral on July 25 1866, he carried out special duties with various boards until asked to serve as Governor of the Naval Asylum, Philadelphia, which post he held until 1871. He passed away on April 12 in Philadelphia in his 79th year.

The third incumbent to take on the mantle of command had probably the most trying and difficult assignment undertaken by the *Susquehanna,* that of blockading the port of Mobile, Alabama. Commodore Robert Hitchcock was an extremely capable and experienced seaman who quickly realized he had been dealt a bad hand when he arrived off Mobile. Not only was the *Susquehanna* in dire need of a major refit, but his squadron was understrength

James Lardner pictured here c1867 as a Rear Admiral on the retired list.
US Naval Historical Center

and the vessels he had were not up to the job. The successful escape of the Rebel commerce raider *Florida* brought matters to a head and resulted in an official inquiry, which exonerated Hitchcock.

The *Susquehanna* was to prove Hitchcock's last sea-going command. With the decommissioning of the ship in May 1863 his next assignment was on ordnance duty during 1864–65. This was followed by appointment to command the post-war Norfolk Navy Yard. A spell of special duties from 1870 to 1873 preceded his retirement from the service and Hitchcock passed away in Cold Springs, New York, on March 24, 1888.

The steamer's last wartime master was Sylvanus Godon. A veteran of the Port Royal engagement he took over the ship following the *Susquehanna's*

14-month overhaul in New York. He had the honor of leading a division of Admiral Porter's fleet in the successful attack on Fort Fisher in early January of 1865, before sailing in command of a special squadron for the *Susquehanna's* final mission, to seek out the Rebel ram *Stonewall*.

Receiving orders to leave Havana, Godon commenced his peacetime duties, assuming command of the South Atlantic Squadron on the Brazilian station until 1868. Appointed commandant of the New York Navy Yard, he held that post until retirement on June 18, 1871. Of his 41 years of naval service, 21 had been spent at sea, more than any other officer of his grade. He passed away full of years and honors, while in Blois, France on May 10, 1879.

Finally there is Amos Burton, whose journal, published in New York in 1863, was very much the inspiration for this book. There is scant information regarding the remainder of his service career, other than the honorable discharge from the Marine Corps granted on May 26, 1864 at Philadelphia, his four-year period of enlistment fulfilled. The National Archives hold no pension records; apparently he never registered a claim. Likewise the Massachusetts State Archives, which holds statewide registrations of births, marriages and deaths, have no records pertaining to Burton's family history or background. One possible explanation of course is that he enlisted under an assumed name, but after reading his journal one gets a feel for the character of the man and this seems unlikely. Whatever the circumstances, Amos Burton has, to all intents and purposes, vanished into the mists of time.

Despite the hemorrhage of those officers who 'went South' to fight under the Stars and Bars, the ultimate triumph gained by the Union Navy belongs to those capable and resolute officers and men of the 'Old Navy' who remained loyal to the flag; aided by the thousands of volunteers who answered their country's call to arms. The deep-water Navy has received scant recognition for the fine service that it gave to the Union. I hope this book has gone a little way in redressing the balance.

*** **The End** ***

SEA SONNETS

Amos Burton kept a journal; other sailors also utilized their free time in literary pursuits. There were three 'amateur' poets serving aboard the *Susquehanna* along with the young marine, who occasionally found the time to put pen to paper. Here are four examples of their efforts; three are fairly serious, dealing with battle and the loss of a comrade, while one is an amusing work, dripping with sarcasm for an officer who was obviously something of a martinet.

THE BATTLE OF HATTERAS

There's a lone, dreary spot, where the white, foaming billows
Dash with fury upon North Carolina's sand shore;
Who's sad, mournful strains often sweep o'er the pillows
Of those who will hear their wild echo no more.
There, 'mid that seclusion and free from intrusion,
Has Liberty's sons shared the blessings of peace;
'Till the vile seeds of discord sprang up in profusion
Around their loved homes, bidding harmony cease.

They strove to demolish that glorious temple
Which the great founder, Washington, raised with such care;
But their polluted hands will yet be made to tremble,
And their homesteads will ring with the cry of despair.
On that once happy shore, near an arm of the ocean,
Their treason-stained hands have a battlement reared;
Despising their long-hallowed love and devotion,
And at freedom's just laws they've defiantly sneered.

But the hour is approaching when dire retribution
Shall fall on their heads with a terrible blow;
For there's yet loyal hearts to the old Constitution,
Who'll defend it until their last life blood shall flow.
Behold, in the distance, yon proud arks of freedom,
As they shine through the first golden ray of the morn,

As they boldly advance on the vile haunts of treason,
To conquer or fall is the oath they have sworn.

Look at those noble ships, as they form line of battle,
In front of that boasted stronghold of the foe,
See their cannon's red flash and hear the loud rattle,
At whose mighty summons those traitors must bow.
Long and fierce raged the contest, till death and disorder
Appal'd their vain hearts as the sight met their eyes;
On the ramparts they've raised a white flag, asking quarter,
Where the flag of the Union now gloriously flies.

James Eggo, 1861

The same balladeer composed the next offering, a lament for one of the *Susquehanna's* seamen, Simon Huttleston, drowned while assisting the gunboat *Harriet Lane* that had run aground shortly after the end of the fighting at Hatteras Inlet, it has no title.

The tumult and noise of the battle is hushed,
And the dark veil of night has o'ershadowed the scene;
But how oft when the heart with victory flushed,
That the sad freaks of fate will at times intervene.
Thus the lot fell to one who had gallantly shared,
In the glory of that ever-memorable day,
To drop like a flower that from blast had been spared,
Till the last snows of winter had melted away.

The perils of battle had scarcely been passed,
E'er another had threatened the *Harriet Lane*;
On a shoal where she had by misfortune been cast,
And despite of their efforts seemed doomed to remain.
No ray of cheer broke through that night's awful gloom,

But Boreas sang loudly his harsh notes of glee,
And conspiringly bent on the noble ship's doom,
Dashed with violence 'gainst the storm-troubled sea.

But humanity reigns in the mariner's heart,
The boats from the ship *Susquehanna* were lowered,
The crew of the tempest-rocked vessel to save,
But one of our men was swept overboard;
And in that dark abyss found a watery grave.

From the yawning gulf rose a shriek of despair,
Which rang high above the fierce howl of the storm,
And e'er the frail boat to the spot could repair,
For ever from our view sank that once manly form;
Still the boats kept around her a vigilant guard,
Till the bright beams of morning dawned o'er the main,
When the roar of the tempest was no longer heard,
And the ocean's blue bosom heaved gently again.

Now the vessel is saved and the storm lulled to rest,
But one of a boat's gallant crew is no more;
May his soul be permitted to dwell with the blest,
Where no tempests are heard nor the billow's loud roar.
When the sad news shall fall on his poor widow's ears,
In the midst of her sorrow may God be her guide;
He can soothe her affliction, and dry all her tears,
For her husband for ever is torn from her side.

After the capture of Port Royal the Union sailors killed in the fighting were buried in a cemetery on Hilton Head. First Class Fireman George Caldwell composed the following for those who had fallen in battle.

AN ELEGY TO THE FALLEN BRAVE

We have lain them to rest on that fair Southern shore,
Where the Port Royal bay in its majesty flows,
While ship-mates and friends their loss do deplore,
And drop a tear where their ashes repose.

The evening shades fell slowly o'er the earth,
The stars looked down from heaven on land and sea;
Hushed were all sounds of revelry and mirth,
And still the busy hum of industry.

It is an hour when better thoughts will spring,
From memory's waste of scenes that's passed away.
A soft and holy feeling to the heart will spring,
Of joy and sorrow in Life's weary way.

Look on those mounds, though rude the hands that reared,
The mould above those forms, whose toils are o'er:
Unlearned, unlettered, nor death nor danger feared,
When lullaby was the wild ocean's roar.

Their country called them from humble walks of life,
To meet her foes, that rank rebellion spread,
O'er our fair land; nor parents, children, wife,
Could keep them back, but to battle sped.

They nobly fell, as heroes only fall;
They gave their lives their country to maintain,
The sun's bright gush of life or night's sable pall,
Shall never wake them to earths toils again.

Sleep on, ye brave! a long and silent sleep,
Far from thy childhood's home and friends that's dear,
While thy sad fate thy mourning ship-mates weep,
And strangers o'er thy grave will drop a silent tear.

George Collins was the unfortunate sailor shot dead one night by trigger happy Union pickets while ashore on outpost duty in the Cooper River. Seaman James Eggo marked his tragic death thus.

LINES ON THE DEATH OF GEORGE COLLINS

The tyrant, Death, has snatched away
Another of as brave a crew
As ever joined the fray,
Or wore the unstained garb of blue.

Not in the battle's deadly strife,
Nor in the ocean's angry swell,
But by a friendly hand, of life
Bereft, our gallant ship-mate fell.

A fatal bullet pierced the heart
Of one that loved his country dear,
And one from whose kind heart would start,
At comrade's fate, "the silent tear;'

And one whose muse would oft inspire
gay feelings to the lonely heart.
But that heart, which glow'd with genial fire,
In Southern soil now lies to rest.

In duty's path he nobly fell,

A martyr to our glorious cause:
But sad, alas! the tale to tell,
He died not by his country's foes.

He can no more her laws defend;
His merry song no more we'll hear:
May Heaven the balm of comfort send
To all on earth who held him dear.

We will finish on a lighter note. An amusing incident revolving around the appropriation of a broken wardroom chair landed George Eggo – who among his other duties had assumed the mantle of ship's barber – in trouble with the captain, and inspired him to write down this humorous rhyme.

On board the US ship *Susquehanna*,
To you shipmates I wish to tell,
About five days of my confinement,
All against the Captain's goodwill.

On the thirteenth of October,
About the hour of nine,
The ship's corporal and sergeant of the guard
Looked for the ship's barber to find.

They took me to the mast sir,
For what cause I knew not what;
I expected to get justice,
But justice was forgot.

There I first met my lieutenant, sir,
To pieces ready me to tear,
About a silly trifling thing
As an unlegged wardroom chair.

There I received my sentence, sir,
Five days under the sentry's charge with care.
But I was put on full ration, sir,
Both me and the wardroom chair.

On the sixth day I was brought to the mast
Expecting to be freed,
But for to get my liberty
Twelve hours brightwork had to clean.

Now all you ship's barbers
Take warning from me with care,
Never meddle with such a trifling thing
As an unlegged wardroom chair.

*** *FINIS* ***

BIBLIOGRAPHY

American Heritage Picture History of the Civil War – *Bruce Catton*
Bonanza Books, New York

Battles & Leaders of the Civil War – Volumes II and IV;
Castle, Book Sales Inc. Secaucus, New Jersey.

By Sea and By River (Naval History of the Civil War) – *Bern Anderson;*
Da Capo Press, New York.

Combined Operations of the Civil War – University of Nebraska Press.

Dictionary of American Naval Fighting Ships – Volume VI;
Naval History Division, Department of the Navy, Washington DC.

Early American Steamers, Volume V – *Heyl;*

Fighting Men of the Civil War – *William C. Davis*
Salamander Books, London and New York.

History of the United States Navy – Volume II, 1775 – 1894

National Encyclopedia of American Biography – Volume IX;
James White & Co. New York, 1899.

"Old Bruin" – Commodore Matthew Perry – *Samuel Eliot Morison;*
Atlantic Monthly Press, Little, Brown & Company.

Records of Living Officers of the US Navy – *Lewis Hamersly,* 3rd edition;
J. B. Lippincott & Co. Philadelphia, 1878 (US Naval Academy Museum Library).

The Blockade – *Editors of Time–Life Books;*
Time–Life Books, Alexandria, Virginia.

The Civil War – *Douglas Welsh;*
Bison Books, Greenwich, Connecticut, USA

The Coastal War – *Peter Chaitin*
Time–Life Books, Alexandria, Virginia.

The Cruise of the *Susquehanna* – *Amos Burton;*
Edward O. Jenkins, New York, (1863).

The Image of War –Volumes III and IV. 'The Embattled Confederacy';
'Fighting for Time'. National Historical Society.

The Official Records of the War of the Rebellion (Naval) – (Various volumes)

Warships and Naval Battles of the Civil War – *Terry Gibbons;*

<u>Officers and Crew of the USS *Susquehanna* – Commodore R B Hitchcock commanding</u>

ABBOT Walter, *Ensign*
ADAMS Frank G, *Mate*
ARNOLD Edward H, *3rd Assistant Engineer*
BEALS Joseph, *Surgeon*
BUEL, R H, *3rd Assistant Engineer*
BURNAP George I, *Second Assistant Engineer*
BUTTERWORTH James, *3rd Assistant Engineer*
CHURCHILL William L, *Acting Master*
DOUGHTY G Morris, *Carpenter*
FENDALL Jr. P R, *Captain of Marines*
HERBERT John C, *Sailmaker*
KEMPFF Louis, *Lieutenant*
LIVINGSTON George B, *Acting Master*
MILLER Charles, *Boatswain*
NELSON Henry C, *Assistant Surgeon*
PARKMAN John E, *Commodore's Clerk*
PRATT Edwin B, *Mate*
RAMSDEN Frederick T H, *3rd Assistant Engineer*
SEWELL George, *Chief Engineer*
SICARD Montgomery, Lieutenant Commander – *Executive Officer*
SIMPSON Robert G, *Paymaster*
THOMPSON William H, *Paymaster*
WAUGH Edward L, *Gunner*
ZEREGA Alfred L B, *Acting Master*

-

<u>Petty Officers</u>

FREEMAN M Fuller, *Master-at-Arms*
HOGAN Edgar, *Surgeon's* Steward
HOLLINGSWORTH R H, *Ship's Steward*
WHITE Jason, *Yeoman*

Boatswains Mates

BLISS, Isaiah

LANE John

SMITH Charles

Gunner's Mates

DEMPSEY Thomas

PRUDEN Martin

Carpenters Mates

DOUGLASS William

STEWART David

Quartermasters

HARDING Jeremiah

NICHOLS John

SMITH Seth

SUTTON William

Captains of Forecastle

BROWN John

JACKSON William

Coxswains

BOWDEN, F H, *Armourers Mate*

BOWEN William, *Captain of Hold*

BRYAN William, *Captain of Maintop*

BUCK James P, *Cooper*

CROSS Nelson H, *Commodores Steward*

DEPERINE Luigi, Band Master

FARREL James, *1st Launch*

GIVENS John, *2nd Cutter*

GOULDING Thomas, *Gig*

HANDFORD John, *Captain of Afterguard*

HARRISON Henry, *Armourer*
HART John, *Commodore's Cook*
HURST Henry, *Captain of Foretop*
JOHNSON Lewis, *1st Cutter*
MARTIN James, *Captain of Maintop*
McLAUGHLIN William, *Captain of Afterguard*
POMBA Arseino, *Officer's Steward*
REESE Thomas, *Sailmaker's Mate*
RICKS David, *Officer's Cook*
SANDBERG Frederick, *Ship's Corporal*
SNEA Andrew, Painter
STANTON John, *Captain of Hold*
WILLIAMS Edward, *3rd Cutter*
WILLIAMS George A, *Barge*
WILLIAMS George, *Captain of Foretop*
WINKLEY George, *2nd Launch*

First Class Fireman
BELL John, *Engineer's Yeoman*
CALDWELL, GW
FERNALD William H
HATTON Hugh
KING Edward
LYONS Daniel
MURPHY Timothy
POOR James W,
SMITH James
WHEELER, DG

Second Class Firemen
BARKER Thomas
CAMPBELL Alex
DARBY Isaac
EICHORN George
FULSOM William
HART William N
HICKEY Matthew
HOGAN Matthew
JAMISON John
McMAHON James
O'DONELL Henry
O'DONELL Martin
QUIN Thomas
SMITH James
WALSH David

Seamen
ALSON Robert
CARONDERS Edward
CROWLEY John
DAVIS Robert
DAY William
DRISCOLL Daniel
EGGO James
FINK Gustave
FORMENOY Matthias
GORDON Alex
HARRINGTON Robert
JACKSON Robert
JOSE Antonio
MAYO Sylvester
McCABE Edward
McGRATH Peter
McGUIRE Bernard
MERCHANT Samuel

NEVINS James
NILES Amos
O'SULLIVAN Michael
PRATT Charles
ROCK Peter
SINCLAIR Jason S
STOCK John
WELDON Charles
WHITCOMB George F

Ordinary Seamen

ALBBANI William
ANDERSON Charles H
ARMSTRONG William E
ASHTON James H
BAGALA Louis
BAKER James
BARRY John
BLUFF Harry
BOTTS Thomas A
BRAG Henry
BROWN James
CAHILL John
CAPEHART Walter
CARR James
CASTIN James
CAULKER Simon
CHANDLER William
COPEDA Leon

Coal Heavers

CONDON John
COONEY Richard
COPEDA Boon
CUNNINGHAM William
DE BREE John
DEVELIN James
DONNELLY John
DOUGHTY David
DRISCOLL Cornelius
DUGAN Charles
DWYER Patrick
ENGER Tallas
FALLEN Patrick
FERNANDI Antonio
FLANDLEY Michael
FORD Arthur
FURLONG August
GOTTSCHAL, K Ernest
GOWDY, T F
HAMILTON George S
HANLON Dennis
HEMENWAY Frederick
HOARD John
HUBBARD Ashbel
HUMPHREY Moore
JEFFERS Matthew
JOHNSON Samuel
JOHNSON William A
KELLY William
KILMARTIN Daniel
KINGSTON Thomas
LAMB John H

Landsmen

LANG Andrew
LLOYD Isaac
LOGAN George

LOVETT George
MANSFRED Dennis
MARRON Richard
McBRIDE Joseph B
McBRYAN Philip
McCOY Francis
McCRISTLE Thomas
McCUNE Patrick
McDONOUGH Stephen
McGRADY Patrick
McGRAN Edward
McKENNA John
McNALLY Edward
McRENNON John
MERKELS August
MICHELI, Guilhelmo D
MORGAN James
MORRIS James
NELSON William S
O'DONNELL John
ORLANDINI Antonio
OSTRANDER Benjamin
PALMER John C
PILLSBOROUGH Richard
PINCKNEY Adam
PINCKNEY Moses
POWELL Robert
PRICE William
QUICK John
QUINN Henry
REYNOLDS James
ROGAN James
ROGERS James
RUDO Andrew
SCHULTZ Damon D
SCOTT Robert
SHERIDAN Edward J
SIDDONS William E
SMITH Charles
SMITH David S
SNELL George
STITT John
SUMMERVILLE Thomas
SYNETT John
TAYLOR George
THOMAS Reuben G
THOMAS William M
THORNTON Thomas
VAN PELT Orin
WELSH Edward
WESSENDORF, L
WILKINSON Thomas H
WILLIAMS Edward
WILLIAMS Henry H
WILLIAMS John

Musicians

BALBI Caesar L
CABONA Andrew
DIDONATO Marcellino
MAZZARO Nunedo
RINALDI Salvator
SAGNELLI Alramo
TORTONA Francisco
WALSH John W
WASSARI Emanuel

Boys

BATTIGUE James
CARNES William E
HARVY Robert E
JACKSON Adam
JACKSON John
KENNEY Henry A
MANNING Isaac
RIVERS Robert
SMITH Albert T
SOULE Charles E
WESSON George H

Marine Guard

SHULDT John, *Orderly Sergeant*

Duty Sergeants

LAYPORTO S S
ROY Joseph

Corporals

CASSIDY Patrick
MEREDITH Henry
O'NEIL Philip
SEMOUR George

Musicians

BAXTER Woolsey
WALSH Michael

Privates

ALLISON Charles
BASSLER, S S
BOZARTH David
BULLNAGER Christian
BURTON Amos
CARPENTER, L C
DAILY Michael
DAYLY John
FAWKES Nicholas
FULLEN James
GILLEN Charles
GROGAN Henry
HARTMAN Augustus
HAYES William
KELLY James
KLEIBER Charles
LOOP Henry
LYNCH John
MILLER Edward W
MILLER Peter
MITTON Moses F
MORRIS James L
MORRIS John T
MULLEN Jonathan
O'BRIEN John
O'NEILL William P
PALMER William H
PAWLE Nicholas
QUIGLEY Thomas H
SHORT Henry
SMITH Charles
TOOMEY James
TREHEARN Andrew

INDEX

INDEX OF UNION VESSELS

INDEX OF CONFEDERATE VESSELS

INDEX OF FOREIGN VESSELS

Figurehead and Cutwater of the *Susquehanna*

An unknown artist designed this carving of a bird with eagle-like features and stylized flowers, fruit and acorns for the prow and cutwater for both the *Susquehanna* and her sister ship *Powhatan.* It is likely to have been an attempt to create a motif using images of native American fauna and flora.
National Archives

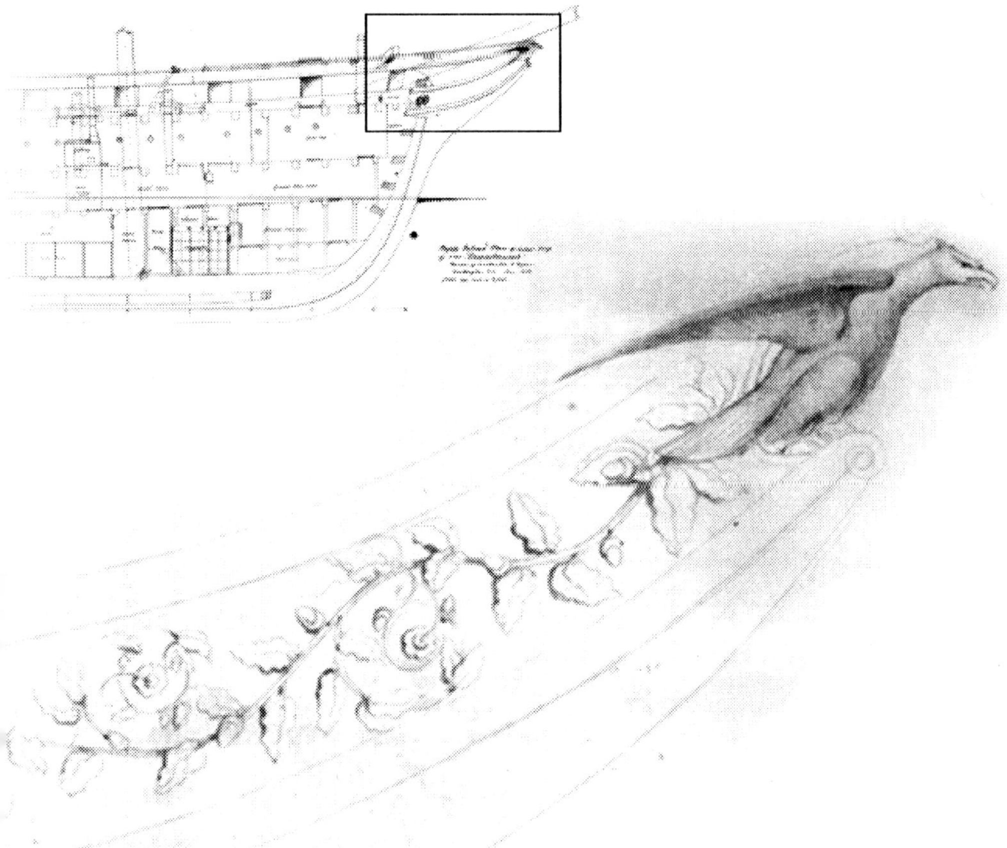

TECHNICAL SPECIFICATIONS OF THE STEAMSHIP *SUSQUEHANNA*

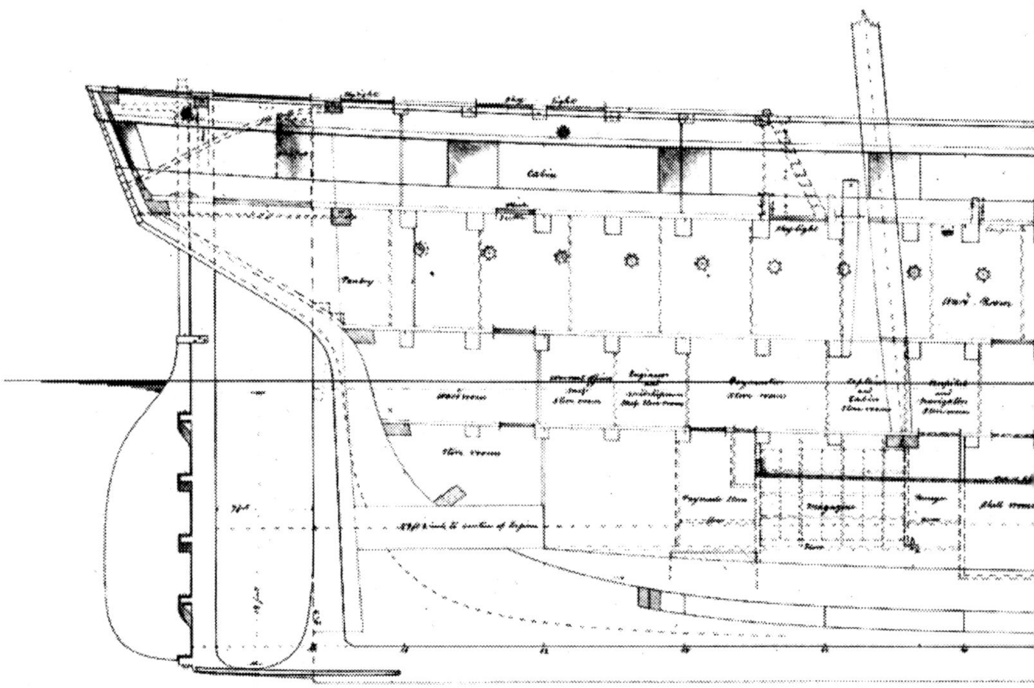

Owner and builder

United States Navy

Side-wheel steamer, First-class wooden sloop; bark rigged

Laid down in 1847 and constructed in Philadelphia Navy Yard

Launched April 5, 1850

Cost - $697,212

Tonnage – 2,436 tons

Average draft of water – 18ft 6 ins.

Dimensions

Breadth of beam – 45 ft

Length on deck – 256ft 6 ins.

Depth of hold – 26 ft.

Draft – loaded, 20 ft 6 ins; light, 18 ft

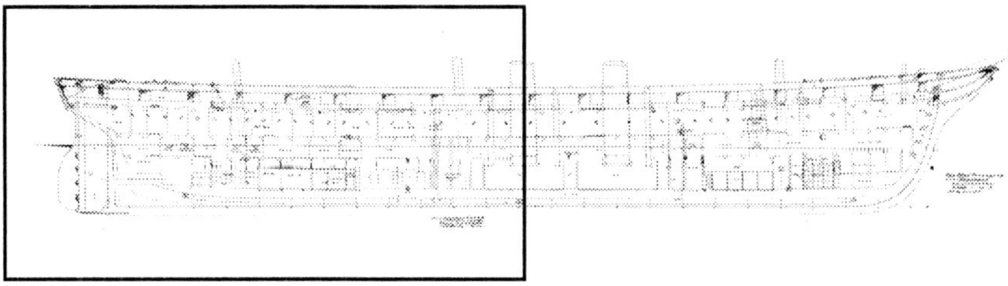

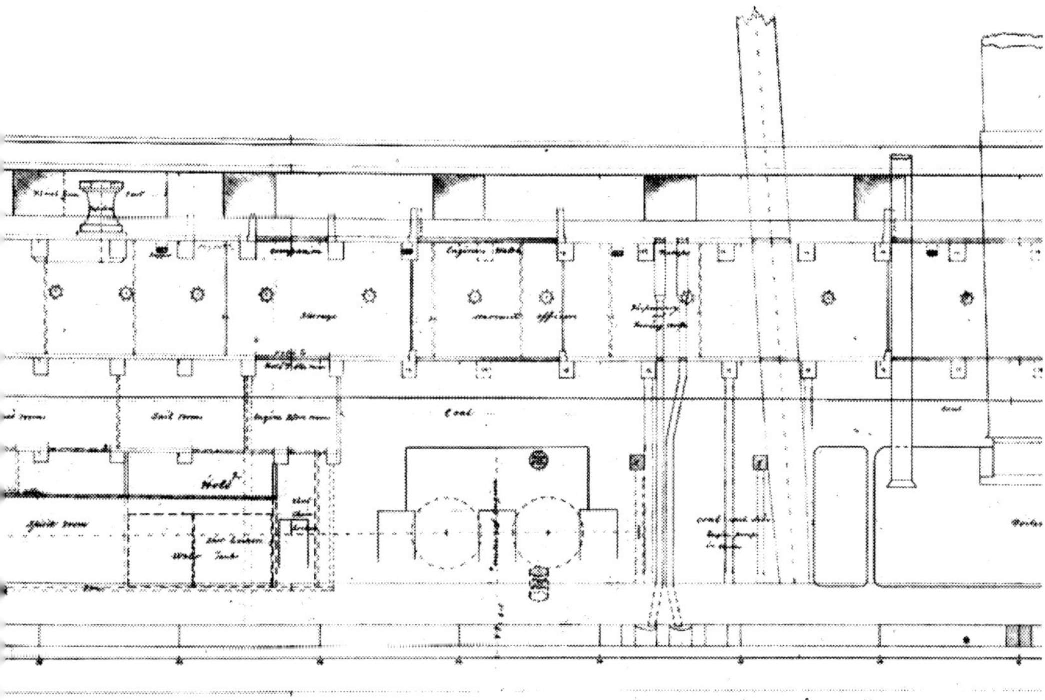

Engines

Two inclined engines designed by Charles W Copeland and built by Murray and Hazlehurst at the Vulcan Works, Baltimore, Maryland.

Diameter of Cylinders – 5 ft 10 ins.

Length of stroke – 10 ft.

Average number of revolutions – 12

Paddle Wheels

Diameter of Wheels – 31 ft. 2 ins.

Length of Paddles 9 ft 6 ins.

Depth of Paddles 17 ins. each, or 2 ft 10 ins.

Number of Double Paddles in each Wheel – 26

Dip of Wheel – 6 ft.

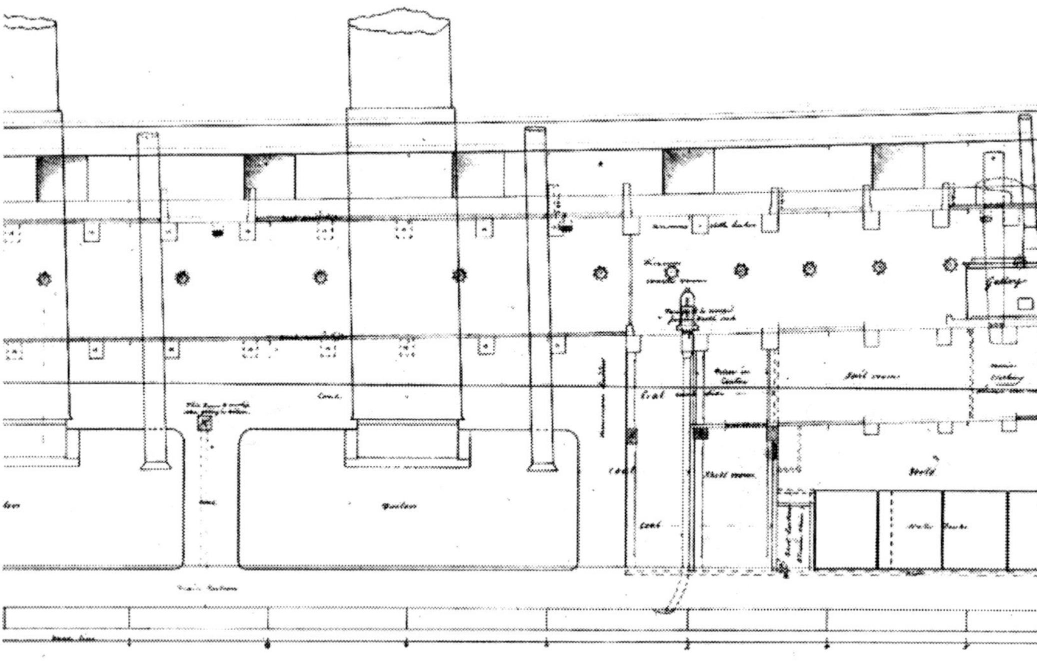

Boilers

Four copper boilers (back to back), also designed and built by Charles Copeland and Murray and Hazlehurst.

Average pressure of steam – 10 lbs.

Coming off at – 6 lbs.

Whole amount of Fire Surface – 8,652 sq ft.

Whole amount of Grate Surface – 342 sq ft.

Ratio of Fire Surface to cubic foot of Cylinder – 16 1/4 to 1

Ratio of Fire Surface to Grate Surface – 25 to 1

Area of First Flues – 82 sq ft.

Area of 2nd and 3rd Flues, each – 52 sq ft.

Coal Consumption

Bituminous coal per hour – 3,270 lbs.

Coal per hour to a square foot of grate – 9 1/2 lbs.

Water evaporated by 1 lb. of coal – 8 lbs.

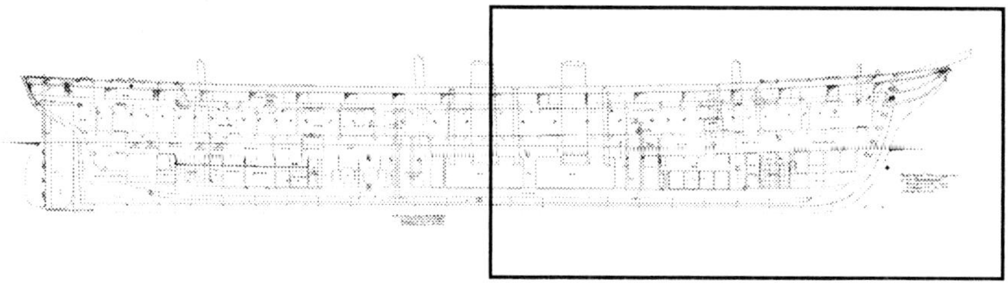

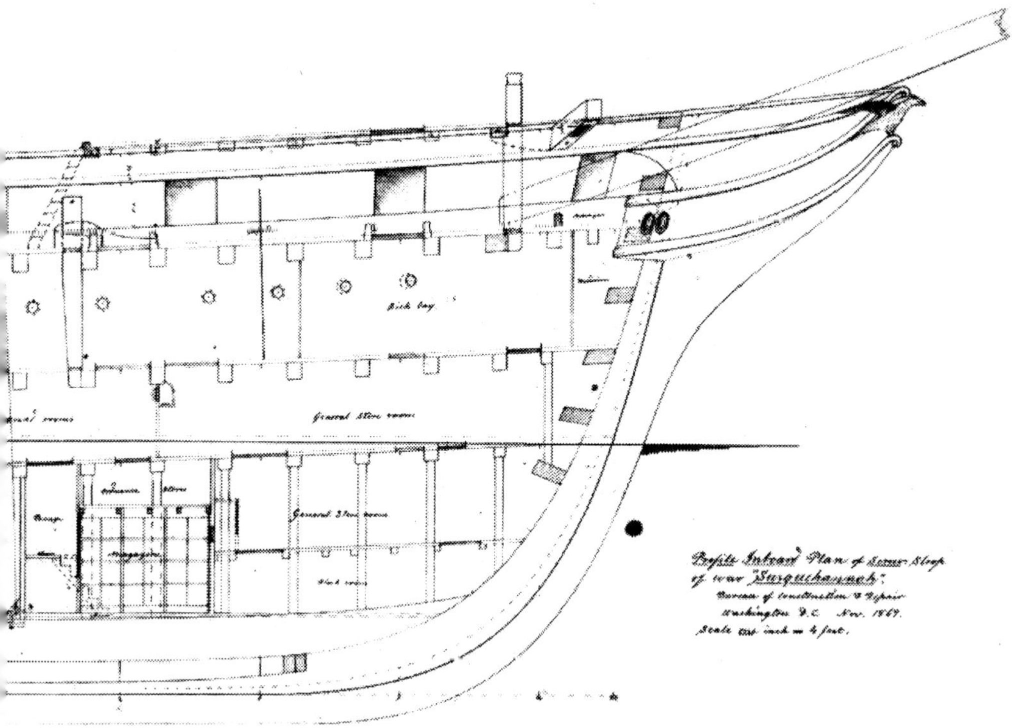

Note: The results were obtained on her first run from Philadelphia to Norfolk. The steam chimney is attached to the boilers, and the steam from each admitted by a regulating valve, so arranged that one may be used at pleasure.

Smokestack

Area of Chimney – 54 sq ft.

Height of Chimney above Grate – 65 ft.

Speed

Maximum, 12.5 knots; average 8 knots

Battery

June 8, 1863: 2 x 150-pdr Parrot Rifles, 12 x 9-inch Dahlgren smoothbores, 1 x 12-pdr Rifle: **August 4, 1864**: add 1 x 12-pdr Rifle; **January 13, 1865**: 2 x 100-pdr Parrot Rifles, 12 x 9-inch Dahlgren smoothbores; **March 31, 1865**: Similar to August 4, 1864; **December 31, 1865**: 2 x 11-inch Dahlgren smoothbores, 12 x 9-inch Dahlgren smoothbores, 1 x 30-pdr Parrot Rifle, 2 x 12-pdr Rifles.